MW01105223

CONVERSATIONS ON PEIRCE

AMERICAN PHILOSOPHY

Douglas R. Anderson and Jude Jones, series editors

CONVERSATIONS
ON PEIRCE

Reals and Ideals

DOUGLAS R. ANDERSON
CARL R. HAUSMAN

FORDHAM UNIVERSITY PRESS   NEW YORK   2012

Chapters 1 and 2 are revised versions of essays originally published in *Transactions of the Charles S. Peirce Society* and are published here by permission of Indiana University Press.

Fordham University Press has no responsibility for the persistence or accuracy of URLs for external or third-party Internet websites referred to in this publication and does not guarantee that any content on such websites is, or will remain, accurate or appropriate.

Fordham University Press also publishes its books in a variety of electronic formats. Some content that appears in print may not be available in electronic books.

Library of Congress Cataloging-in-Publication Data is available from the publisher.

Printed in the United States of America
14 13 12   5 4 3 2 1
First edition

Contents

Preface

Philosophical discussion proper only succeeds between intimates who have learned how to converse by months of weary trial and failure.

—William James to H. N. Gardiner, November 14, 1901

Carl Hausman was initially my teacher and later my colleague for several years prior to his retirement. Together we have explored the issues in this book in a wide variety of settings. We have co-taught classes on Peirce and American philosophy; we have co-written essays and talks; and we have spent countless hours in coffee shops arguing and sketching our ideas for each other. I remember, for example, a long spring afternoon when the two of us worked our way through an example of a Peircean "object" provided by Chris Hookway. We did not reach agreement, but the version of the argument Carl later published revealed its trial by fire in our discussion. Our philosophical styles are a bit different; I tend to work historically, and Carl's work is more thematic and directly argumentative. But we share a great many philosophical interests, and our interpretive study of Peirce is among these.

The chapters of the present text track conversations Carl and I explicitly opened in 1991 when we co-taught a seminar on Peirce's thought. I was then interested in Peirce's various claims that he was an "objective idealist" or "Schellingean." I was curious to see how this idealist history informed Peirce's pragmatism. Carl, on the other hand, was attracted by Peirce's ability to hang on to a non-foundationalist yet rich conception of truth and to an evolutionary cosmology that provided grounds for genuine creativity. Consequently, he was led to focus on the constraints on human reasoning and creative endeavors. During the fall of 1991 we therefore began a conversation—or "discussion"— concerning whether Peirce was an idealist. I argued for the claim and tried to see Peirce's work in light of German and American idealist thought of the nineteenth century; Carl argued against it on the condition that being an idealist entailed the absence of non-mental constraints on human reasoning. In short, he worried that the lack of secondness or otherness with which Peirce occasionally charged Hegel might reappear in Peirce's own idealism. The result here is a collection of essays—some older, some newer—that have developed out of this generative conversation on Peirce.

The initial debate led us into an ongoing dialogue regarding Peirce's conceptions of realism and idealism. And this, as the chapters here reveal, led to future conversations with each other and with other colleagues. I went off in exploration of what Peirce called his scholastic realism, where general ideas and possibilities are to be considered as real as any physical object. Carl's focus on the non-idealist strands of Peirce's thought led him to explore what we call Peirce's metaphysical or scientific realism—his claim that human reasoning is constrained by something other than mind, something "extramental." The chapters here represent our own takes on Peircean thought and are not meant to provide a systematic or an exhaustive account of Peirce's notions of idealism, realism, inquiry, and so on. Nor do we claim radical novelty for all the ideas herein; many good Peirce scholars have taken up these issues in ways similar to our own. What we do offer is an angle on these issues marked by our ongoing discussions and by our shared philosophical interests. Each essay was written to stand alone. Here we have arranged them around themes—perception, inquiry, religion, historical setting— but always with an eye toward the initial issue concerning the ways in which idealism and realism affect the development of Peirce's philosophy. We hope that taken as a whole they might exemplify something of a Greek philosophical endeavor in which friends engage in serious reflection together. We do intend these chapters, at the least, to invite others into our discussion and we hope to make some initial suggestions about the ways in which Peirce was—and was not—both an idealist and a realist.

One important upshot of our conversations is to see that though Peirce in many ways looks like a straightforward transitional figure between modern and contemporary philosophy, he is more than this. His scholastic realism in particular, as John Boler, Susan Haack, and others have tried to show, stands in deep opposition to the nominalistic tendencies of both modern philosophy and most twentieth-century analytic philosophy. In embracing his realism, one is forced to rethink the most basic philosophical conceptions. What is real, what is continuity, what is an individual (a thing), and how is it that we know anything? Peirce's own explicit transformations of such basic concepts are well known—his reconceptions of truth, inquiry, semiotic theory, and God, for example. But the relation of these reconceptions to Peirce's realism and idealism has not always been well documented. One of our aims is to explore some of those relations here.

Perhaps the most fundamental reconception that Peirce made was that of a "relation." As is well known, the moderns had difficulty handling relations because, like the Parmenides figure in Plato's dialogue of that name, they individualized or "thingified" relations and treated them straightforwardly as other entities in the cosmos. Others of course treated them simply as useful fictions. For Peirce, relations are first and foremost instances of real generality. As he points out in his basic semiotic work, signs or representamens are general in nature—they mediate between an object and an interpretant, and they cover a multiplicity of particulars. Semeiosis, for Peirce, involves exemplary instances of relations. Without a thoroughgoing reconception of the nature of relations, Peirce suggested, all of the problems of modern philosophy remain intact and, argue as we may, we will remain stuck with the disjunctive dilemma of Cartesian foundationalism or Humean skepticism. For Peirce, a realistic reconception of relations is pragmatic, and practical, because it makes better sense of our actual scientific practices as well as of our actual normative hopes in both ethics and logic. It is in any case an avenue worth exploring given the dead ends of modern thought so openly exposed by the likes of Martin Heidegger and John Dewey. We would invite readers to join the conversation we have enjoyed for the last twenty-five years.

DOUG ANDERSON

Acknowledgments

We thank the following for permission to include in this book modified versions of essays they originally published: Value Inquiry Book Series and Rodopi Press for Hausman, "Peirce's Dynamical Object: Realism as Process Philosophy," which appeared in *Process Pragmatism*, ed. Guy de Brock, 2003; Indiana University Press for Hausman and Anderson, "The Telos of Peirce's Realism," which appeared in *Transactions of the Charles S. Peirce Society* 30, no. 4 (fall 1994) and for Anderson, "Who's a Pragmatist: Royce and Peirce at the Turn of the Century," which appeared in *Transactions of the Charles S. Peirce Society* 41, no. 3 (summer 2005); *American Catholic Philosophical Quarterly* for Anderson and Groff, "Peirce on Berkeley's Nominalistic Platonism," which appeared in vol. 72, no. 2 (fall 1998); *International Philosophical Quarterly* for Anderson, "Realism and Idealism in Peirce's Cosmogony," which appeared in vol. 32, no. 2 (June 1992); and Kluwer/Springer Publishing for Anderson, "Peirce's Agape and the Generality of Concern," which appeared in *International Journal for the Philosophy of Religion* 37, no. 2 (summer 1995). We also thank all of our former students, who have pushed us to consider further our own philosophical takes on things. Special thanks go to Steven Miller, who not only joined our conversation but had the patience to help shape this book.

Abbreviations

In this volume, citations for Peirce's work are noted in line rather than in endnotes. The following rubric explains these references. In those cases where the abbreviation is followed by two sets of numbers, the first of these indicates the volume number. In citations of *The Collected Papers of Charles Sanders Peirce* (CP) the second number refers to the paragraph. In citations of other woks, the second number refers to the page.

CP   *The Collected Papers of Charles Sanders Peirce.* Edited by Charles Hartshorne and Paul Weiss (vols. 1–6) and by Arthur Burks (vols. 7–8). Cambridge, Mass.: Harvard University Press, 1931–58.

EP   *The Essential Peirce.* Edited by Nathan Houser and Christian Kloesel. 2 vols. The Peirce Edition Project. Bloomington and Indianapolis: Indiana University Press, 1992–98.

MS   The Charles S. Peirce Papers. 30 reels of microfilm. The Houghton Library. Cambridge, Mass.: Harvard University Library Microreproduction Service, 1963–66.

N   *Charles Sanders Peirce: Contributions to* The Nation. *Part Two: 1894–1900.* Edited by Kenneth L. Ketner and James E. Cook. Graduate Studies 16. Lubbock, Texas: Texas Tech University Press, 1978.

NE   *The New Elements of Mathematics*. 4 vols. Edited by Carolyn
     Eisele. The Hague and Paris: Mouton; Atlantic Highlands, N.J.:
     Humanities Press, 1976.

RLT *Reasoning and the Logic of Things: The Cambridge Conferences
     Lectures of 1898*. Edited by Kenneth Laine Ketner. Cambridge,
     Mass. and London: Harvard University Press, 1992.

SS   *Semiotic and Significs: The Correspondence between Charles S.
     Peirce and Victoria Lady Welby*. Edited by Charles S. Hardwick.
     Bloomington: Indiana University Press, 1977.

W   *Writings of Charles S. Peirce: A Chronological Edition*. Edited by
     Max Fisch, Nathan Houser, Christian Kloesel, et al. 8 vols. to
     date. The Peirce Edition Project. Bloomington: Indiana Uni-
     versity Press, 1982–.

CONVERSATIONS ON PEIRCE

CONVERSATION I

PRAGMATISM, IDEALISM, REALISM

ONE

PEIRCE ON BERKELEY'S NOMINALISTIC PLATONISM

Doug Anderson and Peter Groff

Peter Groff and I began this piece with a discussion of nominalism in the work of William James. As early as 1915 John Dewey had argued that James was more nominalistic than was Peirce, and that this had some effect on their particular versions of pragmatism. This led us to a consideration of Peirce's attribution of nominalism to a variety of modern thinkers. We came to focus on Berkeley because his work so clearly exemplified the ambiguity of Peirce's response to the British tradition.[1]

The exemplary role that Bishop Berkeley played in Peirce's conception of pragmatism is suggested by Peirce's frequent references to Berkeley's proto-pragmatic practice. "It was this medium [the river of pragmatism]," Peirce said, "and not tar water, that gave health and strength to Berkeley's earlier works, his *Theory of Vision* and what remains of his *Principles*" (CP 5.11). On another occasion he remarked: "In 1871, in a Metaphysical Club in Cambridge, Massachusetts, I used to preach this principle as a sort of logical gospel, representing the unformulated method followed by Berkeley, and in conversation about it I called it 'Pragmatism' " (CP 6.482). This continuity in pragmatic practice has been noted by a number of commentators. However, although he sought to appropriate Berkeley's proto-pragmatism, Peirce also consistently resisted what he saw as the nominalistic features of Berkeley's earlier works. He went so far as to identify Berkeley as one of the four great nominalists of the modern period (CP 4.1). Peirce's double-edged response to Berkeley's work was of both historical and contemporary importance to him. On the one hand, Berkeley worked in the tradition of nominalism that Peirce believed took its impetus from Ockham's response to the Scotists: thus, Berkeley was for Peirce an important link in the British tradition that developed and maintained an alliance between "scientific" philosophy and nominalism. It is an alliance that is still maintained by both physical realists and some neo-pragmatists in American thought.[2] Peirce took this alliance, which informed the work of nineteenth-century scientific philosophers such as John Stuart Mill and Peirce's contemporaries Karl Pearson and T. H. Huxley, to be both accidental and mistaken. Thus, the historical interest led directly into Peirce's own immediate interest: pragmatism and the aims and methods of scientific inquiry. Peirce hoped to bring his own version of scholastic realism back to life as an important ally of science and pragmatism. As Peirce argued:

> There are certain questions commonly reckoned as metaphysical, and which certainly are so . . . which as soon as pragmatism is once sincerely accepted, cannot logically resist settlement. These are for example, What is reality? Are necessity and contingency real modes of being? Are the laws of nature real? Can they be assumed to be immutable or are they presumably results of evolution? Is there any real chance, or departure from real law? (EP 2:420)

Berkeley was important to this project because 1) his thinking had a pragmatic streak in it that led in the direction of, though never arrived at, a version of scholastic realism; and 2) his work revealed some difficulties in maintaining a marriage of pragmatism and nominalism, a fact Peirce hoped would not be lost on his pragmatic contemporaries William James and F. C. S. Schiller.

The focus on Berkeley clearly raises a number of important issues in interpreting Peirce's own thinking. We limit our discussion here, however, to examining what Peirce had in mind when he identified Berkeley's idealism as a nominalistic Platonism. Our thesis is that Peirce saw Berkeley as a kind of mirror image of Scotus. Scotus, Peirce argued, marked out a position that was just the breadth of a hair from nominalism. As we see it, Peirce understood Berkeley's nominalistic idealism to be a hair's breadth from realism. Thus, by examining this assessment of Berkeley, we can hope to see more clearly just what was at stake for Peirce in retaining his realist stance over against the likes of Pearson, James, and Schiller.

Peirce often identified himself as a Scotistic or scholastic realist, but he just as often noted that Scotus's realism was as close as one could get to nominalism without being a nominalist.[3] He maintained that Scotus was "inclined toward nominalism" (CP 1.560) and that Scotus's realism was separated from nominalism "by a hair" (CP 8.11). Through his notion of a formal distinction, Scotus raised the possibility of saying that a quality, for example, was real without also being an independent existent. Despite his praise of Scotus, Peirce eventually found himself moving beyond Scotistic realism: "Even Duns Scotus is too nominalistic when he says that universals are contracted to the mode of individuality in singulars, meaning as he does, by singulars, ordinary existing things. The pragmaticist cannot admit that" (CP 8.208).[4] Ultimately, even the hair's breadth that kept Scotus a "realist" was insufficient for Peirce, who acknowledged that he maintained an "unqualified" realism (MS 641, p. 12).

It was an analogous problem that led Peirce to view Berkeley's thought—despite its emphasis on ideas—as nominalistic.[5] Berkeley, even more than Scotus, was unable to see the importance of generality.[6] For Peirce, part of the question was "whether *laws* and general *types* are figments of the mind or are real" (CP 1.16). Berkeley leaned toward the first option, and as a nominalist saw all reals as "singulars," as existent things. What remains important in assessing Berkeley, however, is that his nominalism remained intact while his pragmatic thinking was enroute to a broader, more inclusive conception of the real; he simply did not pursue the avenue he opened in the direction of realism.

Peirce's objections to Berkeley's thought are, as noted, to be found in part in his identification of Berkeley as a nominalistic Platonist. "Berkeley," he stated, "is an admirable illustration of this national character, as well as of that strange union of nominalism with Platonism, which has repeatedly appeared in history, and has been such a stumbling block to the historians of philosophy" (CP 8:10). Peirce suspected this "strange union" began with earlier medieval thinkers, including Abelard and John of Salisbury (CP 8:30), and he believed it represented the inability of nominalists to make a distinction between existence and reality:

> Individualists [nominalists] are apt to fall into the almost incredible misunderstanding that all other men are individualists, too—even the scholastic realists, who, they suppose, thought that "universals exist." It is true that there are indications of there having been some who thought so in that greater darkness before the dawn of Aristotle's *Analytics* and Topics, when such grotesque weldings of doctrine as that of nominalistic Platonism are heard of, and when Roscellin may possibly have said that universals were *flatus vocis*. (CP 5.503)

For Peirce, the "real is that which is not whatever we happen to think it, but is unaffected by what we may think of it" (CP 8.12; see also 5.430); existence, on the other hand, "is a special mode of reality, which, whatever other characteristics it possesses, has that of being absolutely determinate" (CP 6.349; see also 5.503). Berkeley, as did other nominalistic Platonists, failed to make this distinction, and thus found himself forced to collapse the real into the existent. The conflation left him with inadequate resources, as Peirce saw it, for dealing with meaning, communication, and most centrally, the practice of inquiry, all of which require the real generality of relation and sem-eiosis, or sign activity.

Peirce's assessment of Berkeley's nominalistic Platonism can be approached from two distinct, though related, directions, one with an epistemological emphasis, the other with an ontological emphasis. The first has been developed insightfully and in some detail by Cornelis de Waal. We begin with a brief look at this approach before turning to the second.

De Waal, following Peirce, points out that one pragmatic difference between nominalism and realism is marked by the respective ways in which they describe the locus of constraint on finite thinkers. As de Waal puts it, "nominalism and realism are two rival hypotheses that try to give an account of the constraints upon the mind."[7] Both the nominalist and the realist look for a way to account for this constraint. As de Waal shows, for Peirce, the nominalistic answer is that the mind must be constrained by something external to it—something that is "independent" of mind by being actually separated from it. The commonsense notion that material objects serve as external constraints on thought is perhaps the most common version of such nominalism. Peirce states the nominalist's case as follows:

> Where is the real, the thing independent of how we think it, to be found? There must be such a thing, for we find our opinions constrained; there is something, therefore, which influences our thoughts, and is not created by them. We have, it is true, nothing immediately present to us but thoughts. These thoughts, however, have been caused by sensations, and those sensations are constrained by something out of the mind. This thing out of the mind, which directly influences sensation, and through sensation thought, because it is out of the mind, is independent of how we think of it, and is, in short, the real. Here is one view of reality, a very familiar one. And from this point it is clear that the nominalistic answer must be given to the question concerning universals. (CP 8.12)

Thus, in searching for that which is independent of the mind, nominalists—and materialists especially—seek it in that which is external to and not like the mind. Thus, as de Waal points out: "It appears that the nominalist assumes that the only way in which something can be independent of the mind is by being *external* to it."[8]

Although Berkeley was a nominalist, he was a nominalist of a peculiar stripe. He rejected the most common form of nominalism—materialism—by asserting that taking material things as the constraining, external others is superfluous from a pragmatic point of view:

> I say it is granted on all hands—and what happens in dreams, frenzies, and the like, puts it beyond dispute—that it is possible we might be affected with all the ideas we have now, though there were no bodies existing without resembling them. Hence, it is evident the supposition of external bodies is not necessary for the producing our ideas; since it is granted they are produced sometimes, and might possibly be produced always in the same order we see them in at present, without their concurrence.[9]

After rejecting material bodies in this fashion, Berkeley sought to locate the constraint on our ideas—the real—elsewhere, in something that seems to have more natural affinity with our ideas. He therefore turned to the divine spirit, or God's ideas: "[I]t remains therefore that the cause of ideas is an incorporeal active substance or Spirit."[10] More generally, as Fraser puts it, "[i]n and through God, or Active Reason, the material world becomes an intelligible world."[11] In some ways, this is, for Peirce, a step in the right direction: it moves toward his own realism, which locates the independent in the "final opinion" of inquiry, which "is independent, not indeed of thought in general, but of all that is arbitrary and individual in thought" (CP 8.12; see also W 2:239 and Turrisi, p. 143).[12] However, as de Waal shows, from Peirce's perspective Berkeley's move, while overcoming materialism, does not get beyond nominalism. The difficulty is that God, or God's mind, remains an external entity—like matter, it stands over against our minds with no clear route of access. Here Peirce, framing a Berkeleyan ontology, found the epistemological dimension of Berkeley's nominalistic Platonism:

In the usual sense of the word *reality*, therefore, Berkeley's doctrine is that the reality of sensible things resides only in their archetypes in the divine mind. This is Platonistic, but it is not realistic. On the contrary, since it places reality wholly out of the mind in the cause of sensations, and since it denies reality (in the true sense of the word) to sensible things in so far as they are sensible, it is distinctly nominalistic. (CP 8.30)

So, despite the fact that Berkeley shifted the locus of constraint to the divine mind, thus making thought or reason central to the intelligibility of our ideas and moving in the direction of Peirce's realism, he remained a nominalist. As de Waal remarks, "the danger of this approach . . . is that it situates reality again outside our reach. Even though reality is now by definition conceivable, it remains utterly unknowable unless we either have a direct and independent access to the mind of God, or can distinguish intuitively which ideas are imprinted upon our mind by God and which are fictions of our fancy."[13]

To be sure, Berkeley suggested several ways by which we might come to know the divine mind, but each of these from Peirce's perspective requires the introduction of an element of real and imperceptible generality into Berkeley's scheme: analogy, symbol, relation, and so forth.[14] In replying to objections to his principles, for example, Berkeley stated that we know God by way of those ideas of ours which disclose the general "order and concatenation" of ideas, for they are "the immediate effects of a FREE SPIRIT."[15] He developed this solution further in the fourth dialogue of *Alciphron*, where he discussed the possibility of these effects being signs of God.[16] Berkeley also introduced his conception of a "notion" of God, which, because it cannot be mediated by ideas, appears to exhibit a reliance on intuition. It is, de Waal points out, precisely his intuitionism at this juncture that allows Berkeley to remain nominalist—to keep God external to finite minds. From Peirce's perspective, Berkeley, whether he relies on intuition or knowledge through effects, fails to be consistent. Peirce notably rejected intuition as being inadequate to our actual experience of cognition (W 2:193–211). But even on Berkeley's own terms, a notion, as distinct from an idea, seems to require a self-consciousness or self-awareness; thus, to know God notionally, we must either experience our own God-consciousness, or work analogically from our own self-awareness to an awareness of God. The former seems experientially false, except perhaps for mystics; moreover, if it were true, it would seem to depend on a continuity of minds, which, as Peirce saw it, would endorse the very realism Berkeley intended to avoid. The latter returns us to a semiotic process, as is the case with our knowing by way of effects. Peirce's complaint about knowing by way of effects and/or analogy is, once again, that generality is already at work in these operations and that, therefore, if Berkeley wants to hold on to this way of knowing, he must give up his insistence that all things are singular existents. Not only God but also the ways of knowing God are themselves imperceptible; thus, where epistemology is considered, Berkeley's nominalistic Platonism seems to have to move beyond its own limits.

In his review of Fraser's *Berkeley*, Peirce stated his concern for the epistemic inadequacy of Berkeley's nominalism in terms of his rejection of that which is "absolutely incognizable" (CP 8.16). As did Ockham, Berkeley began with the belief "that reality is something independent of representative relation" (W 2:240). Consequently, Berkeley's God and the divine ideas, in being external, individual existents, seem to be in principle unknowable and, therefore, inadequate as the conditions for knowing, as the loci of constraint on finite thought. God, in effect, becomes "a thing in itself, a thing existing independent of all relation to the mind's conception of it" (CP 8.16).

Although this is not the place to pursue Peirce's general rejection of the notion of a thing in itself, this way of framing the issue reveals how for Peirce the epistemological concern is linked to Berkeley's ontology; this opens up the second approach to Peirce's assessment of Berkeley's nominalism. As Peirce saw it, Berkeley put himself in an ontologically odd position with his shift to idealism. He introduced something "real" that is not perceptible, creating an internal tension in his thought, one that later critics such as Hume would work to their advantage. Peirce noted this tension:

> Of course, many things that are Real are not capable of being directly perceived. Berkeley himself admits this; for he makes spirits,

or Minds, to be Real, notwithstanding his *esse est percipi*. In #89 of the second edition of his *Treatise concerning the Principles of Human Knowledge* he further acknowledges that there are real Relations between things. (MS 641, p. 23)

In terms of Peirce's own categories or modes of being—firstness, secondness, and thirdness—Berkeley's rejection of materialism and adoption of idealism appear to generate a metaphysics that involves both the firstness of qualities and the thirdness of laws or general ideas. Peirce said as much in his own overview of metaphysical systems:

> The Berkeleyans, for whom there are but two kinds of entities, souls, or centres of determinable thought, and ideas in the souls, these ideas being regarded as pure statical entities, little or nothing else than Qualities of Feeling, seem to admit Categories First and Third and to deny Secondness, which they wish to replace by Divine Creative Influence, which certainly has all the flavor of Thirdness. (CP 5.81)

Berkeley was moving in the direction of Peirce's own triadic ontology and offers "the flavor of Thirdness," Peirce's category of real generality.[17] However, Berkeley did not follow his own lead; his move toward realism was stunted by his fundamentally nominalistic outlook, leaving him with a nominalistic Platonism—a Platonism in which the divine spirit and its ideas are taken to be existent individuals, devoid of generality. So, his transition from an emphasis on secondness (matter) to an emphasis on firstness and thirdness (ideas and divine spirit) is stifled by his retention of secondness—actual existence—as the category through which everything is to be made intelligible.

Berkeley's nominalism, of course, began with his rejection of the reality of abstract general ideas. His claim was that all ideas are actual sensations and that these are all particular existents. What we call "abstract general ideas" have no status; they are entirely dependent on particular ideas, having no reality of their own. They are for Berkeley mere signs of particulars: "it seems that a word becomes general by being made the sign, not of an abstract general idea, but of several particular ideas, any one of which it indifferently suggests to the mind."[18] To bring this point home, Berkeley denied that we can "frame an abstract, general, and consistent idea of a triangle."[19] Berkeley brought this same commitment to his idealism; if there are no referents for what we call general signs, then the ideas of God must also be particular and existent. As we noted earlier, "Berkeley's doctrine is that the reality of sensible things resides only in their archetypes in the divine mind . . ." and at the same time "it denies reality (in the true sense of the word) to sensible things in so far as they are sensible . . ." (CP 8.30). Thus, Berkeley's thinking is analogous to the nominalistic Platonism Peirce found in Fredigisus's claim that "darkness is a thing" (CP 5.215, n. 1); for Berkeley, divine archetypes are things (see MS 641, p. 14).

Peirce responded to Berkeley at this juncture by appealing once again to his own modes of being and to his distinction between reality and existence.[20] He responded specifically to Berkeley's denial of the reality of a triangle in general:

> Berkeley and nominalists of his stripe deny that we have any idea at all of a triangle in general, which is neither equilateral, isosceles, nor scalene. But he cannot deny that there are propositions about triangles in general, which propositions are either true or false; and as long as that is the case, whether I have an *idea* of a triangle in some psychological sense or not, I do not, as a logician, care. I have an *intellectus*, a meaning, of which the triangle in general is an element. (CP 5.181)

Despite his implicit attempts to outflank himself by using his conception of a "notion," Berkeley, through his nominalism, confined himself to the "psychological sense" of an immediate, existent sensation.

Peirce took Berkeley's emphasis on one mode of being—existence —to produce other unwelcome consequences across the range of his philosophical concerns. One such problem arises if we consider how Berkeley's nominalistic Platonism might address cosmology or, in traditional terms, the question of God's purpose. Insofar as God's ideas are existents, they are also specified and determinate, or what Peirce sometimes called concrete. What, then, might the divine mind's purpose or telos be in Berkeley's world? On his grounds, in its specificity this telos can have no inherent generality. Again, in traditional terms, Berkeley's divine mind has foreknowledge precisely because its telos, as an idea, is already determinate—it is fixed. There is no free play here under a general heading as we suppose there is, to use a Peircean example, when one of us wants to make an apple pie. The real generality of our aim, "apple pie," allows it to be specified in any number of ways (see CP 1.341).[21] It was just this conception of real generality that enabled Peirce to adopt an evolutionary cosmology and what he called a developmental teleology, ideas he took to be reasonably consistent with late-nineteenth-century science (CP 6.156). As he saw it, Berkeley's nominalism left no room for development or growth, because it required the world to be determinate at the outset. He lodged his complaint to his contemporaries in somewhat dramatic fashion:

> Get rid, thoughtful Reader, of the Ockhamist prejudice of political partizenship that in thought, in being, and in development the indefinite is due to a degeneration from a primal state of perfect definiteness. . . . [T]he unsettled is the primal state, and . . . definiteness and determinateness, the two poles of settledness, are, in the large, approximations, developmentally, epistemologically, and metaphysically. (CP 6.348; see also 6.189f. and MS 641)

Berkeley, who was in the tradition of the Ockhamists, at least on this score, left no room, as Peirce saw it, either for individual creativity or for development in the cosmos.[22]

Another consequence of Berkeley's nominalism was the limitation it placed on our ability to understand semeiosis. On the one hand, Peirce routinely praised Berkeley for his pragmatic insight "that every thought is a sign" (CP 5.470; see also W 2:173, 241). In one such instance he again revealed his ambiguous attachment to Berkeley:

> Every competent critic will recognize in me a disciple of Berkeley, although I am utterly opposed to his Nominalism, and although his denial of Matter, bad enough in his own day, has become ridiculous in ours. His attack on infinitesimals is of a piece with his Nominalism. But the Truth of Berkeleianism lies in his hinging

all philosophy,—all *Coenoscopy*, to borrow Bentham's excellent
word,—on the concept SIGN. (MS 641, p. 18)

Berkeley began by noting that our ideas are themselves signs[23] and
then played this into his idealism so that, as Fraser maintained, "Natural causation is natural symbolism, dependent on, and expressive of,
the perfect reason and will of God."[24] Our world, literally, becomes a
world of signs.

This pervasiveness of semeiosis was, of course, attractive to Peirce.
But again Berkeley's nominalism interfered with his insight. For
Peirce, signs *are* general, but for Berkeley they bear no generality (see,
for example, CP 6.344 and Turrisi, p. 149). At best, from Peirce's
perspective, Berkeley can generate a semeiotic of indexicality or reference, though even this, as Peirce saw it, involves relation and therefore generality. Realism, in admitting generality, offers a considerably
more powerful semeiotic. For the realist, "general conceptions enter
into all judgments, and therefore into true opinions" (CP 8.14). The
consequence of Berkeley's nominalistic Platonism, then, is not only
an impoverished semeiotic but the loss of the ordinary features of
human reasoning: "But the sense of Berkeley's implication would be
that there is no truth and no judgments but propositions spoken or
on paper" (CP 8.26, n. 9).[25] It is precisely this consequence that made
Peirce resist the alliance of nominalism and science.

There were a variety of key ideas that Peirce thought important for
late-nineteenth-century science and for which he believed Berkeley's
nominalism made no room: continuity, growth, evolution, and perhaps most important, species and law. As Peirce saw it, the "most
important reals" of our everyday world "have the mode of being of
what the nominalist calls 'mere' words, that is, general types and
would-bes. The nominalists are right in saying that these reals are
substantially of the nature of words; but their 'mere' reveals a complete misunderstanding of what our everyday world consists of" (CP
8.191). The wider quarrel Peirce had with Berkeley's nominalistic Platonism that is evidenced in these examples is that it was unable to do
what it set out to do: to establish an adequate constraint on our ideas

that is not completely foreign to them, and to make our ideas—our world—intelligible. The central reason Peirce saw for this failure was the inadequacy inherent in Berkeley's reliance on existence as the single category or mode of being. Peirce took his own realism to be more inclusive and thus more adequate for addressing human experience. As Edward Moore notes, the distinction between reals and existents is crucial: "firsts are real (5.118), seconds are real (6.349), and thirds are real (5.122). But only seconds *exist* (5.429)."[26]

In Berkeley, Peirce saw both a kindred, pragmatic spirit working his way back toward a scholastic realism, and a nominalistic Platonist foreshadowing Peirce's nominalistic, scientistic contemporaries who "recognize but one mode of being, the being of an individual thing or fact" (CP 1.21). Peirce had a genuine historical interest in Berkeley, but his interest was more than historical. Berkeley served also as a marker of nominalism's failure, and was thus useful in Peirce's own battles with the likes of Karl Pearson, whose nominalism led to the assertion that "it is we who make the Laws of Nature" (MS 641, p. 22). In concert with his assessment of Berkeley's nominalistic Platonism, Peirce was able to say in response to Pearson, as we will detail in chapter 8, that with his three modes of being, he embraced a realism that is inclusive of the nominalist's existents, that maintains an independent constraint on individual thought in the "would be" final opinion of an indefinite inquiry, and that authorizes science's quest for laws that are of nature and not of our making.

Peirce's resistance to Berkeley as a nominalistic pragmatist reveals his insistence on the linkage between pragmatism and scholastic realism. When we turn to the historical development of pragmatism in its American setting, the notion of scholastic realism becomes a useful tool for assessing similarities and differences between Peirce's outlook and those of other self-professed pragmatists.

TWO

WHO'S A PRAGMATIST
Royce, Dewey, and Peirce at the Turn of the Century

Doug Anderson

This essay grew out of conversations concerning the philosophical simi-larities among the early pragmatists, including Royce. Often their differ-ences seem exaggerated and their shared beliefs overlooked, in large part because of contemporary pragmatists' tendency to self-identify as Royce-ans, Jamesians, Deweyans, and Peirceans. These conversations led me to reread the early pragmatists, attending to the ways in which they influ-enced one another.

[Pragmatism] is, so far, a house at war against itself concerning not incon-siderable questions; but perhaps this will not endanger its stability, and it certainly renders the discussions more interesting.

Charles Peirce, *The Nation* 3 (1905): 233

I. Introduction

Ultimately, it may not matter much who is or is not a pragmatist. There are some reasonable political motivations at any given time for wanting or not wanting to be counted as among the pragmatists, depending on whether pragmatism is or is not in vogue. But if we ask how the question "who is a pragmatist?" was answered by Josiah Royce, Charles Peirce, and John Dewey in the early years of the twentieth century, we find some interesting answers that we can use to help sketch a picture of where their respective philosophical commitments lay. It is an interesting heuristic tool. Seeing how they answered the question helps us sharpen the boundaries and borders among their respective outlooks. The foci of my particular query are Royce's, Dewey's, and Peirce's notions of a method of inquiry and their respective assessments of what Peirce called his "scholastic realism." Here I follow Peirce, who in a 1905 letter to Mario Calderoni wrote, "Pragmaticism [the "first kind of pragmatism"] is not a system of philosophy. It is only a method of thinking." It is a method, he stated, that also "best comports" with his common sensism and, consequently, his scholastic realism (CP 8.206–08). And in 1904 Peirce similarly wrote to William James: "The most important consequence of it [pragmatism], by far . . . is that under the conception of reality we must abandon nominalism" (CP 8.258). My hunch is that though there are clear continuities among their views, Peirce explicitly marked out and developed a strong middle ground between Royce's "absolute pragmatism" and Dewey's "instrumentalism." Holding this middle ground was important precisely because it allowed Peirce to capture a wider range of human experience and natural history than he believed was captured by Royce or Dewey in their more extreme moments.

In his recent essay "Peirce's Place in the Pragmatist Tradition," Sami Pihlström maintains that there were many more affinities among the early pragmatists than is sometimes acknowledged. Here he follows in the tradition of John E. Smith, Max Fisch, and Stan Thayer, among others. I agree with Pihlström's observation and thus begin by answering my own question with the claim that all of the above are pragmatists, and I would add to the mix without hesitation William James and F. C. S. Schiller. What is interesting to me is that

not all the early pragmatists answered in this fashion. I am not referring here to Peirce's well-known renaming of his own position as
"pragmaticism." On the contrary, it appears that Peirce was more inclusive than his pragmatic kin. Royce, after first rejecting pragmatism
as James and Peirce initially presented it, later commandeered it by
transforming it into what he believed was its only workable form: absolute pragmatism. Dewey in turn traced the development of Royce's
thought, arguing that Royce, contrary to his claim, had never been a
pragmatist.

Royce initially attacked the pragmatic method in *The Religious Aspect of Philosophy,* where he argued that inquiry—the quest for truth
and the avoidance of error—could not be conducted in the absence
of an absolute judge. His argument there was a reduction to the condition of the possibility of error, and it was of a sort that Peirce would
have classified as *a priori.* For Royce, *"The conditions that determine
the possibility of error must themselves be absolute truth,"*[1] and the central condition he found was the actual presence of an "absolute
judge" whose judgment was inclusive of all finite judgments. The
"truth" he claimed to find was this: *"All reality must be present to the
Unity of the Infinite Thought."*[2] Part of what I hope to show is that
though this "truth" underwent extensive reconstruction over the
course of Royce's career—much of it under the influence of Peirce's
thought—it was never fully abandoned. And it is just this unrecon-
structed part of Royce's outlook that established the border between
his thought and Peirce's regarding method of inquiry and scholastic
realism. The target of Royce's criticism at this juncture was a Thrasy-
machus-like character that he created who argued that only a *"possible* judge" was requisite for making a distinction between truth and
error—that is, error could be understood as what an ultimate judge
"would" reject in the long run of inquiry. Royce argued that in the
absence of an actual and absolute judge, such a pragmatic Thrasymachus would be set adrift in inquiry, never knowing where he was
headed. In Peircean terms, the Thrasymachus character believed "the
real is that which any man would believe in, and be ready to act upon,
if his investigations were to be pushed sufficiently far" (CP 8.41, W

5:22). As a pragmatist, Peirce believed the true and the real were best understood in relation to the consequences of inquiry. In "What Pragmatism Is" he maintained that

> thought, controlled by a rational experimental logic, tends to the fixation of certain opinions, equally destined, the nature of which will be the same in the end, however the perversity of thought of whole generations may cause the postponement of the ultimate fixation. If this be so, as every man of us virtually assumes that it is, in regard to each matter the truth of which he seriously discusses, then, according to the adopted definition of "real," the state of things which will be believed in that ultimate opinion is real. But, for the most part, such opinions will be general. Consequently, *some* general objects are real. (CP 5.430, W 5:22)

Royce argued that no such long-run investigation could get off the ground without an *a priori* commitment to reality's *presence* in the unity of Infinite Thought. And at least for much of his career, he conceived this unity of thought, as had Berkeley, as an ultimate individual, not as a general. Royce did not identify the model for his pragmatist-like Thrasymachus. However, it is difficult not to agree with Peirce that the argument as stated is a direct attack on pragmatism, particularly Peircean pragmatism. In response Peirce wrote with his usual irony, "But I must with shame confess that if I understand what the opinion of this poor, Royce-forsaken Thrasymachus is, I coincide with it exactly" (CP 8.41).

Initially we see then that Royce set his idealism over against pragmatism; but that is not where he left the issue. In the years between the 1885 publication of *The Religious Aspect of Philosophy* and his 1903 Presidential Address to the American Philosophical Association, Royce's thought underwent some dramatic shifts after he had read and listened to the arguments of Peirce. In *The World and the Individual*, we see traces of Peirce's ideas of continuity, generality, and pragmatic meaning allowing Royce to construct a more dynamic account of the finite person's relationship to the whole of things. By 1903, then, Royce had come to see himself as a kind of pragmatist, and it was in his Presidential Address that he began to answer the question, "who's a pragmatist?" The strategy he employed was provocative and straightforward. He identified what he called "pure pragmatism"— which he tacitly aligned with the work of James, Schiller, and Dewey— as the view that whatever beliefs meet one's subjective needs and thus "work" are true. This view is what Royce often raised when stating his concern for the "mutability of truth." Whether and to what extent James, Schiller, or Dewey actually held such a view is not important at this juncture. What is important is that Royce used this description as a way of taking pragmatism in his own direction. Using arguments similar to those in *The Religious Aspect of Philosophy*, he maintained that no one who was a "pure pragmatist" could engage in meaningful dialogue concerning truth and error, and the consequence of this was that though pure pragmatism might be stated or believed by some-one, it was not a tenable *philosophical position*. In practical terms, Royce argued, one cannot be a practicing pure pragmatist; "a pure pragmatist," he claimed, "is . . . self-refuting."[3] His reductive argu-ment cleared the ground for him to identify himself as a pragmatist of a different sort, an "absolute pragmatist." "We must be pragma-tists," he argued, "but we must also be more than pragmatists."[4] Royce began by pointing out that he, like the "official" pragmatists, saw philosophy's importance as bringing thought to bear on the con-duct of life, and he had a wealth of evidence to present of having done so, from his earliest ethical writings to his later work on loyalty, community, and race issues. However, his absolute pragmatism pro-vided the grounds for entering into the quest for truth in what he believed was a legitimate way not available to the pure pragmatist. With absolute pragmatism as the only viable—workable—form of pragmatism, Royce implicitly excluded others from the pragmatic camp; in being pure pragmatists they could not effectively engage in inquiry and therefore were not able to make sense of philosophy's commitment to the conduct of life.

Royce's answer, then, was that he was a pragmatist, but that James, Schiller, and Dewey, strictly speaking, were not. At best, they were offering an impractical pragmatism. Given his acknowledged debts to

Peirce, Royce, it seems, counted Peirce among the absolute pragmatists and not among those who claimed pure pragmatism as their own. He at least seems to have been correct in believing that Peirce shared his concern about the mutability of truth in the outlooks of some other pragmatists. However, this agreement does not by itself bring Peirce into Royce's camp, as I will try to show in a moment. First, however, let us turn to Dewey's response to the question at hand.

Dewey, of course, employed and defended the ideas of both James and Peirce in the early twentieth century. Indeed, though it is often remarked that Peirce's influence on Dewey developed gradually, Dewey was early on familiar with three of Peirce's series of essays: the so-called "cognition" series, the "Illustrations of the Logic of Science" that included the "Fixation of Belief" and "How to Make Our Ideas Clear," and the *Monist* series on cosmology of the 1890s. A close reading of *Democracy and Education* reveals a wide range of affinities with these Peircean essays. Moreover, Dewey's 1916 essay "The Philosophy of Peirce" shows that Dewey already had an excellent grasp of Peirce's core thought as well as an insightful understanding of the differences between Peirce and James. It was also in 1916 that Dewey took Royce to task for trying to identify himself as a pragmatist. For Dewey, Peirce, James, and Schiller were pragmatists but Royce was not; rather, Royce, he argued, was initially a moral absolutist who found that a metaphysical absolutism was needed to sustain his ethics. As Frank Oppenheim suggests, this aligns Dewey with the mainstream reading of pragmatism that excludes "Royce completely from the pragmatic tradition or at best gives him minimal notice."[5] Comparing an early and a more recent work of Royce, Dewey declared that "what the transition from the voluntarism of the earlier essay to the intellectualism of the later exhibits, is not a change from pragmatism to absolutism, but a recognition of the objective absolutism latent in any ethical absolutism."[6]

The key issue for Dewey had to do with Royce's conceptions of reality and truth. As we have seen, Royce's absolutist metaphysics committed him to a reality and truth that are, in some way, already actualized. That is to say, reality for Royce was a fixed, unified whole and the story to be told about it—the truth—was equally fixed and whole. Such conceptions satisfied Royce's inclination for an *a priori* method, and a consequence of this, as I will try to show in a bit, was that "inquiry" for Royce became a matter of re-establishing or de-scribing the nature of this unified whole. This certainly foreclosed on Dewey's more open, experimentalist approach to inquiry. It made the immediate act of judgment, rather than the judgments of the long run of inquiry, crucial to truth determination. As Dewey put it, taking Peirce as the authoritative pragmatist, "It is the *act* of Acknowledge-ment which is emphasized. There is no reference to determination or measure by consequences. Now Peirce repudiated just such a position."[7]

Thus Royce and Dewey, in quite different ways, sought to exclude each other from the camp of functioning pragmatism. At the same time, both men included Peirce among the pragmatists, in part be-cause James had identified Peirce as the originator of the movement but also in part because they saw strong likenesses between Peirce's thought and their own. In one feature of pragmatism, Royce and Dewey actually stood closer together than either did with Peirce—that is, they both addressed social issues directly in their roles as pro-fessional philosophers. This was something that Peirce both by inclination and by intent for the most part avoided. This emphasis on the practical may be at least one reason that Peirce in turn identified both Royce and Dewey as pragmatists; ironically, perhaps, he was more inclusive than they in answering the question, "who is a prag-matist?" Given the mainstream accounts of pragmatism, we may have a temptation to jump to the conclusion that Dewey was more right than Royce—but Peirce had good reasons for seeing both of them as pragmatists, but not pragmaticists.

In a 1905 letter draft to Schiller, responding to Schiller's own at-tempt to define pragmatism, Peirce wrote: "I would let it grow and then say it is what a certain group of thinkers who seem to under-stand one another think, and thus make it the name of a natural class in the Natural History fashion" (MS L390, p. 3). Interestingly, Peirce's move, in acknowledging the developmental nature of pragmatism, seems more pragmatic in spirit than that of Schiller, who attempted a knockdown definition along more medieval lines of genus and difference. In this response we can see the traces of Peirce's realism and his commitment to the real generality of "pragmatism." Pragmatism, as a method of thinking, is a general class that is produced naturally and historically. As such, it takes on a life of its own. It embodies real generality precisely because it is able to hold together such different thinkers as Royce and Dewey. It acknowledges real possibility just insofar as pragmatism remains open to growth and development in the future. In short, Peirce in his very defining of pragmatism revealed his commitment to both real generality and real possibility. Thus despite the fact that Peirce felt compelled, because of *particular* unwanted affiliations, to rename his own view "pragmaticism," he included all the usual suspects as pragmatists. In his letter to Calderoni, he explicitly identified James, Schiller, Royce, and Dewey as members of the pragmatic movement (CP 8.205). Furthermore, as we noted, he here indicated that pragmaticism was to be understood as an initial version of pragmatism, not as a fundamental alternative. The upshot is that Peirce saw the thought of Royce and Dewey both as continuous with his own and at the same time as bearing marks of distinction. In finding where Peirce might locate these marks of distinction—the borders between his thought and theirs—we can get a clearer sense not only of where he stood, but why.

II. Royce and Peirce

Pihlström maintains that Royce "developed a mixture of pragmatism and Hegelian idealism . . . that was closer to Peirce's views than were most other classical formulations of pragmatism."[8] As I will try to show, when all is said and done, this seems in some ways an accurate statement. There were some important respects in which Royce's later outlook was "closer to Peirce's views" than were the views of Dewey and James. Royce acknowledged his debts to Peirce, and as John Hermann Randall suggests, Peirce pointed Royce in the direction of two central ideas: "the mathematical notion of an infinite series, and the notion of a community of interpretation."[9] But, as I will also try to show, Pihlström's claim stands in need of some qualification.

My specific agreement with his claim grows from the belief that two central features of Royce's work—one epistemological and one ontological—were highly influenced by his dialogue with Peirce, and that this influence brought Royce's philosophy steadily to look more and more like a Peircean view. As many commentators have pointed out, Royce modified his theory of inquiry from an immediate relationship between an individual inquirer and an absolute judge of truth to an ongoing interpretive act by a community of inquirers whose final claims would constitute the truth of the whole. On the ontological side, Peirce's scholastic realism, in some ways, merged well with Royce's idealistic commitment to the reality of relations, classes, and communities.

My qualification of Pihlström's claim is that Royce remained a step—or as Peirce liked to say, "a hair's breadth"—away from Peirce's pragmaticism both epistemologically and ontologically. Consequently, there were some features of Peirce's pragmaticism that were *better* captured by Dewey's instrumentalist pragmatism. I will turn to a consideration of this claim in the second half of this chapter. My present aim is to try to show how Royce remained a hair's breadth from becoming a pragmaticist even as Peirce openly embraced him as a pragmatist.

I take as given, then, the fact that Peirce influenced Royce's thought in some important ways; my focus will be on the several ways in which, despite this influence, Royce set himself apart.[10] My hope is that marking these points of difference will help bring into relief a few key features of Peirce's middle-ground pragmatism.

If we return to Peirce's review of *The Religious Aspect of Philosophy*, we can begin to trace the points of resistance between Peirce and Royce. Royce's resistance to the Thrasymachus character's probabilism at root revealed his distrust in an inductive, experimental method that lived with no up-front guarantee of success. Thus, in his review, Peirce argued that "Dr. Royce and his school, I am well aware, consider inductive reasoning to be radically vicious" (CP 8.43, W 5:226). He further noted, foreshadowing later disagreements, that "they often deny this . . . and say they rest entirely on experience" (CP 8.43, W 5:226). In short, from Peirce's perspective, Royce's deductive, dilemma-driven reasoning was apriorist as a method; it was not "scientific" in the sense articulated in "The Fixation of Belief." For Peirce, "Induction gives us the only approach to certainty concerning the real that we can have" (CP 8.209). My suggestion is that even as Royce's epistemological and ontological outlooks changed drastically in the next thirty years under the influence of Peirce's thought, he never overcame this initial fear of the fundamental instability of induction. To make a brief case, I turn first to Peirce's reviews of *The World and the Individual* and then to a look at the method of inquiry and the ontological commitments expressed in Royce's later logical writings.

Both in his published reviews and in private correspondence, Peirce openly praised much of the content of Royce's *The World and the Individual*. He especially praised Royce's more synechistic understanding of the World that overcame and replaced his earlier radical fragmentation of individuals from each other and from God. As Royce put it in *Studies of Good and Evil*: "The nature-experience, so our hypothesis supposes, is, in at least a considerable degree, relatively continuous with ours. That is, there is experience in nature which closely resembles human experience; there is other experience which less resembles ours, but which need not be lower; there is conscious experience still more remote from ours; and so on."[11] Peirce also endorsed Royce's developing pragmatic description of the meaning of ideas: "in the same pragmatistic spirit, Prof. Royce holds that the Internal Meaning of an idea is a Purpose, obscurely recognized in consciousness, partially fulfilled in being recognized but mainly unfulfilled and ill-understood in itself. The external meaning lies in the fulfillment of the purpose" (CP 8.119). His difficulties with *The World and the Individual* had to do with the fact that, as Peirce saw it, Royce did not alter his method to match these developments in ontology. As he wrote to James in 1902: "I have been studying Royce's book.

The ideas are very beautiful. The logic is most execrable. I don't think it good taste to stuff it so full of the name of God" (CP 8.277).

Royce was still in the habit of employing his reductive dilemmas to establish absolute truths which, he believed, no thinking person could disavow. He argued this way even as he was laying the groundwork for his later community of interpreters. Peirce labeled Royce's method "a mere apotheosis of the dilemma" (CP 8.48). Royce's adherence to his old method must have baffled Peirce just insofar as Royce seemed to embrace his pragmatic conception of meaning. "Now by the internal meaning or purpose of an idea," Peirce wrote, "Prof. Royce, if we rightly gather his intention, understands all the experiments which would verify it. . . . This internal meaning calls, then, for more and more definiteness without cessation" (CP 8.115). From Peirce's angle, this must have looked as if Royce had made his peace with the probabilist Thrasymachus. Yet despite his transformed understanding of the meaning of an idea, Royce continued in his practice to employ his old method of inquiry, and it was this practice that Peirce found execrable:

> It follows, that deductive, or mathematical, reasoning, although in metaphysics it may oftener "take the stage" than in the drama of special research, yet after all, has precisely the same *role* to enact, and nothing more. All genuine advance must come from real observation and inductive reasoning. Yet Dr. Royce cannot free himself from the Hegelian notion that the one satisfactory method in philosophy is to examine an opinion and to detect in it some hidden denial of itself,—which is nothing but the *reductio ad absurdum*. (CP 8.110)

And for Peirce this "Hegelian" method is nothing but a version of *a priori* reasoning, for "Absolute idealism depends, as Hegel saw that it did, upon assuming that position at the outset" (CP 8.130).

Royce's lingering Cartesian fear of induction was closely coupled with an ontological/cosmological feature of his conception of God or the Whole both in his 1897 lecture "The Conception of God" and in *The World and the Individual* (1899–1901). That is, Royce still considered God in an Augustinian way as a unifying, eternal Individual who actually and, as it were, "presently" transcended and incorporated all finite existence. As Royce maintained in the introduction to his text, we inquire because we seek "a passage to absolute determinateness," and part of our quest is "to know what the whole individual Being called the World is; and who the Individual of Individuals, namely, the Absolute, or God himself is."[12] Insofar as this God in its eternality was the alpha and omega of "what is" in its determinateness, all inquiry—even inductive inquiry—could be seen from a divine perspective as *a priori* and deductive. That is, induction could be construed simply as the explication over time of "what is" by finite inquirers. Such a World is in principle already closed. Such an ontological scheme—offered both as an assumption of and as a result of Royce's method—stood beyond what Peirce believed we either *did* or *could* know with certainty. Indeed, Peirce thought that scientific inquiry, rather than revealing to us a closed and fixed Whole, suggested a developing World that was synechistic but still tychistic, always harboring an element of chance.

For Peirce, tychism was a subordinate correlate of synechism. Not only is the universe constituted of real generality but also of real vagueness. There are real possibles that stand outside already developed habits of nature, such that, as Peirce saw it, the habits or laws of nature were themselves open to change. As he wrote to Christine Ladd-Franklin in 1891: "The tendency to form habits or tendency to generalize, is something which grows by its own action, by the habit of taking habits itself growing. Its first germ arose from pure chance" (CP 8.317). As William James wrote to Peirce, it was just this feature of tychism that most fascinated him; and it was precisely James's affinity for tychism, leading to battles over the import of spontaneity, freedom, and pluralism, that kept Royce and James perpetually at odds. Throughout his later work, Royce often mentioned Peirce's allegiance to real chance with a sound of hesitancy. In *Studies of Good and Evil*, for example, Royce described Peirce's notion of chance "by scientific thinking, as standing for the merely 'individual' or 'internal' element of our experience, or for the limitations of the individual point of view."[13] Thus, chance is a contingency of finitude and not a real feature of the Absolute. Later in the same text Royce indicated that his differences with Peirce's cosmological essays centered on the reality of "objective 'chance,' and whether all natural law is, in the last analysis, a product of evolution."[14] Royce was therefore a Peircean realist of law but not of possibility. "On the topic of chance," Oppenheim observes, "a marked difference in their thinking persisted almost to the end."[15] I would argue that this difference persisted all the way to the end. Thus, Royce's adherence to his early method, which, as he believed, yielded some absolute truths, had to do with his belief that these truths would keep the World from being loose-ended in just the way Peirce portrayed it.

Peirce read Royce's work closely and noted not only his residual commitment to the method of reductive dilemma but also his resistance to the reality of chance and possibility. As he wrote in his 1897 review of "The Conception of God," he believed Royce disregarded "genuinely possible worlds" and in the end was "still unwilling to admit an element of blind force in the universe" (N, p.152). Out of respect for each other as thinkers, Royce and Peirce usually spoke plainly in their correspondence. Thus, both in his 1902 reviews of *The World and the Individual* and in a 1902 letter to Royce, Peirce urged Royce to "revolutionize" his method. "The time is ripe," he said, "and you are the very man to accomplish the great achievement of covering that distance [between philosophy and science]. Yet you could not do it with your present views of logic, antagonistic to all that is possible for progressive science. My entreaty is that you will study logic" (CP 8.117).

As Mary Mahowald insightfully suggests, "in general the relationship of Royce to Peirce may be characterized as one of deference, his relationship to James as one of friendship."[16] Thus, when Peirce entreated Royce to study logic, he did so. And, as Oppenheim points out, from "1902 to 1905 and thereafter, with Peirce as mentor, Royce engaged with him in a quasi-correspondence course in logic."[17] The results, as anyone who has studied *The Problem of Christianity* (1913) or Royce's later logical writings knows, are impressive. Royce gave Peirce's ideas of community, semeiosis, and interpretation a fully social context, taking them in fruitful directions Peirce would not have done on his own. Furthermore, Royce's discussions of relation, class, and order offered a new way of thinking about metaphysical categories. But again, it is to the points of difference that I turn my attention.

Royce openly acknowledged his pragmatic turn in *The Problem of Christianity*: "As to certain metaphysical opinions which are stated, in outline, in the second volume of this book, I now owe much more to a great and unduly neglected American logician, Mr. Charles Peirce, than I do to the common tradition of recent idealism."[18] And in his 1916 lectures on metaphysics he told his students, "I follow Charles Peirce in proposing a third mode of knowledge, interpretation, which has the character of a triadic form of knowledge and requires distinctly a social relation to make it such."[19] The focus on the triadic relation, on the social context of developing knowledge, and on the importance of interpreting the world gave all of Royce's later work a distinctively Peircean flavor. From this it might be easy to draw Pihlström's conclusion that Royce stood closer to Peirce than did other pragmatists. Indeed, these were all the reasons why Peirce rightly included Royce as a member of the natural class of pragmatists. Nevertheless, a close reading of *The Problem of Christianity* and the later logical writings reveals Royce's non-pragmaticistic claims and suggests that we, and Peirce himself, might need to turn to Dewey, and perhaps to James, to draw a more complete picture of Peirce's own version of pragmatism. To bring the Roycean side of my project to a close, then, let me turn to a brief look at some of his later logical writings, with an emphasis on the 1912 *Principles of Logic*.

Royce opens the *Principles* by stating the importance of developing a method of inquiry. He walks the reader through Peirce's three stages of inquiry and the importance of statistical reasoning for modern research. His account of the stages, however, subtly shifts emphases in a non-Peircean direction. He downplays, for example, the ampliative nature of abduction, describing it primarily as the tendency to classify. He aligns induction once again with the "pragmatists"—here meaning his negative construal of James and Dewey—and he associates it with the

temptation to speak of truth in terms of probability, suggesting a slippery slope to the "mutability of truth." Finally, he asserts the importance of deduction in constituting theories, and indirectly, for asserting
existences, in stark contrast to Peirce's earlier warning, aimed directly
at Royce, arguing that "all that necessary reasoning can do is to keep
an initial hypothesis consistent with itself; it cannot prove any matter
of fact" (N, p. 151). Royce's resistance to chance is here paralleled by an
implicit fear of the spontaneity of abduction and an attraction for the
stabilizing comfort of deduction. The upshot is that even as Royce
openly tries to bridge the distance between philosophy and science as
Peirce had urged, he reverts to his original practices. Having laid out
the importance of interpretation and statistics, Royce then turns to
making scientific method ultimately dependent on some *a priori* absolute truths. "And thus a general review of Methodology," he argues,
"leads us to the problems of the Science of Order."[20]

The "Science of Order," it turns out, is not interpretive, because
its "problems" lead us to ask about the conditions of scientific inquiry, setting us up for a transcendental argument. Science, Royce
maintains, initially must deal with individuals; then it must come to
grips with relations, and relations, he argues, "are impossible unless
there are also classes."[21] All of these—individuals, relations, and
classes—in turn depend even more fundamentally on types of order:
"to be reasonable," for Royce, "is to conceive of order systems, real
or ideal."[22]

Now Royce sees a pragmatic element in our "will to order" just
insofar as our classifying activities follow our chosen purposes. But
our selective establishment of classes and orders itself must, he argues, be underwritten by a more general tendency to employ classes
and types of order. Once again, we find Royce turning to a dilemma:
either order is real, or our thought is unintelligible; either the world
is itself determinately orderly, or it is unintelligible. Thus, he claims,
"the act of defining at least some norms or principles of classification
is an act whose logical value is not only pragmatist, but also absolute."[23] As Oppenheim describes, then, Royce continues to employ

"his dialectical 'reflective method' which led to performatory contradictions that opened one's inner door to an experience of absolute truth."[24]

In "The Fixation of Belief" Peirce had begun by asking what method of settling opinion would satisfy someone who was interested in what he called "the logical question"—that is, how can we learn what we don't know from what we do know? He then moved through the methods to show that the scientific method best met the conditions of the logical question. However, he left his conclusion in a hypothetical condition—if one seeks to address the logical question, this method appears to be the most reasonable. He employed dilemmas, but not to generate absolute truths; the concluding paragraph of the "Fixation" is instructive because it calls for an existential commitment to the scientific method. In short, the method is operable in practice even if not absolute, so long as we have no living doubts about it. Nevertheless, committing to this method of inquiry leaves the method itself as another strand on a cable of mutually sustaining beliefs.

In principle, the method, just as its results, is open to criticism and further revision. This is the model that Dewey would develop so elaborately, incorporating as he went more and more historicist features. And it is here that Royce remains an apriorist. From the point of view of the other pragmatists, Royce argues, "the logical hypothesis: 'that there are classes, relations, and order-systems,' would be true merely insofar as the acts of conceiving such objects, and of treating them as real, have, under the empirical conditions under which we do our thinking, a successful result." That is, "the logical existence and validity of classes, of relations, and of various types of order, would stand in the same position in which all the 'working hypotheses' of an empirical science stand."[25] The pragmatists, he complains, "are disposed to admit a maximum of the empirical and the contingent into the theory of order."[26] Even if he does not admit a "maximum" of contingency and the empirical, Peirce admits *some*, and this stands in sharp contrast to Royce's absolutism.

Thus, even in his most pragmatic accounts of reasoning, Royce remained tied to his earliest method: "[W]e have already indicated that, so far as the existence of classes and of relations in general is in question, and in so far as the validity of certain logical laws is concerned, we are obliged to maintain a position we may characterize by the term Absolute Pragmatism."[27] For Royce, the reduction to the order of orders, classes, and relations meets the criterion for absolute knowledge—in denying them, one must admit them. "In sum," he argued, "an absolute truth is one whose denial implies the reassertion of that same truth."[28]

Regarding method, Royce remained at least a hair's breadth from Peirce's pragmaticism. Instead of finally bridging science and philosophy as Peirce had urged, Royce left science to rest on *a priori* philosophical claims. Though it is not my aim to develop it here, let me sketch the *a priori* method's presence in two examples. One is Royce's conception of statistics in *The Principles of Logic,* in which he describes the need for statistical reasoning as a function of our finitude.[29] The world about which we inquire, he intimates, is a fully determinate continuum in which there is not room for real vagueness or chance that might make statistical analyses appropriate to the world itself. We employ statistics only because *we* cannot have an immediate, absolute vision of the world. The same can be seen in *The Problem of Christianity* when Royce redefines the World in terms of a developing community of interpretation. Mahowald is right in asserting that "in regard to interpretation, God, and Community, the mature writings of Royce definitely show a more pragmatic strain than did his early works."[30] Even so, Royce wrote to Reginald Robbins in 1914 of his theory of community as influenced by Peirce: "Here is a theory that allows for the endless variety of individual 'interpretation,' and for endless change, growth and fluency, while 'absoluteness' is nevertheless a 'chronosynoptic' and universal, above all and in all the flow and the tragedy of this world whose unity means that it 'contains its own interpreter.' "[31] The variety and plurality are made available by Royce's scholastic-realist take on community and the

Whole—interpretation is a historical process carried out by real individuals and communities with differing angles of vision on the Whole. Nevertheless, the variety and growth to which he alluded remain absolutely constrained by the progress of the Absolute; in other words, however infinite the interpretation process might be, it is always determined by the dictates of the Absolute itself. Royce never came around in his ontological and cosmological speculation to admitting real chance and real possibility. Thus, if we were to have an absolute rather than a finite point of view, the world would appear necessary to us. Possibility in Royce's scheme must be construed as a function of our finite and fragmented perspective. In the end, he captured well enough Peirce's emphasis on real generals, but he stayed shy of admitting real possibles that might in spontaneous fashion alter the habits of nature.

Reading Royce as a pragmatist helps us to see the ways in which he appropriated and developed Peirce's synechism, the reality of generals, the methodological and ontological importance of community, and semeiosis as a living and systematic process. Focusing on the ways in which he was not a pragmaticist, though the results may seem obvious to some, helps direct us toward the affinities between Peirce and Dewey and James. More than Royce, for example, Dewey was committed to "the free, the indeterminate, the growing, the potential factor in reality."[32] Moreover, Dewey clearly recognized and understood Peirce's scholastic realism and focused much of his work on the role habits play in cultural development. Such likenesses are often eclipsed because Peirceans, Jamesians, and Deweyans like to highlight differences to mark out their own ground of conversation. Seeing the limits of the identity of "absolute pragmatism" and "pragmaticism" forces us to consider the ways in which Dewey and James stood closer to Peirce than did Royce. Royce and Peirce were at odds on some difficult questions: Is the pragmatic, experimental method itself open to criticism and revision? Is it tested only in its use? Do the habits of nature ever evolve in spontaneous ways involving real chance, such that the world is not the determinate continuum Royce envisioned?

As isolated philosophical issues, these may not seem all that important. However, from a pragmatic point of view, our answers to such
questions hold important consequences for conduct in science and
ethics. Peirce and Royce, for example, must ultimately hold decidedly
different accounts of scientific experiment, artistic creativity, and education. For as Dewey rightly stated in describing Peirce's scholastic
realism, "not only are generals real, but they are physically efficient."[33] As helpful as Royce is in showing us some potential fruits of
Peircean pragmaticism, we must look to others in the natural history
of pragmatism to offer complementary fruits in the practices of science, politics, and art.

III. Peirce and Dewey

If Royce's absolute pragmatism is akin to Peirce's pragmaticism in
some ways, Dewey's early instrumentalist pragmatism is akin in other
ways. We have already seen that Royce tried to exclude the "pure
pragmatists"—James, Schiller, and, presumably, Dewey—from the
camp of genuine pragmatists, and that Dewey, in turn, argued that
Royce had never been anything but an apriorist idealist. In this second part of the chapter, I want to sketch Dewey's two central affinities
with Peircean realism—his belief in the reality of habits and in the
reality of possibility. I will also suggest how Peirce sought, as was the
case with Royce, to distance himself from certain aspects of Dewey's
early logical theory in order to hold to the middle ground I described
earlier.

Dewey's assertion that for Peirce generals are real and physically
efficient leads into an assessment of the role of habits in our experience. In his 1903 essay "Logical Conditions of a Scientific Treatment
of Morality," Dewey argues that "the generic propositions or universals of science can take effect, in a word only through the medium of
the habits and impulsive tendencies of the one who judges."[34] At this
juncture in the text, he inserts a footnote asserting the proximity of
Peirce's ideas to his own. I quote it here at length:

So far as I know, Mr. Charles S. Peirce was the first to call attention to this principle, and to insist upon its fundamental logical
import (see *Monist*, Vol. II, pp. 534–36, 549–56). Mr. Peirce states
it as the principle of continuity: A past idea can operate only so
far as it is physically continuous with that upon which it operates.
A general idea is simply a living and expanding feeling, and habit
is a statement of the specific mode of operation of a given psychical continuum. I have reached the above conclusion along such
diverse lines that, without in any way minimizing the priority of
Mr. Peirce's statement, or its more generalized logical character,
I feel that my own statement has something of the value of an
independent confirmation.[35]

I do not doubt that Dewey arrived here along "diverse lines"—
indeed, this fact would help confirm Peirce's synechistic view of the
independent reality of ideas in a cultural history. However, inasmuch
as Dewey read widely among Peirce's early essays, one should not dis-
count some measure of more direct influence. The two avenues are
not mutually exclusive.

The reference Dewey makes is to Peirce's "The Law of Mind,"
where habits are the tendencies of a person to act in certain ways according to general ideas of one sort or another. The idea only receives
its agency in the habits of the thinker or "the one who judges," as
Dewey put it. The essential point is that habits are not merely resulting descriptions of previous behavior; they are real tendencies of a
"psychical continuum"—a "personality," in Peirce's vocabulary—to
act in certain ways under certain circumstances. Thus, a personality
is a growing matrix of continuous habits together with a capacity for
spontaneous or impulsive action. This spontaneous action is the
locus of the reality of possibility. At least at the level of human experience, then, Dewey and Peirce agree that continuity and possibility are
real and that general ideas are both open to modification and revision
and are generally efficacious through the real habits of actual
inquirers.

As did Peirce, Dewey knew the history of the nominalist-realist debate from the ancients to Roscelin to Abelard. Moreover, he agreed
with Peirce's assessment that Ockham's nominalism underwrote

much of the development of British empiricism. He also agreed that the central relevant questions regarding nominalism and realism at the end of the nineteenth century had to do with the status of natural or scientific laws and with the efficacy of ideas and habits in human experience. In his sketch of the history of nominalism and realism, Dewey pointed out that the idea of a universal or real general had evolved from that of essence to that of static general. But with the advent of scientific thinking this changed. "With recent thought," Dewey argued, "the universal becomes law, or method."[36] This was a turn that was clearly at the heart of Peirce's own updated "scholastic realism." "For Peirce," Dewey later argued, "understands by the reality of a 'general' the reality of a way, habit, disposition, of behavior."[37] Dewey's focus naturally fell on the work of habits in human experience. Despite his later rejection of Royce as a pragmatist, he saw the pragmatic school as open to creative development: "The pragmatic movement is still so loose and variable that I judge one has a right to fix his own meaning, provided he serves notice and adheres to it."[38] Thus, as early as 1903 Dewey identified his own version of the doctrine as "instrumentalist pragmatism" or "the doctrine of what Mr. James calls the 'Chicago School.'"[39]

In his description of instrumentalist pragmatism, Dewey openly avowed its disinterest in ontology and traditional versions of metaphysics: "Philosophy is a mode of knowing wherein reflective thinking is much in play. It is hence self-contradictory for an instrumental pragmatism to set up claims to supplying a metaphysics or ontology."[40] Moreover, unlike Peirce and Whitehead, Dewey did not find it interesting or useful to develop a speculative cosmology. Thus, to find realism in Dewey's work, as noted earlier, we must look elsewhere—specifically we must look in his descriptions of human experience. Here we find the two affinities described at the outset: reality of habit and of possibility.

Students of Dewey's work have long emphasized the importance of "habit." From his earliest psychological writings to his later ethical writings, Dewey highlighted the importance of habits in human behavior. Habits, for Dewey, are human attitudes or lived beliefs. They are general in nature, which is to say they govern particular actions by bringing a kind of rule or law to bear within a lived situation. And, as Dewey repeatedly pointed out, habits have efficacy—they affect our everyday actions in the world. Thus, human habits are akin to Peircean "reals"; it was, indeed, for this reason that Peirce occasionally identified natural laws as "habits" of nature. As we noted above, Dewey wrote: "Peirce understands by the reality of a 'general' the reality of a way, habit, disposition, of behavior; and he dwells upon the fact that the habits of things are acquired and modifiable."[41] Peirce made this connection explicit in the last of his 1878 *Popular Science Monthly* essays, with which Dewey was closely familiar: "That every belief is of the nature of a habit, in so far as it is of a general character, has been shown in the earlier papers of this series" (EP 1:198). Thus, Peircean beliefs as habits are both general and malleable—they can be modified, thoroughly revised, or, in some cases, fully rejected. This squares with Dewey's basic ideas regarding social transformation. The trick is not merely to try to alter specific actions, but to tailor human habits that might bring about and oversee ameliorative actions in a general way. One side of Dewey's focus on growth and education was the ability to transform our habits for both self and community development. As he put it: "If education were conducted as a process of fullest utilization of present resources, liberating and guiding capacities that are now urgent, it goes without saying that the lives of the young would be much richer in meaning than they are now."[42]

Peirce's pragmaticistic realism and Dewey's instrumental pragmatism are thus closely aligned in their descriptions of belief-habits as real generals. These habits govern much human conduct and, therefore, are crucial to the development of selves and communities. Indeed, both Dewey and Peirce focused much of their own work on how we can go about transforming our habits of reasoning—how by way of inquiry we can learn. As Dewey argued, "Pragmatism as attitude represents what Mr. Peirce has happily termed the 'laboratory habit of mind' extended into every area where inquiry may fruitfully be carried on."[43]

Habits, precisely because of their efficacy as real generals, are not, however, unqualified goods. As both Peirce and Dewey point out, well functioning habits—such as the laboratory habit of mind—can allow us to be productive in daily affairs. This is what Peirce tried to show in "The Fixation of Belief." And, as Dewey put it in "Reconstruction in Philosophy,"

> *If* ideas, meanings, conceptions, notions, theories, systems [all real generals] are instrumental to an active reorganization of the given environment, to a removal of some specific trouble and perplexity, then the test of their validity and value lies in accomplishing this work. If they succeed in their office, they are reliable, sound, valid, good, true.[44]

At the same time, habits, when not functioning well, can routinize our lives—for Peirce, perhaps, the cosmos as well—to the point of paralysis. For Dewey, the aim of human conduct thus becomes to maintain useful habits and to modify or jettison those habits whose consequences are stifling. Again, for Dewey,

> A life of complete routine, a condition of fossilized habit, though it be one in which every act corresponds quickly and accurately to some familiar feature of the environment, is not one that we desire. We want change, variety, growth.[45]

But if growth is not only desired but to be made possible, then habits, as real generals, must allow for rejection and revision. Development depends on possibilities—a world of thoroughly fixed habit would indicate the sort of necessitarianism against which Peirce argued in the 1890s. Thus, as Dewey rightly points out, Peirce

> dwells upon the fact that the habits of things are acquired and modifiable. Indeed, he virtually reverses Aristotle in holding that the universal always has an admixture of potentiality in it.[46]

For Peirce, both cosmic and personal habits have an admixture of potentiality for a kind of self-revision or self-overcoming. For him the universe, even as it grows more orderly, always retains elements of spontaneity—growth and development are constrained but never finished in Peirce's cosmology. In the personal realm, or the Deweyan realm of experience, the coupling of habits and potentiality is central. The very purpose of education has to do with enabling growth through employing and transforming habits. Herein lies the second "realistic" feature shared by Peirce and Dewey—the reality of possibility.

The closest Dewey gets to sharing Peirce's ontological realism of the possible appears in *Experience and Nature*:

> Against this common identification of reality with what is sure, regular, and finished, experience in unsophisticated forms gives us evidence of a different world and points to a different metaphysics. We live in a world which is an impressive and irresistible mixture of sufficiencies, tight completenesses, order, recurrences which make possible prediction and control, and singularities, ambiguities, uncertain possibilities, processes going on to consequences as yet indeterminate.[47]

Just as for Peirce, a mixture of order and spontaneity constitutes the world of human experience. But in the early days of pragmatism, Dewey focused primarily on possibility's role in the development of human selves and communities. This selective emphasis made good sense against the necessitarian background of absolute idealism and scientistic mechanism that ruled the intellectual scene at the time.

For Dewey, *instrumentalist* pragmatism was about transforming the world of our experience, and he was not shy in adopting his own version of what Royce in derogatory fashion referred to as "pure pragmatism":

> The popular impression that pragmatic philosophy means that philosophy shall develop ideas relevant to the actual crises of life, ideas influential in dealing with them and tested by the assistance they afford, is correct.[48]

Dewey's philosophers were not *a priori*–driven deductivists; they were artists and healers whose work hinged on experimental method, on creating and testing hypotheses to deal with the crises of existence. "A pragmatic intelligence," Dewey wrote, "is a creative intelligence, not a routine mechanic."[49] This was an outlook that Peirce too embraced, though for somewhat different reasons. For both Peirce and Dewey, the notions of growth, development, and creativity were underwritten by the reality of possibility and potentiality.

In his 1893 "The Superstition of Necessity," Dewey alluded in a footnote to the similarity of their outlooks regarding possibility and indeterminacy:

> This article, as the title may indicate, was suggested by Mr. Peirce's article upon "The Doctrine of Necessity Examined." As, however, my thought takes finally a different turn, I have deemed it better to let it run its own course from the start, and so have not referred, except indirectly, to Mr. Peirce's argument. I hope this will not be taken as a desire to slur over my indebtedness to him.[50]

Regardless of the depth of indebtedness, what Dewey and Peirce share is a belief in two ways in which habits have an "admixture of potentiality" such that creative intelligence can overcome the fixity of those that are deleterious. First, the generality of habits allows us to creatively embody or instantiate them in particular actions. Second, aims, ends, or ideals are a kind of habit-belief according to which we conduct our lives. For both Dewey and Peirce, these aims are not only general but vague in the sense of not being fully defined even in their generality. Such habit-beliefs are thus open to growth and development even as they are pursued experimentally; and, in the extreme, if they fail to yield desired outcomes, they are open to rejection and replacement by other ideal belief-habits.

The first of these two claims is perhaps the less controversial. Recall from chapter 1 Peirce's example of an apple pie. As an aim or end, an "apple pie" is general. Making an "apple pie" can be achieved successfully in a wide variety of particular instantiations. Thus, the individual organism (the pie baker) is free to bring new meaning to what it means to be or to make an apple pie. The idea—as aim or telos—grows; and the person who creates the new instantiation can likewise be said to grow, since her or his habits have been modified in an expansive way. "Hence," Dewey claimed, "the free, the indeterminate, the growing, the potential factor in reality. Meaning, significance is never just predetermined. It is always hanging upon the operation of the psychical, of the peculiarly individual."[51] This is akin to what Peirce called a "developmental teleology," a teleology not fully fixed by the pre-existing state of affairs.

Creativity in this first mode takes place *within* the generality of the belief-habit. The second mode—that of the vagueness of the real habit—suggests the full reviseability of the meaning of the belief-habit itself. It is transformative, not just expansive. Dewey's way of stating it was to align it with chance: "The vagueness or lack of determinateness in our end, the irrelevancy of actual end to conscious intent, chance, are all names of the same thing."[52] He pushed toward the Peircean ontological account—toward what Peirce called tychism. Still, Dewey focused on action—the indeterminacy and vagueness of a belief-habit or end-in-view is cashed out in our inability to know what will come about under its influence. There is risk and contingency in our world of endeavor. Dewey and Peirce shared Emerson's belief that we "live by experiment." Belief-habits, indeterminate toward the future, may run aground, become thoroughly vacuous and inefficacious, or may lead us into experiences of fuller luminosity. As self-controlled experimentation with belief-habits, creative intelligence works to govern itself in the face of contingency. Without this reality of the possible, without Peircean tychism, inquiry could revert to something like Royce's apriorism.

Creative intelligence, then, is both the ability to bring novelty into play in our worlds of experience *and* the ability to respond usefully to a world of contingency in which our belief-habits are never fully adequate but always stand in need of clarification, revision, or rejection. The pragmatic inquirer is both artist and scientist.

Despite these strong affinities between pragmaticism and instrumentalist pragmatism, the two early-twentieth-century outlooks also provide significant contrast. As noted earlier, Dewey was more akin to Royce than to Peirce in always aiming his philosophy at immediate practical needs. And, as we have just seen, Dewey, at least around the turn of the century, was not inclined to engage at any length in

ontological or cosmological speculation regarding realism and nominalism. He sided with Peircean realism just insofar as it made sense
of his emphases on growth, education, and cultural transformation.
But perhaps the strongest rupture between the pragmatisms of Peirce
and Dewey appeared, as did the rupture between Peirce and Royce,
in the logics that each believed were needed to accompany their versions of realism.

Royce's apriorism tended to follow Royce's affinity for order and
stability. Dewey's experimentalism, admittedly influenced by Peirce's
pragmatic writings, was designed to fit his tendency to honor the
novel, the developing, and the contingent. Peirce counted Dewey
among those who had unsettled the traditional belief in a fixed order
of nature (CP 5.508). However, in a now well-documented letter draft
of June 1904, Peirce openly worried that Dewey's genealogical or "genetic" experimentalism might point in the direction of either a reduction of truth to historical interpretation or a pure relativism of truth's
future: "The effect of teaching that such a Natural History [of
thought] can take the place of a normative science of thought must
be to render the rules of reasoning lax; and in fact I find you and your
students greatly given over to what to me seems like a debauch of
loose reasoning" (CP 8.240). Peirce did not expressly dismiss Dewey's
way of considering logic but suggested that it might open the door
for others to fully relativize logic and truth.

IV. Conclusion

There seems to me, then, truth in Pihlström's claim that Royce and
Peirce may, in some ways, be closely aligned. But if taken too strongly
I think it creates an unbalanced picture. For on Peirce's other side, as
it were, Dewey is equally aligned with a Peircean pragmaticism and
realism. Peirce recognized and gave articulation to the affinities and
differences he saw in both directions. In doing so, he explicitly placed
his pragmaticism and its attendant realism in a middle ground between the potential extremes of dogmatism and relativism—I say
"potential" because it seems clear to me that Peirce did not believe

Royce to be a dogmatist nor Dewey a relativist. Either extreme was for Peirce the end of philosophy precisely because they both, in different ways, close off all avenues of inquiry. The dogmatist has no *need* to inquire and the relativist has no *way* to inquire. Peirce's strong and direct quarrels with Royce and Dewey, as well as with William James (another story), were aimed at keeping them oriented toward this middle ground, the home ground of his pragmaticism.

THREE

TWO PEIRCEAN REALISMS
Some Comments on Margolis

Carl R. Hausman and Doug Anderson

When Joe Margolis's essay "The Passing of Peirce's Realism" first appeared in the Transactions of the Charles S. Peirce Society, Carl and I
read it separately and, for somewhat different reasons, resisted Margolis's assessment of Peirce. We then entered into a discussion of whether
our separate resistances to Margolis's position were of a piece. Despite
our disagreements here with Margolis's reading of Peirce, we both greatly
admire his philosophical work and appreciate his ability to catalyze our
own reflections.

We turn now from considering Peirce's realism in relation to
the work of his contemporaries to a consideration of a com-
mentary by our contemporary Joseph Margolis, who in recent years
has undertaken to bring analytic philosophy and pragmatism into
conversation. Margolis's article "The Passing of Peirce's Realism"
provides us with a close probing of Peirce's views on the reality of
generals. In his attempt to bring Peirce's realism into the context of

contemporary debates, however, Margolis seems to us to overlook an important dimension of Peirce's philosophy; thus he makes some dubious assumptions in his treatment of Peirce's version of realism. He misses Peirce's conception of the integration of the dynamic reality with the dynamic development of thought. One reason for the oversight may be an excessive dependence on the early stages of Peirce's view, especially that which is evident in his 1871 review of Fraser's edition of Berkeley (CP 8.7–38). Margolis tends to treat Peirce's version of realism as a foundationalist and static view of the reality of generals in nature, and he dismisses (as mythical) the crucial role of the evolution of generals into the indefinite long run. Similarly, Margolis ignores Peirce's conception of conditionality, or the "would-be" character of generality. He thus underemphasizes the importance of the would-be function of generals in Peirce's version of scholastic realism and in the epistemological and ontological status of the final opinion. Our major concern in the present chapter is to address these points. We also aim to raise some questions about the larger philosophical issues presented in Margolis's essay.

Before turning to these points in Margolis's critique, we should mention a lacuna that frames and infects Margolis's treatment of the question of realism: his silence about what he means by the term *realism*. One must infer from the discussion that the dominant meaning he presupposes consists in what may be called *external realism,* or the view that inquiry is directed toward a structured system of laws that is real in the sense of existing apart from mental processes and the framework internal to what the consciousness of the inquirer confronts. A second sense of *realism,* and one that is crucial to Peirce, may be called *cosmological* or perhaps more appropriately *cosmic* realism, by which we refer to the view that the universe is or has an aspect that is extramental. Peirce's cosmic realism is not simply the notion of a final opinion (which Margolis recognizes), but is that notion of an infinitely encounterable excess to thought (which is not, apparently, recognized by Margolis). Cosmic realism is developed in an original way by Peirce. To be sure, the two senses of *realism* may overlap, but they are clearly distinguishable, particularly in the context of

Margolis's discussion. One can be a scholastic realist without being a realist about the cosmos. For instance, one can be a Hegelian or Lotzean objective idealist and still affirm scholastic realism. This point is important, because Margolis skirts the dimension of Peirce's philosophy according to which he is committed at once to a form of scholastic realism and also to a unique kind of cosmic realism with respect to his conception of the evolutionary structure of the universe. Understanding Peirce's thought as a whole, as difficult as this may be, requires, we think, seeing that these two forms of realism are inseparable for him. We trust that the significance of this point will become clearer in the main part of our discussion.

I

Margolis's central objection to Peirce turns on the idea that Peirce's realism depends on a final matching of thought, triadically constituted (thirdness in thought), with intelligible reality that is also triadically structured—that is, as thirds making up a system that is antecedent to inquiry. This assumption that matching must take place presupposes the dualism that Peirce rejects: a separation of mind and reality—where reality is understood either as wholly independent but possibly to be matched with thought (apparently Margolis's assumption), or as something independent and unknowable in principle (Kant's thing-in-itself) and thus unmatchable. In Margolis's terms, the dualism he imposes on Peirce is the separation of "human invention of thirdness" and "thirdness in reality at large."[1]

One pillar of Margolis's account is Peirce's challenge, in a Lowell lecture (1903), that his audience try to disbelieve the prediction that if he were to release a stone, then it would fall. Margolis argues that Peirce's example defeats nominalism, but it does not tell us "about the nature of universals as real."[2] However, Peirce's conception of the character of universals lies in his conception of generals, as Margolis indeed emphasizes. This conception is found in many other passages. The example of the "would-falling" of the stone is not intended to state "the nature of universals as real." It simply gives a common-sense justification for recognizing that real generals are operative. Yet in a sense, in the passages in which the challenge is proposed, Peirce does tell us something about the nature of generals as real. He tells us that experience has convinced him that certain objects behave as he predicts they will and that the proposition stating the prediction is a representation, thus indicating that generals are regularities or habits and that our linguistic and conceptual references to them are part and parcel of semeiosis; thus, beliefs about generals can be understood in terms of the semeiotic.

Once this move to the semeiotic is made, the question of the "nature" of what is real turns on what Peirce says about the objects of signs. In turn, the relation of semeiotic objects to seconds is what most directly indicates the character of generals as reals—the constraining conditions (the observed instances of generals) that are irreducible to thought. Margolis recognizes both the role of seconds and the tie with the semeiotic, but he avoids considering at least one essential part of it. What is left out is Peirce's dynamical object—an omission that is to be considered later.

In any case, Peirce's characterizations of universals as generals are found in many different contexts. The overwhelming weight of evidence is that he did not think that generals are real as universals in the sense of invariant, fixed laws that are in every respect independent of and antecedent to inquiry. Generals are subject to growth, not simply in the sense that theoretical inquiry about them changes, but also in the sense that nature, or the complexes of regularities as symbolized in theory, grows. This is clear in his 1890's *Monist* papers on evolution. And it is clear in the sixth Lowell lecture, which followed the lecture with the "would-fall" stone example. Peirce includes himself among those who hold that "uniformities are never absolutely exact, so that the variety of the universe is forever increasing" (CP 6.91). And a bit later, he says that even Platonic forms, with which he sometimes compares his own view of generals, can grow: "The evolutionary process is, therefore, not a mere evolution of the existing universe, but rather a process by which the very Platonic forms themselves have become or are becoming developed" (CP 6.194). It seems clear that the life of generals is dynamic in the universe and is linked to interpretation, but interpretation that is constrained by something not wholly dependent on mental activity in inquiry. Generals gain actuality insofar as they are instanced in seconds. This is one feature of Peirce's "scholastic realism." At the same time, generals grow within a system that is constrained by the dynamical object that is the regulative condition of inquiry.

In spite of his recognition of Peirce's evolutionism, Margolis seems to us to be unclear about whether he sees that, for Peirce, generals "in nature" evolve and are interactive with mental processes while at the same time they are partially independent of thought insofar as they are constrained by seconds. Thus, when he objects to Peirce's approach to the congruity between evolution of science and evolution of the cosmos, he does so on the ground that Peirce turns from the notion of triadic development in science to the notion of an intelligent and living cosmos. "Nature only appears intelligible," Peirce maintains, "so far as it appears rational, that is, so far as its processes are seen to be like processes of thought" (CP 3.422). And this, Margolis says, is a myth.³ But this objection does not apply to the other dimension of Peirce's conception of the cosmos, that according to which there is an extramental, transhuman reality that pressures human intelligence through experiences of seconds, which, in semeiotic terms, are experiences as reactions to the conditioning of the dynamical object. Presumably because the cosmos that is independent of human thought is understood by Peirce as humanlike in being intelligent, Margolis characterizes Peirce's solution to the relation of thinking to reality (what is "out of mind") as a *"deus ex machina."*⁴ And what is more significant is that Margolis claims that there must be an "antecedent and continuous correspondence between the triadicity inhering (somehow) in cosmic evolution (which therefore harbors real universals)."⁵ But such bifurcation is precisely what Peirce's evolutionism excludes. What Margolis takes as "continuous correspondence" is in Peirce's view more accurately termed "growing harmony"—the attunement of human abductive progress with the objects of inquiry—and what Margolis rightly calls the "triadicity" inhering in "cosmic evolution" is, as already suggested, dynamic. Being dynamic is hardly a condition associated with a harbored system of antecedent, real universals. Thus, as pointed out, Peirce goes so far as to say that even Platonic forms can come into being. Furthermore, precisely because of this triadicity, the objects of inquiry, "in nature," are continuous with inquiry and thought in general and not separated from the cosmos.

Thus, contrary to Margolis's view that Peirce believed that there was a "disjunction between brute existence (secondness) and the intelligible structure of the real world (thirdness)," a proper modified constructivism sees the intrusions of secondness as inseparable from the spontaneity of qualitative occasions (firsts) and the growth of generals or of thought—seconds are the constraints that force thought onward. Peirce's constructivism, then, does more than "rely entirely and only on the self-corrective efforts (reflexively perceived) of human communities." If this were not so, then Peirce's constructivism would be subject to the question that should be asked of Margolis's "viable" theory of constructivism: to what measure can the corrective efforts of communities appeal? If there are no such measures in some way independent of communities, then what does "corrective" mean? Peirce has a twofold answer: 1) a condition, if not a measure, is present in the constraints that sooner or later are effective on communities at large; these are pragmatically, at least, correctives for problem solving and for suggesting connections within larger contexts of systems so that communities can change (for better or worse); 2) there is a projected hope of a would-be long run, which justifies the very attempt to engage in corrective measures.

The crux of the matter seems to lie in two considerations. The first has to do not only with Margolis's overlooking Peirce's dynamical object, but also with his omission of Peirce's conception of the continuity that pervades the universe. In light of this continuity, human abductive action is integral to the growth of generals—even understood as Platonic forms. To this extent, Peirce is a constructivist. Yet the realism is there because of the role of external constraints, the

eruption of seconds—what are understood semeiotically as dynamical objects. Thus, extrahuman structured cosmic life neither awaits
the discovery of inquirers nor creates intelligible structures independently of the contribution of human inquiry. There is an interaction,
an interaction that is constituted in a community of inquirers, that
is present neither between an antecedent structure and inquiry nor
between a separately growing cosmos and thought (human or extrahuman), but instead between inquiry or thought in general and the
constraints of the dynamical object. This, we think, is what we might
call "a modified constructivism" or "unique Peircean realism" or
"evolutionary realism." The second consideration tied to the crux of
the issue with which we are dealing can be seen in Margolis's own
recognition of (at least something like) Peirce's modified constructivism or unique realism, but which he denies is Peirce's view:

> If the triadic structures of intelligible reality were, in some mea-
> sure, artifacts of human construction, generated (as thirds) in the
> very process of man's inquiry and survival (as seconds and among
> seconds)—then, easily enough intelligible reality would not be
> "something entirely independent of thought." Science might still
> be said to be "objective," to "correspond" to reality, because both
> structures would, in some measure, be social constructions
> —subject all the while to the "brute action" of existing things
> (secondness).[6]

This denial is also indicated in Margolis's claim that Peirce's view
does not give a place for the contribution of inquiry itself to the function of laws or regularities described in scientific inquiry—for example, when he says that constructivism is "fatal to Peirce's project."[7]
Yet Margolis's own suggestion is a version of Peirce's linking of inquiry with communities of inquirers who develop theories under the
constraints both of their own systems of thought and of the resistances (seconds) that prompt abductive leaps. The difference between
Peirce and Margolis with respect to constructivism is that Peirce takes
seconds seriously and moves to his unique metaphysical or evolutionary realism that does not stop short of hypothesizing a way of ac-
counting for seconds. This can best be seen in Peirce's conception of

the semeiotic structuring that has effective outcomes in relation to both immediate and dynamical objects: that is, respectively, the object as interpreted (Margolis's "social construction") and the object as effective in "brute action" or constraints on the construction of the immediate object.

Consideration of "Peirce's project" in terms of his semeiotic helps illuminate the relation of the evolution of generals to the reality-condition of constraints that are experienced in seconds. What Peirce identifies as immediate object, the object as interpreted, is the referent of a sign that is understood in terms of an interpretant. The immediate object, then, is a complex of respects in which the initiating object—or the "thing" (referent) with which a process of semeiosis begins—is interpreted. These respects are like Platonic forms. Consequently, it is reasonable to regard the systems of generals (which include laws) that serve as the objects of inquiry as systems of these complexes of generals, or immediate objects. Immediate objects, or complexes of generals that are the outcomes of interpretation, thus can be looked on as the socially constructed structures that Margolis proposes. But what can be said about the objectivity of the reality structure, which Margolis marks off from the "artifacts of human construction"? This question, in a sense, should not arise, for the immediate object is the reality structure from the vantage point of inquiry or interpretations. What remains that can for Peirce be thought of as reality that is independent of both the inquiry and its objects— the community of scientists with the referents of their theories, which are "socially constructed"—are the constraining conditions of seconds, as Margolis himself suggests. Within the semeiotic account, seconds are the resistances conditioned by the dynamical object. The dynamical object belongs to that dimension of Peirce's thought that is independent of mind (and social construction).

It is significant that when Margolis pursues what to him is a non-Peircean view, he compares Peirce's view with Putnam's internal realism. The internal realism of Putnam, as Margolis says (and we think rightly), collapses into constructivism and the historicity of thinking. However, the point we have been trying to press is that Peirce can

hold on to the proposed view without affirming a complete constructivism, because he hypothesizes a condition of constraints on the part
of something that is not internal to the constructions. This condition,
the dynamical object, is absolutely indispensable in Peirce's thought,
and it is contrary to Peirce's thought as a whole to overlook it, even
if the notion of the dynamical object is complex and not easily
understood.

Margolis, then, does not give sufficient credit to Peirce's subtle way
of affirming the extraconceptual condition that in principle provides
a control on the evolution of immediate objects. Because of the evolutionary structure of the immediate objects of inquiry, Peirce's modified constructivism or evolutionary realism has the advantage that it
does not "fail to be hospitable to frequent conceptual incommensurabilities."[8] Incommensurabilities, Margolis thinks, are consistent with
"a strong constructivism." But Peirce's evolutionism also implies reason for being so hospitable. It is open to a tolerance for divergences
in our systems of generals. And Peirce's tolerance has the chief advantage that it also implies reason for expecting incommensurabilities to
teach us something—for instance, that new hypotheses are needed
and that at least one of the incommensurabilities needs to be abandoned—a possibility that seems missing from Margolis's strong
constructivism.

According to the evolutionism affirmed by Peirce, then, there is no
independent, pre-established structured reality. Thus, what is commonly said to be the Peircean notion of a convergence of thought
toward a final, true opinion is not convergence toward a pre-fixed
structure to be matched, but convergence toward a reality that is dynamic. And as this reality constrains inquiry, it suggests the hypothesis that it is developmental. Experience presents inquiry with laws or
regularities, many of which tend to be rigid while at the same time
undergoing divergences, sometimes followed by the origination of
new regularities, the general drift seeming to be toward what would
be a final harmony if inquiry were to continue into the infinite future.

In connection with Peirce's insistence on the would-be future, we
should point to what appears to be another oversight in Margolis's

view. In not adequately acknowledging Peirce's insistence on the
would-be condition of the final opinion, Margolis ignores Peirce's re-
peated appeals to an infinite long run, which as infinite will not be
reached. There is some justification for this neglect, because Peirce on
a few occasions refers to the future that will be. In his argument Margolis quotes statements by Peirce that employ the future tense. Yet
Peirce most often used the conditional, even calling attention to his
own view as a conditional idealism (see EP 2:419). This not only
seems more consistent both with his references to a future that is infinite and with his insistence on fallibilism, but is also confirmed by
the fact that in his writings there are more references to the would-
be as compared to the will-be character of final opinion, especially in
his later work. This is a point that Margolis skirts. In any case, the
idea of an infinite long run precludes the assignability of a time when
a final judgment *will* be reached. However, this notion of a long run
that lies in an infinite future suggests Margolis's objection that Peirce
invokes myth.

Apparently, the reason Margolis balks at seeing the extent to which
his own proposal echoes Peirce is that he believes his proposal to be
in conflict with the idea of inquiry's approaching a final opinion, or
a point at which thought terminates in final truth. "Constructivism
is fatal to Peirce's project: for it undermines the idea of progressive
fallibilism that, from the side of inquiry, asymptotically approaches
an opinion matching the independent structure of the world."[9] However, the claim that fallibilism is inconsistent with "convergence" follows from Margolis's dubious assumption that evolution is headed
toward a reality that is a frozen, independent, and structured world
rather than an ideal limit. Moreover, as Cheryl Misak points out, even
if we hope for a "will-be" final judgment, our hope too is fallible.
And "since we can see that our hope is tenuous, we construe truth in
terms of what *would be* the upshot of inquiry."[10]

What evolution develops toward is indeed an ideal. Yet Peirce refers to the ideal limit as in the infinite future. He also holds forth
the expectation that seconds and departures from laws are infinitely
integral to the future. Thus, actuality would continue to be instanced

in seconds, which continually occur in the infinite long run. "At any assignable date in the future there will be some slight aberrancy from the law" (CP 1:409); and, as we have noted earlier, "the variety of the universe is forever increasing," and still further, Reason "is something that never can have been completely embodied" (CP 1.615). Peirce's fallibilism, then, does not require an actual final end against which it can be measured, as if there were a state of infallibility in the future, after all.

Of course, these statements about increasing variety in the universe do not demonstrate the notion of convergence, and they seem to conflict with the hope of sufficiently developing a perfected inquiry. They are, however, the outcome of two supporting considerations. First, science seems to progress; even if the instances of the convergence of theoretical systems are local, or relevant to finite contexts, the larger context of changes in science does seem to show a general increase in the interconnections of many of its conclusions. Biochemistry is a product of two former disciplines; genetic theory works with both biological concepts and basic concepts in physics. Thus, when Margolis asserts that "Peirce must explain, from within the space of a working science, just what the evidence is that the real structure of a 'mind-independent' world has been discerned or progressively approached," we surely have reason to assume, at least "within the space of two working sciences," that there is progress—the discovery of DNA and recent discoveries of disease-genes illustrate advances in science.[11] Common-sense realism, although probably not philosophically respectable from the perspective Margolis assumes in his critique, supports the idea of progress toward at least provisional limits.

Moreover, additional support is suggested by a second consideration. A metaphysical commitment in cosmology is unavoidable if we do not stop short in our critical reflections on the meaning of our views of the cosmos and the place of humans within it. It is unavoidable in strong constructivism, because if one holds to the constructivist view advocated by Margolis, one supposes that the universe or world—which constructivists, or at least prominent ones, do not hesitate to cite—either must be one of open chaos, so that the constraints of seconds are purely random; or one must suppose that there is no world, no universe, to which constructions can refer, the consequence being some form of linguistic and conceptual insulation, or some form of linguistic idealism. In either case, there is a tacit if not explicit metaphysical commitment on the part of strong constructivism.

The Peircean critical reflections that lead to agreement with common sense, the metaphysical assumption that accords with the ideal, and the rationale for attempts in science to harmonize theories developed in different disciplines, we think, are more reasonable—or "more plausible," to use a more fashionable expression—than the other options, particularly if the role of constraints on thought from seconds is recognized. At this point, Margolis undoubtedly would charge our counterproposal—which we make in what, we believe, is a Peircean spirit—with being the myth and *deus ex machina* to which he refers. Let us then turn to this issue of invoking "myths."

II

The claim that we have a myth is apparently associated with another claim: Margolis asserts that the idea of approximation to a future of regularity "'cannot' serve as a regulative notion, unless it functions thus everywhere in the short-run science; and it cannot function thus except on the grounds internal to the work of the human mind (by way of hypothesized thirds)."[12] However, the work of the human mind, which is perhaps most directly obvious in Peirce's semeiotic, is exactly what Peirce regards as integral to the growth of generals—generals "in reality" which are generals in thought.

We have indicated earlier that, for Margolis, the ideas of an infinite long run and of a reality that is independent of thought but not pre-structured would be labeled as myth-making, and perhaps as incoherent. Margolis concentrates primarily on Peirce's scholasticism. However, Peirce's scholastic realism, as noted in chapter 1, plays an epistemological and ontological role in his more broadly conceived philosophy of science.[13] Thus, in conjunction with scholastic realism, Peirce needs his phenomenology and in turn his metaphysics in order to account for major components in his thought, namely, its idealistic dimensions, its anti-nominalism, and its realism (epistemological with respect to method in science). Yet Margolis shies from the metaphysics that Peirce incorporates into his system. Any Peircean move in the direction of metaphysics is rejected as myth. The question, however, is whether metaphysics, or some hypothesis or abduction about the cosmos (or its absence), can be avoided. Margolis and many constructivists presumably believe that they avoid it. However, in assuming their purity, they ignore their own myths. They assume that what does not fit their sights is mythical, and apparently assume that "we"—the company of antimetaphysicians, if not everyone— will find it distasteful to trust myths.

Of course, with respect to what has been stressed in our considerations of Margolis's critique, our proposed introduction of the idea of a dynamical object would leave Margolis unconvinced, because the idea not only introduces metaphysics but also raises again the question whether, in resorting to myth, Peirce fell back on something suspiciously like a thing-in-itself, which he rejected. Further, the idea of an infinite future raises questions of what can be meant by *infinite* in what to some looks like an improper use of a mathematical notion in a nonmathematical context. These questions indeed are raised. And it is these fundamental issues that deserve to be addressed. The question of the adequacy of Peirce's realism seems to us to need focusing on the proper locus—a locus that is central to the whole of Peirce's thought, rather than a segment that is severed from the metaphysical or cosmological underpinnings that Peirce gave it. More attention needs to be given to these central issues—the dynamical object and the infinity of the future—if a fair analysis is to be given of the contribution of Peirce's special evolutionary realism to contemporary controversies over realism and antirealism. And the kind of attention that is philosophically appropriate should be properly prescinded from historically driven criticism. By *historically driven criticism*, we refer to Margolis's practice of restricting the criteria that are deemed appropriate for a critique of another's thought to those rules and acceptable data that are available in the professional circles of one's own historical context. After all, whether one's philosophical conclusions are reducible to just such historically localized perspectives is one of the points at issue.

Just as important, it seems to us, however, is the point that myth-making can hardly be avoided in any attempt to probe the limits of thought. Margolis presumably believes that his constructivism is free of metaphysics and myth-making. Yet it seems to us that Margolis's own robust attempts to force a subtle thinker up against the contingency-morass that is endemic to so many twentieth-century thinkers raise the question of what he too must face if he were to reflect on the context of his strong constructivism.

In his case, as with the contemporary way of thinking with which he aligns himself, he rises to his own mythical levels when his social constructions are given the status of ultimates—thus raising them to a level at which they replace the gods. Whether metaphysics or myth-making, reflection concerning all features of the cosmos we take to be part and parcel of philosophical work.

FOUR

THE DEGENERATION OF PRAGMATISM
Peirce, Dewey, Rorty

Doug Anderson

In the previous two chapters we have explored Peirce's relationship to other early pragmatists and one contemporary attempt to merge Peirce's pragmaticism with the analytic tradition. In this chapter I explore the ways in which John Dewey's pragmatism stands between Peirce's pragmaticism and the neo-pragmatism of Richard Rorty. Our conversation on these matters began with the publication of Rorty's Philosophy and the Mirror of Nature *and* Consequences of Pragmatism. *The difficulty was that at the same time that Rorty's work led readers to a tradition of pragmatism, it quite intentionally distorted the nature and meaning of that tradition.*

P ragmatism has reached its most recent state of notoriety, for better and worse, through the writings of Richard Rorty, who claimed that he drew his inspiration, in part at least, from William James and, even more emphatically, from John Dewey. Some years ago Cornel West, describing in *The American Evasion of Philosophy* the trajectory of the development of the political dimensions of pragmatism, provided external evidence to corroborate Rorty's self-placement in the pragmatic tradition. My task in this chapter is akin to West's, though I operate from a rather different angle of vision. My purpose is to provide a diagnostic descriptive overview of the present state of pragmatism, much in the way that Rorty himself addressed the history of philosophy. The difference is that I will examine the development of Rorty's pragmatism from the perspective of Peirce's pragmaticism. Through my descriptive diagnosis I hope to show that Rorty's pragmatism emerged from an apparent ambiguity in the pragmatism of Dewey and James, and that Rorty then presented us with a false dichotomy between a static realism of the sort adopted by British empiricism and the kind of nominalistic historicism that he himself adopted. The upshot is that, from Peirce's perspective, Rorty's version of pragmatism is a degenerate one.

I employ the term *degeneration* deliberately because of an ambiguity it bears within the framework of Peirce's writing. In discussing his category of "thirdness," Peirce described triads that are composed monadically or dyadically as degenerate thirds or triads (CP 1.473). The point is that these other forms of thirds are both real and important, though not genuine. Their degeneracy consists in a shift in emphasis. In this sense, Dewey's pragmatism might be understood from Peirce's perspective as significant and pragmatic, though not fully akin to Peirce's pragmaticism. Degeneration can also suggest a full loss of relation, and it is in this latter sense that Peirce might have identified neo-pragmatism as degenerate from the vantage point of his pragmaticism. Given this distinction, Dewey's pragmatism may be understood as once removed from Peirce's but still within the tradition; Rorty's neo-pragmatism, on the other hand, might not be recognized by Peirce as standing in the natural history of pragmatism.[1]

In 1898 James identified Peirce as the founder of pragmatism. In 1877–78 Peirce had published two essays, "The Fixation of Belief" and "How to Make Our Ideas Clear," that laid the groundwork for his pragmatism, though he did not use the term in print. By 1903 "pragmatism," as evidenced by work in the *Monist* and *The Hibbert*

Journal, had become a popular topic of discussion, and Peirce began to a feel a need to distance himself from what he perceived to be the more subjective versions of the movement being offered not just by James and F. C. S. Schiller but also by those outside philosophy who were adopting it uncritically—in what Peirce called "literary pragmatism." It was in this intellectual environment that Peirce first encountered Dewey's work. After reading *Studies in Logical Theory,* in 1904 Peirce drafted a letter to Dewey, as noted in chapter 2, stating his concern that replacing "the Normative Science" of logic with a "Natural History" of logic might have important and unwanted consequences (CP 8.239):

> Although I am strongly in favor of your Pragmatistic views, I find the whole volume penetrated with this spirit of intellectual licentiousness, that does not see that anything is so very false. Of course you will understand that I should not write in such underscored terms to any man with whom I did not feel a very deep respect and sympathy. I am simply *projecting upon the horizon,* the *direction* of your standpoint as viewed from mine. (CP 8.241)

Dewey never relinquished this "genetic" or genealogical method of reasoning that stirred Peirce's concern, but he also never relinquished his belief that inquirers are constrained by the real—he had a working conception of truth and warranted assertibility that he carefully documented in *Logic: A Theory of Inquiry.* Rorty, however, openly dismissed the need for secondness in inquiry since the world is "well lost," and he took pragmatism beyond the horizon in the direction Peirce projected: to the place where it is not clear "that anything is so very false." Peirce's fear of the "natural history" and "genealogy" turned on the unstated implication that there are no real constraints on human inquiry. Indeed, inquiry, for Rorty's pragmatism, reduces to a sort of twentieth-century gnosticism—a knowing without constraint. Put another way, Peirce feared that an extreme genealogical view of logic made inquiry a matter of sheer creativity with no element of discovery; in today's parlance, it would become a full-blown constructivism.

As I have noted throughout, Peirce was a three-category realist, maintaining that there are, in his terms, real firsts, seconds, and thirds in the cosmos:

> Next, I ask, what are the different kinds of *reals*? They are 1st those whose being lies in the substance of the thought itself, mere ideas, objects logically possible, the objects of pure mathematical thought for example. 2nd those whose being consists in their connexions with other things, existents, reacting things. 3rd those whose being consists in their connecting two or more other things;—laws, generals, signs, etc. In short the real is the ultimately undeniable. (MS L387b, 00350)

I want here to focus on the second two categories of reals. The first of these was presented as a hypothesis in "The Fixation of Belief":

> There are Real things, whose characters are entirely independent of our opinions about them; those Reals affect our senses according to regular laws, and, though our sensations are as different as are our relations to the objects, yet, by taking advantage of the laws of perception, we can ascertain by reasoning how things really and truly are. (CP 5:384)

Peirce later came to see that this picture did not speak adequately to science's quest for laws because it suggested a focus on "colors, sounds, smells, tastes, and resistances to pressure" (MS L387b, 00349). This led him to propose in more detail what he had hinted at as early as 1871 in his review of Fraser's edition of *The Works of George Berkeley* (CP 8.7–38, W 2.462–86): "that *Thirdness* is operative in nature" (CP 5.96).

His claim was that laws are habits of existents and, though they are not themselves existents, they are real because they are at work independently of what any one mind or any finite set of minds thinks about them. In short, then, the cosmos has habits that are instantiated by seconds or existents, and it is precisely these that science seeks to know. Such habits, when understood as generals or laws, yield predictability within ranges because they tell us what would be—not what will be—the case, under given sets of conditions. They have, Peirce said, "a sort of *esse in futuro*" (CP 5.48).

For Peirce, both orders of reals—existents and generals—place constraints on inquiry. However, his account of our access to them was not naïve. First, he suggested that these reals "forced" themselves on us in experience. In this much, he saw an element of direct encounter with reals: "Nothing is more completely false than that we experience only our own ideas. That is indeed without exaggeration the very epitome of *all* falsity" (CP 6.95). Second, as Hausman has argued at length in his *Charles S. Peirce's Evolutionary Philosophy*, these reals were for Peirce not static but dynamic. Indeed, Peirce, as I noted earlier, included himself among those who believed that "uniformities are never absolutely exact, so that the variety of the universe is forever increasing" (CP 6.91; see also 6.194). This dynamism precluded Peirce from holding any simplistic notion of "the end of inquiry."[2] Moreover, he recognized that we do not see these reals as with a "mirror of nature," but that we interpret them. The semeiotic nature of inquiry emerges from a continuity with perception itself: "abductive inference [the first step in inquiry] shades into perceptual judgment without any sharp line of demarcation between them" (CP 5.181, EP 2:227). The upshot is that fallible interpreters, as inquirers, make inroads into the truth—to understanding the "would bes" of the world—through a method of inquiry, but that no finite community of inquirers ever achieves a whole picture. It was his insistence on these realisms that led Peirce to decide to rename his own version of pragmatism *pragmaticism*, in distinction from versions that tended toward nominalism (see CP 5.414). And it was from this vantage point that he measured all other versions of pragmatism.

Dewey shared Peirce's transactional notion of experience and, indeed, as John E. Smith has pointed out, offered an even more radical reconception of experience: "he made paramount the idea of *transformation* and construed experience in terms of its role in resolving problematic situations or in transforming the indeterminate, unsatisfactory situation into a determinate and non-problematic one."[3] Dewey's emphasis on transformation has the capacity for being misleading; indeed, it seems to me plausible that both Peirce and Rorty were to some extent misled by it. What we must not overlook is that, for Dewey, the transforming takes place only within the context of an experiential transaction of the sort Peirce had indicated.

"Experience," Dewey maintained, "is 'double-barrelled' in that it recognizes in its primary integrity no division between act and material, subject and object, but contains them both in an unanalyzed totality."[4] If we reflect on this transactional totality with which Dewey begins, we find a point of ambiguity on which Rorty drew in constructing his own pragmatism, but which, if carefully examined, reveals Dewey's affinity for Peircean realisms, as I argued in chapter 2. On the one hand, Dewey denied that there is a fixed "world of things indifferent to human interests because it is wholly apart from experience."[5] At first blush, this seems to suggest to some that the world is merely a result of our construction. But this in fact is not Dewey's point. Rather, he wanted to show, along the Peircean lines indicated above, that the empiricist's epistemological concern about whether an experiencer can reach some external world is unnecessary because it is *in* experience that we do find nature:

> Since the seventeenth century this conception of experience as the equivalent of subjective private consciousness set over against nature, which consists wholly of physical objects, has wrought havoc in philosophy.[6]

Dewey rightly identified the nominalistic conception of nature as contributing to the problem. The transactional totality is simply the primal meeting of inquirer and nature; as Dewey saw it, "naive experience already has in its possession" that which the philosophical schools achieve only "by a long and tortuous course."[7] In spirit it is also akin to Peirce's Schellingian three-categoried ontology in which knower and known appear together in nature.

What is real for Dewey is what constitutes the transactional totality that is experience. In analysis of the totality, we find a reflective distinction between "the process of experiencing" and the "subject-matter experienced."[8] It is at the level of this distinction within experience that the question of Peirce's realisms comes back into play, although Dewey's own interest was to continue to focus on the instrumental, transformative dimension of knowing. Again an apparent ambiguity arises that must be worked through. On the one hand, Dewey says "that the *ways* in which we believe and expect have a tremendous effect upon *what* we believe and expect."[9] The process of experiencing determines in large part the nature of the subject-matter of experience: "We discover that we believe many things not because the things are so, but because we have become habituated through the weight of authority, by imitation, prestige, instruction, the unconscious effect of language, etc."[10] Contrary to Rorty's oft-repeated suggestion, for Dewey, "nature speaks." The method of "natural history" weighs in at this juncture. On the other hand, in maintaining his emphasis on transaction between process and subject-matter, Dewey kept afloat the Peircean belief that experience involves secondness and an interpretive act. In retaining the element of secondness, Dewey clearly adopted something like Peirce's realism of secondness, of existents and factual generals, within the context of experience: "It is not experience which is experienced, but nature—stones, plants, animals, diseases, health, temperature, electricity, and so on."[11] There is no mere process of experiencing that simply manufactures or constructs a "world." Thus, despite the appearance of a pure historicism, Dewey argued minimally for something more. As would Rorty's later response, many of the initial responses to Dewey's presentation of his account of experience failed to acknowledge this realist strain; these responses prompted Dewey to add the following note to the text of *Experience and Nature*:

> Because of this identification of the mental as the sole "given" in a primary, original way [as is true for some empiricisms and some idealisms], appeal to experience by a philosopher is treated by many as necessarily committing one to subjectivism. It accounts for the alleged antithesis between nature and experience mentioned in the opening paragraph. It has become so deeply engrained that the empirical method employed in this volume has been taken by critics to be simply a re-statement of a purely subjective philosophy, although in fact it is wholly contrary to such a philosophy.[12]

As noted in chapter 2, where Dewey stood concerning the status of thirdness and the reality of nature's laws and orders is not immediately apparent. Peirce openly claimed that nature is itself shot through with reason, with habits. What inquiry does is to provide interpretive articulations of these habits as laws or generals. We then employ these laws to organize experience and make predictions. Dewey's emphasis was on this organizational and transformative element in inquiry. Indeed, in a way he downplayed the importance of the philosophical question of the reality of thirds altogether:

> For the only possible alternative interpretations are either the (highly unsatisfactory) view that the conceptions [of experienced subject-matter] are mere devices of practical convenience, or that in some fashion or other they are descriptive of something actually existing in the material dealt with. From the standpoint of the *function* that conceptual subject-matters actually serve in inquiry, the problem does not need to be "solved"; it simply does not exist.[13]

Despite this seeming indifference in talking from the standpoint of function, Dewey nevertheless indicated his resistance to a thorough-going nominalism. This is important to note, since at times he seemed to argue as if he were a nominalist and at other times as if he were a Peircean scholastic realist.

The latter, as I indicated in chapter 2, is suggested by Dewey's various claims that there are "ways of being" in nature that knowers come to know. In *Logic*, for example, he indicated his belief in the reality of generals when he stated that "racing and burning are *ways* of acting and changing" that "are exemplified in singulars but are not themselves singulars."[14] In *Experience and Nature*, echoing ideas he espoused just after the turn of the century, he made the same point in a more Peircean fashion: "Unless nature had regular habits, persistent ways, so compacted that they time, measure, and give rhythm and recurrence to transitive flux, meanings, recognizable characters, could not be."[15]

The first or nominalist alternative also appeared, however, in Dewey's suggestions that the experiencer creates the thirdness or meaning of experienced subject matters. In *Logic,* for example, he claims that "the sameness of the singular object" and the determination of an item's "kind" are "products of the continuity of experiential inquiry."[16] This may seem to suggest that Dewey believed there is no continuity in nature as experienced subject matter. Such an interpretation seems further evidenced by Dewey's various descriptions in *A Common Faith* of the human construction of continuity in a world where none exists. In *Experience and Nature* this nominalistic bent seems even more apparent: "Knowledge or science, as a work of art, like any other work of art, confers upon things traits and potentialities which did not *previously* belong to them."[17] The suggestion is that we construct, artfully as it were, the laws and habits that are attributable to real existents. Subjectivism and historicism appear again as possibilities, this time at a second level after the realism of seconds has already been adopted. On this reading, Dewey appears to be a traditional scientistic nominalist of the sort Peirce most wished to challenge.

These appearances are important to show because readers often cast Dewey's work as falling squarely into either naïve realism or nominalism. In particular, Rorty divided Dewey's work according to these alternatives and suggested there is a "good" Dewey (the nominalistic one) and a "bad" Dewey (the realistic one); he then developed his own work in line with his "good" Dewey. Despite appearances, however, judging from what Dewey actually said, it seems most accurate to see Dewey's position as akin to Peirce's dynamic realism. There are, Dewey said, real habits in nature as subject matter. However, these are not known in a simple reflective manner; again, the process of experiencing is not a mere mirror of nature.[18] On the one hand, our understanding of the habits—the laws—is always mediated; it is always interpreted in a historical context. On the other hand, insofar as inquiry is transformative, we, as inquirers, add meaning to nature's habits. The meaning adds an instrumental dimension to the habits or ways of acting that they did not previously possess. Thus, like Peirce, Dewey held a realism of thirds that is unlike traditional realisms in not "fixing" the nature of these thirds in themselves and in maintaining that inquiry does bring something to the meaning of these laws. For both, real generals are neither merely discovered nor simply constructed. The transactional nature of inquiry means that within primary experience there are reciprocal constraints of the process on the subject matter and of the subject matter on the process. It is precisely this reconstructed realism that Dewey and Peirce shared and that gave them a common pragmatism; it is also this realism that sets their work apart from that of Rorty. To revisit my conclusion in chapter 2, in shifting his focus away from explicit concern with this realism while still maintaining it, Dewey offered, from a Peircean perspective, a mildly degenerate form of pragmatism, but one that still bears a strong family resemblance to Peirce's pragmaticism.

From Peirce's perspective, Dewey's emphasis on the functional rather than the disclosive dimension of inquiry with respect to laws or generals suggests the horizon at which pragmatism may become nominalistic and constructivist to the point of making science a matter of sheer imagination. Rorty seemed to see the same possibility in Dewey's emphasis and pushed his own version of pragmatism in this more fully degenerate direction. In introducing Rorty, however, I should begin with an important distinction drawn by John E. Smith. For Smith, there are two Rorty characters: 1) "rorty," the philosopher "who acutely captures the central drift of Pragmatism and brings it to bear on recent discussion in an illuminating way"; and 2) "Rorty," who "is doing something quite different in latching onto Dewey and onto the idea of 'overcoming' the tradition in order to get rid of Platonism and metaphysics or what he sometimes calls 'Philosophy.' "[19] The object of my diagnosis is Rorty, not rorty, though it is important to keep in mind that Rorty is, to some degree, informed by rorty.

Rorty's version of pragmatism takes its leave from the apparent ambiguities in Dewey's dealing with realism that arise at both the levels I have discussed. For Rorty, the hints that Dewey can be read as denying both levels of realism together with Dewey's open emphasis

on transformation indicate that there is the "good" Dewey I have
mentioned—nominalist with a disinterest in metaphysics—as well as
the "bad" Dewey who "*wanted* to write a metaphysical system."[20] As
Rorty saw it, Dewey simply "wanted to have things both ways."[21] He
believed, however, that Dewey's emphasis on the transformative nature of inquiry could define pragmatism in absence from metaphysical, and especially realist, considerations. Philosophy need only be
critical and transformative, not "metaphysical" or systematic; in
Rorty's way of speaking, it becomes "therapeutic" and "edifying."[22]
Despite his attempt to remain a-metaphysical, however, Rorty slid
back into describing the nature of pragmatism along the lines of the
nominalist and constructivist hints he saw in Dewey's writing.

   The backsliding began with Rorty's full opposition to Peirce and
his realisms: "his contribution to pragmatism," Rorty said, "was
merely to have given it a name, and to have stimulated James."[23] The
hyperbole here is heightened by the fact that Rorty (as well as rorty)
seems to miss the dynamic nature of Peirce's realism. Rorty saw all
realism in terms of his notion of Platonic stasis and hinted at the need
to replace it with a nominalistic pragmatism: "But conformity to *social* norms is not good enough for the Platonist. He wants to be constrained by the ahistorical and nonhuman nature of reality itself."[24]
In Rorty's vision, the "nature" of reality is nothing more than the
story expressed by some society of conversers; pragmatism on his
view is the belief that philosophy is conversation that constructs sto-
ries about the way things are. Thus, in the preface to *Contingency,
irony, and solidarity* Rorty made the following plea:

> A historicist and nominalist culture of the sort I envisage would
> settle instead [of for a meta-vocabulary] for narratives which con-
> nect the present with the past, on the one hand, and with utopian
> futures, on the other.[25]

Through his strident anti-Platonism, Rorty rejected all possible versions of a realism of thirds, including the dynamic version that Peirce
and Dewey identified and defended.

   Rorty did not, however, end his assault on realism at the level of
thirds; he occasionally points to the more radical claim that existents

are likewise unreal. His outlook moved beyond a nominalism in which atomistic things constrain our beliefs to a picture in which the world is lost to us. His now well-known essay "The World Well Lost" states that appeals to secondness are forever doomed, insofar as any description of "world" is either vacuous or fixed by some constructed theoretical account of the world.[26] For Rorty, experience *is* of experience—or language—only; there are no natural constraints on inquiry, only social ones of our own making. And unlike Peirce and Dewey, he did not seem to admit that even social constraints are *natural*. To employ the terms Peirce used in "The Fixation of Belief" to describe the development of inquiry, for Rorty there is only "the social impulse"; there are no brute experiential constraints (CP 5.378, W 3:250). This denial of seconds marks another feature of Rorty's version of pragmatism:

> [A] third and final characterization of pragmatism . . . is the doctrine that there are no constraints on inquiry save conversational ones—no wholesale constraints derived from the nature of the objects, or of the mind, as of language, but only those social constraints provided by the remarks of our fellow-inquirers.[27]

In short, Rorty's constructivism reaches all the way down. The history of social conversation is the *only* source of constraint on the further conversation that constitutes his pragmatic philosophy.

With these brief sketches in place, we are now in a position to say something about the degenerate pragmatisms of Dewey and Rorty as viewed from the vantage point of Peirce's pragmaticism. Dewey's emphases on transformation and "natural history" in inquiry in their initial appearance made Peirce restless, because they suggested the possibility of the absence of real constraints on thinking. In digging more deeply into Dewey's work, however, I find his insistence that transformation itself only takes place in and through a transaction between an inquirer and an environment that are mutually affecting. He did not argue for inquiry as a mirroring of nature but as a process that developmentally comes to grips with that which constrains it. His emphasis was on the control this process gives us because we come to interpret nature's habits, but he did not dismiss the regulative conception of truth that Peirce placed behind the possibility of control.[28] Control and stability involve a developmental engagement with the subject matter of experience. Indeed, Dewey's own notion of amelioration suggests the possibility of a directionality in inquiry. Moreover, at the level of thirdness, Dewey clearly believed that there are habits of nature, ways of acting, that constrain not only inquiry but how we generally conduct ourselves in the world. Thus, from the seat of Peirce's pragmaticism, Dewey's pragmatism is degenerate in the honorific sense. It clearly shifts the points of emphasis and focus; it tempers the interest in Peirce's cosmological evolutionism and calls into question his theism. Nevertheless, it shares the central reconception of experience and inquiry as transactional and developmental. Both Peirce and Dewey believed in inquiring and knowing, though not in the closure of either inquiring or knowing. Peirce's fallibilism and Dewey's sense of the instability of experience point to the inquirer's ongoing struggle to interpret and articulate the dynamic subject matter of experience. Inquiry is historical, but it is not fully historicized or merely constructed. Pragmatism in their terms is well captured by Peirce's suggestion that inquirers are engaged in a "critical common-sensism" (CP 5.505ff, EP 2:346–59).

As Smith points out, the greatest irony of his two Rorty characters is that while rorty seemed to understand pragmatism relatively well, Rorty seemed to miss completely what is central to the pragmatisms of Peirce and Dewey: the reconception of experience.[29] Bernstein, in his review of *Philosophy and the Mirror of Nature*, zeroes in on this peculiarity in Rorty's thinking:

> But there is a variation of this Either/Or that haunts this book—
> *either* we are *ineluctably* tempted by foundational metaphors and
> the desperate attempt to escape from history *or* we must frankly
> recognize that philosophy itself is at best a form of "kibitzing."[30]

Rorty, perhaps captured by his own analytic background, did not see, or did not want to see, the middle ground-conceptionof experience with which Peirce and Dewey are working. For him, if experience is not a mirror of nature, its subject matter must not be "discoverable" at all—or, perhaps, must not be said to be real. Stanley Rosen, in his perceptive reading of *Philosophy and the Mirror of Nature*, shows how Rorty displayed an unwitting kinship with Platonism in denying the possibility of a metaphysics that gives a complete account of the cosmos. Rosen then points out the point of difference: "The difference between the two is that for Plato, the falsehood of the image [of form] does not cancel its power to convey a perception of the truth."[31] Again, as Rosen's analysis indicates, Rorty seemed unable to understand that "[t]o see with difficulty is not the same as not to see at all."[32] These criticisms all point with irony to the same thing: apparently stuck on the assumption that the universe must follow in all instances the law of the excluded middle, Rorty could not see or would not accept the pragmatic middle ground proposed by Peirce and Dewey, in which experiencing and knowing are transactions between an experiencer and an environment.

Rorty's version of pragmatism, from Peirce's angle of vision, is therefore more radically degenerate than Dewey's. It does not merely attack the cosmology and emphasize the value of inquiry as an instrument of social change, but returns us to the kind of nominalism that Peirce believed to have distorted nineteenth-century conceptions of scientific inquiry. Ironically, then, from a Peircean perspective Rorty appears to be a reactionary who, by argument rather than by experience, reinstituted the subjectivists' conception of experience as of itself and defended a historically outmoded philosophy. From a Deweyan point of view, Rorty reprivatized that which Dewey had struggled to make public. Instead of making sense of our experience of secondness, Rorty treated it as internal to a constructed experience, and as a result he looks more like a traditional sceptical empiricist, say a neo-Humean, than a revolutionary late-twentieth-century philosopher. For Peirce and Dewey, Rorty would not seem to be a pragmatist at all.

In my diagnostic description I have resisted offering the standard sorts of self-referential paradoxes that are normally brought to bear against Rorty's pragmatism. I have done so not because I believe they are pointless, but because Rorty himself rejected them as shallow. So far as possible, I try to meet Rorty on his own terms by presenting a sort of genealogy of pragmatism, but one that inverts the picture offered by Rorty and Cornel West. In our Peircean picture, Rorty's version of pragmatism seems thoroughly degenerate—in missing the reconception of experience, it loses its family resemblance to what *all* the pragmatists believed. Rorty, I believe, will in the long run be better understood as having written the obituary of analytic philosophy than as having written a new chapter in the career of pragmatism. Even as he tried to accommodate himself to Dewey's insights, he resisted Dewey by preferring an analysis of language to the felt pressures of lived experience as a guide to his thinking. Where Peirce and Dewey found themselves engaged with real seconds and thirds, Rorty found himself manipulating linguistic events; these are indeed different worlds and different pragmatisms. This diagnosis leaves us therefore with a present state of pragmatism that is deeply bifurcated. There are two degenerate practices on the contemporary scene that go by the name of pragmatism, the Deweyan and the Rortian; from where I sit, it seems reasonable to say that Rorty and his intellectual offspring are merely masquerading as pragmatists. Given the contingencies of intellectual history, however, at present they seem to have the floor and get to define the territory. Nevertheless, although I agree with Rorty that the future of philosophy is not easily predicted, I am sufficiently pragmatic to venture that, in Thoreau's terms, philosophy—and pragmatism in particular—will "come back to its senses" and see that the transformational is also transactional.

Insofar as for Peirce and Dewey pragmatism in all its guises is closely tied to conceptions of experience, it is important to see how Peirce considered human experience, from its instinctive and perceptual origins to its conceptual and semeiotic expansiveness. In the next section we therefore turn to considerations of some features of his ideas of perception, interpretation, and inquiry.

CONVERSATION II

PERCEPTION AND INQUIRY

FIVE

PEIRCE'S DYNAMICAL OBJECT
Realism as Process Philosophy

Carl R. Hausman

From our many discussions of the realist and idealist strands in Peirce's pragmaticism and from our engagement with contemporary pragmatists such as Margolis and Rorty, our conversations inevitably turned to the way in which Peirce tried to hold a middle ground between sheer mirroring and sheer constructing in the process of human knowing. Thus, in pursuing what Peirce might have meant by representational realism, we were led to consider the semeiotic processes Peirce pointed to in showing how perceptual judgments led back to a point of resistance. This led to various examinations of the dynamical object, one of which follows here.

As noted earlier, Peirce's conception of pragmatism has been interpreted as both a form of objective idealism and a form of realism. Objective idealism, as I understand it, insists that whatever is regarded as real must not only be mind dependent but also constituted by mind in the sense of being ultimately reducible to mental activity. Opposed to idealism is what I think of as ontological realism, which I take to be the view that what is real in relation to thought in general is not itself exhausted by, or actually reducible to, thought. Instead, what is real, although it is necessarily related to thought, maintains an independence insofar as it functions as a constraint on what anyone and every intelligent being thinks. This independence from thought as a whole is what is crucial and is what we tried to address in responding to Margolis. However, whether Peirce's thought depends on an idealistic or a realistic commitment, it surely is a kind of process philosophy, and a kind that seems to me to be unique. An explanation of this claim hinges on an attempt to understand what Peirce considered to be the function of the dynamical object in relation to interpretation in general—to the semeiotic system in which human understanding relates to the world. My aim here is to focus on the way in which the dynamical object distinguishes Peirce as at once a unique realist and a unique process philosopher. Before offering this account of Peirce's process realism, however, let me consider the import of the terms *pragmatism* and *process philosophy*.

The popular understanding of pragmatism is that it is a theory or quasi-theory about inquiry that is governed by concerns for practical action and practical goals. Thus, in this view pragmatism is something like a caricature of the Jamesian theory that what is true is what works. And what works is what satisfies inquirers or anyone who asks about the meaning and truth of an idea. Satisfaction is a form of experience, and thus the reference and test of an idea seems to lie in some conscious experience. Such a notion is at the heart of constructivist versions of pragmatism.

Peirce's early unnamed pragmatism and his later pragmaticism need to be thought of differently. For Peirce, pragmatism is a way of determining the meaning of general terms, and—taking into account his views after the 1880s—it presupposes an epistemology and an ontology concerning truth and what is real for rational communities. My concern, then, is with the ontological dimensions of Peirce's pragmaticism. In this context, one stratum of common ground between

Jamesian and Peircean pragmatism is crucial. Both insist that the determination of meaning must lie in consequences—in future occurrences. For James pragmatism is "*[t]he attitude of looking away from first things, principles, 'categories,' supposed necessities; and of looking towards last things, fruits, consequences, facts.*"[1] And for Peirce the "kernel of pragmatism" is the idea that "the *whole* meaning of an intellectual predicate is that certain kinds of events would happen, once in so often, in the course of experience, under certain kinds of existential condition" (CP 5.468). Thus, for Peirce, reality is determinable in terms of future activity. Reality, then, is evolutionary. This point is central to the relating of Peircean pragmaticism to process philosophy.

With respect to process philosophy, I take the main thrust of its advocates to depend on the rejection of any metaphysical or ontological position that views reality as substantival and static. What is knowable as reality is temporally spread as or in sequences of events. Events are connected by relations, and the only stabilities in the processes of reality consist in these relations.

Taking these ideas as my starting point I turn now to my speculative interpretation. I will openly engage in a good deal of extrapolation from Peirce's view and, though cautiously, I will introduce speculations of my own that go beyond a strict interpretation of Peirce's view. My chief concern, therefore, will not be to suggest and justify a claim about the position Peirce "really" held. Rather, I will employ what he *did* say concerning his realism to suggest what he *might* have said had he gone further in this direction.

I

After describing reality as the object of the final opinion, Peirce raised the question whether the object is independent of all thought in general. His answer, as noted in chapter 1, is not definitive. He maintained that the real is not necessarily ultimately dependent on thought in general. "The opinion which is fated to be ultimately agreed to by all who investigate," he argued, "is what I mean by the truth, and the object represented in this opinion is the real" (CP 5.407, W 3:273). What is important here is the status of the object of this ultimate opinion. Is this object in part and in some way independent, or is it wholly dependent on the final opinion? It is clear that Peirce insists that the final opinion is independent of any finite thought or thoughts of a finite group of inquirers. But what about the object of the ultimate opinion, which is not that of any finite community of intelligent beings?

Peirce continued with the following suggested answer:

> But it may be said that this view [of reality] is directly opposed to the abstract definition which I have given of reality, inasmuch as it makes the characters of the real depend on what is ultimately thought about them. But the answer to this is that, on the one hand, reality is independent, not necessarily of thought in general, but only of what you or I or any finite number of men may think about it; and that, on the other hand, though the object of the final opinion depends on what that opinion is, yet what that opinion is does not depend on what you or I or any man thinks. (CP 5.408, W 3:274)

The independence from finite thought, of course, leaves room for some form of objective idealism. However, in saying that reality is not necessarily independent of thought in general, he inserts an element of doubt about whether some kind of external reality is, after all, independent of thought in general. If it is not necessarily independent, it may also be said that it is not necessarily dependent. As I will try to show later, this final object of opinion is what Peirce later called the immediate object as distinct from the dynamical object. The immediate object is the object as interpreted, which seems to be just what he means here by "the Final Object," that is, the object as finally interpreted. Thus, we are still left with the question of what the object is that is interpreted, or, more precisely, what the condition is that functions as that which is interpreted by the final opinion.

Peirce's discussion here, which is from his 1878 paper "How to Make Our Ideas Clear," indicates, I think, that relatively early he at least nodded toward some form of metaphysical realism—that is, the view that everything that is, is not wholly mind dependent. In any case, I do not think that Peirce, in the final analysis, held a form of pragmatism that unqualifiedly equated reality with mental action, as, perhaps, other pragmatists have done.

The second passage that provides apparent support for viewing Peirce as an objective idealist is the one in which Peirce says that matter is effete mind.[2] However, this in itself is relevant to the issue only if matter is understood to be a nonmental substance that has its own laws, independently of what thought in general thinks. Peirce, of course, rejects this idea. Matter, for Peirce, is physical substance accessible through sense qualities, and it is intelligible by virtue of a lawfulness that is constituted by interpretation, and thus which is attributed to mind. To say that matter in this sense is effete is to say that it is not effective or active for inquirers without falling under interpretation, or theory. But this is not in itself to affirm objective idealism. I think that there still are ways of acknowledging some externality of conditions constraining theory and interpretation in general. It is Peirce's notion of such conditions that will be the main thesis of my discussion.

The third piece of evidence for the claim that Peirce was an objective idealist is his statement that objective idealism is the one intelligible theory of the universe. What may be the weakest counter to the idea that this is conclusive evidence that Peirce believed himself to be an objective idealist is that being the one intelligible theory of anything is not to exclude there being more to the universe than that which is subject to the one intelligible theory. And this "more" may indeed constrain the theory. Moreover, granted that Peirce saw his attempt to make sense of the universe as following the ways of objective idealist theorizing, as mentioned earlier, Peirce explicitly ruled out Hegelian idealism, because it does not do justice to his category of secondness, or the presence in experience of resistance and spontaneity. In "the Hegelian system," he argued, firstness and secondness "are only introduced in order to be *aufgehoben*" (CP 5.79). Secondness thus functions in tension with the claim that all of reality is constituted by mind, or by theorizing itself. The persistence of secondness, it seems to me, must be a thorn in the side of any committed objective idealist.

The responses I have offered to the labeling of Peirce as an objective idealist are telescoped in one central reason. There is a distinction that Peirce makes in the context of his semeiotic, a distinction between the object *as* interpreted, which he calls the *immediate object*, and that which *is* interpreted, which is his *dynamical object*. In short, I think his view of reality was that immediate objects are interpretations of something infinitely resistant to interpretation, and what resists is something that in a sense is other than interpretation or the intelligible mental activity. The substance of what follows is an elaboration on these claims—claims foreshadowed in the opening chapter.

II

The issue here concerning whether Peirce was a realist or an idealist, it must be emphasized, is not a matter of his scholastic realism; nor does it center on his nod toward the kinship between, but also a basic difference between, Platonic forms and his generals—with the understanding that the former are unchanging and the latter are evolutionary. The issue with which I am concerned is whether Peirce was a metaphysical realist, that is, whether he offered an insightful realism in which reality is not construed as wholly constituted by mind or as isomorphic with mind or mentality as such. The question, then, is: did Peirce have a vision of a reality that functions as an extramental condition not exhausted by the interpretants that render it intelligible? The answer lies in the semeiotic distinction. This distinction, as indicated already, is between the immediate and the dynamical object. I think that attending to Peirce's notion of the dynamical object is the only way to distinguish his metaphysical commitments from some form of objective idealism.

Interpretation, then, has two objects, or what perhaps should be called a two-fold object of interpretation: the dynamical object and the immediate object. In 1909, Peirce stated, "I must distinguish between the Immediate Object,—i.e. the Object as represented in the sign,—and the Real (no, because perhaps the Object is altogether fictive, I must choose a different term, therefore), say rather the Dynamical Object, which, from the nature of things, the Sign cannot express, which it can only indicate and leave the interpreter to find out by collateral experience" (CP 8.314). I also describe this distinction by saying that there is one referent of a sign and that the referent has two sides or aspects. Perhaps it is helpful to say that the referent of a sign consists of two interactive objects, the immediate object and the dynamical, or real, object, a distinction to be considered later.

The dynamical object seems to be the object that functions as the beginning of and basis for semeiosis or the interpretive process, for it is that which is to be interpreted. And, as I mentioned earlier, the immediate object is the interpreted dynamical object. It is the outcome of interpreting the initiating object. The dynamical object functions as a condition of constraints on interpretation. The ways it thus constrains is a crucial issue, to be considered in a moment. The brief description of the semeiotic distinction just mentioned, of course, does not characterize any pre-interpreted dynamical object with respect to the qualities or characteristics that it might be thought to have and that need to be specified as interpretation discovers them. As Peirce stated it in considering the dynamical object, it is the "[o]bject as it is regardless of any aspect of it" (CP 8.183).

Interpretation is in a sense creative. It is creative insofar as it does its job according to the ways the mind works, which is to say that it proceeds on the basis of its memories of other objects, its dispositions or forms of perceiving and thinking, and its own prior fund of semeiotic systems. In general, the mind imposes its laws or regularities, or its ways of generalizing, on the matter for interpretation. Thus, it is impossible in principle—it is self-contradictory—to characterize the initiating object of interpretation prior to interpretation, for such characterization presupposes that the object is already interpreted. If one could say just what any given dynamical object is in itself, then, apparently in accordance with a form of representational realism, one would be implying a special access to reality as a determinate condition of theory or interpretation in general.

Nevertheless, Peirce suggested that one may have an acquaintance with a dynamical object within what he called collateral experience, a matter to be considered later. Suffice it to say at the moment that the experience possible with respect to the dynamical object is not determinate and describable until it has entered an interpretive process.

Likewise, it would be contrary to Peirce's notion of the dynamical object to conclude that the object to be interpreted does not play its role in constraining the imposition of intelligence on it, no matter how creative or free from antecedent determinations the interpretive act may be. And no matter how much funded experience, or how many assumptions, instinctive beliefs, and so forth inform interpretation, the object plays its own role in interacting with that ongoing semeiosis. Peirce said that indexical signs and their objects "make an organic pair, but the interpreting mind has nothing to do with this connection, except remarking it, after it is established" (CP 2.299). It is clear that Peirce regarded the dynamical object as having a pre-interpreted, pre-triadic, and yet constraining function with regard to interpretation.

It may now be obvious that, in light of the impossibility of defining a dynamical object without contradicting its status, I will develop and elaborate on what I take to be Peirce's notion of the dynamical object by assuming a functional approach. This approach was more than hinted at a few moments ago when the question was raised about how reality functions in relation to interpretation, and in my observation that dynamical objects and their indexical signs are organically related. Thus, the proper and pragmatic way to understand the term *dynamical object* is to understand the function or functions it has in interpretive experience. Perhaps it would be best, then, to propose to answer the question, "What does the dynamical object *do*?" rather than "What *is* the dynamical object?" However, it will be obvious later that the functional approach will reach a limit, and some commitment to an underlying ontology must be faced. This limit is reached when the functions of the dynamical object are traced to their origins in the condition by virtue of which there are functions—in short, when one faces the question of what *does* the functioning. I believe this approach is at least consistent with the way Peirce thought of what can be said about the two objects of interpretation.

III

The dynamical object might be understood in a variety of ways. David Savan has offered a systematic account of the most basic ways, all understood in terms of kinds of interpretants and signs as they relate to both immediate and dynamical objects. Underlying these are Peirce's three categories. Savan's discussion is helpful, and some of his ideas have influenced my thoughts as they relate to this discussion. However, I am not sure that he gives sufficient emphasis or, for that matter, sufficient attention to the resistance and the demands of the constraints dynamical objects may impose on interpretation. Also, my purposes are somewhat different from his. The different interpretations of dynamical objects that I will summarize are based on my central aim of showing the extent to which the dynamical object can function as an external condition, not wholly subject to the mind and to thought in general.

It seems to me that there are at least five ways of understanding the possible overlapping functions of the dynamical object. I describe these ways of functioning in terms of options for distinct, although interrelated, ways of characterizing them. Let us emphasize that each one of them is properly attributable to a complex understanding of what Peirce meant, or at least what he may have thought ought to be meant, by the idea of the dynamical object.

IV

The first option or way of understanding is that the dynamical object functions as a Kantian thing-in-itself, as a condition external to and independent of all thought, although relevant to thought, even if not, in itself, knowable. This option seems plausible in light of what was just said about the trying and failing to describe and thus the impossibility of saying what the dynamical object in itself is. However, the idea that the dynamical object functions as a thing-in-itself may also seem unlikely, given reasons to be mentioned in a moment. But it is useful to consider how it contrasts with the other four possible functions, which suppose that the dynamical object has an immediate and a direct relation to interpretation.

The first proposal, then, supposes that a dynamical object functions as an external individuality, a thing that exists and is an extra-conceptual cause of the determinations achieved in interpretation. It may be construed as a singular or as a multiple of things-in-themselves, each being an external thing itself for every object of every sign.

If the thing-in-itself were causal, as efficient or as final, it might be equated with the final dynamical object. This approach seems to be suggested by Peirce in statements such as, "The Sign . . . has been, in a mediate and relative way, also created by the Object of the Sign, although the Object is essentially other than the Sign" (CP 8.179). Thus, a final dynamical object would not be internal to semeiosis. But Peirce also suggests that the dynamical object constrains what interpretation makes of it and feeds this into the immediate object, which is the mediating sign for the dynamical object. Thus, Peirce's characterization does not suppose that the dynamical object is, in principle, an unknowable reality. Furthermore, it should be added that Peirce's discussions of the dynamical object treat it as functioning in an experiential presence for interpretation, especially for particular contexts of interpretation. Moreover, what seems to be the most convincing evidence that Peirce did not regard the dynamical object as a thing-in-itself is that, in his early writings, he insisted that the idea of a thing-in-itself is not coherent. What, then, can be said about the other ways of understanding the function of the dynamical object?

The other ways share in seeing the relevance of direct and immediate bearing on experience on the part of the dynamical object. And they suggest that the term *dynamical object* may indicate a single, a unitary and unifying, condition, or a multiple of conditions. In the capacity of functioning as a single condition, however, the dynamical object may be, in fact must be, manifest and effective in a multiplicity of conditions that constrain and propel particular semeiotic situations.

According to the second proposed function, the dynamical object serves as a sense manifold. This might seem to be suggested in Peirce's early paper "On a New List of Categories." In that context, if the dynamical object is a sense manifold, it would be the experience that invites inquirers to form a judgment in the form of a proposition and would be what the proposition is designed to bring to a unity. It seems that a manifold is necessarily a multiplicity, but not a multiplicity of specific or determinate, given pre-interpreted objects.

V

The second possible interpretation of the dynamical object is that it is a sense manifold, an indeterminate sensuous and emotional field ready for semeiotic attention. As suggested earlier, there is some basis for this interpretation in Peirce's early writing, when he begins with a Kantian notion of a sense manifold that needs to be brought to unity in a proposition. The manifold is a supposed presence, and it is the only pre-interpreted field of which there is consciousness. One could, then, conclude that it functions like the dynamical object insofar as it is an object for a sign and as such calls for interpretation. This construes the dynamical object as what Peirce calls the real object, where the term *real* is not limited to spatial location, but may include qualities and laws with their instances. In turn, the interpretation of the real object is an outcome that might be construed as an immediate object—the real object interpreted. However, there are two reasons for rejecting this as an adequate account of the way the dynamical object functions. The manifold that gives itself for interpretation is passive rather than dynamic. That is, the mind in interpreting can make whatever meaning it decides to make, or perhaps is compelled to make because of previously accepted systems of meanings. If there is constraint on the part of the manifold, it seems to be no more than the constraining of an inchoate stuff, in a way, like clay with no determinate shape waiting to be molded into something determinate. The second reason for not accepting the option that the dynamical object functions simply as a sense manifold is that not only is the manifold passive, but it has no even vaguely or incipiently determinate forces that could constrain interpretation one way or the other. Constraints, other than the sheer resistance of mass, must be provided entirely by the interpretive agency.

VI

The third possibility is that the dynamical object serves as an object of an indexical sign and is experienced in a reaction to resistance. This is to assign the real object to the category of secondness; any manifestation of it, then, is a second. The experience of secondness, then, would be the reaction to an impact or a resistance, and the acting referent would be the dynamical object. A toothache, for instance, might be referred to indexically by pointing to it. The object then might be construed as the brute pressure of the pain that is associated with the tooth.

Brute reactions to things that are referred to by signs are instances of secondness and are dyadic relations of signs to objects. Peirce, of course, does consider signs to be indexically related to their objects, as well as to be related to objects by representation and iconicity. Referring to the indexical relation, he says, "The index is physically connected with its object; they make an organic pair, but the interpreting mind has nothing to do with this connection, except remarking it, after it is established" (CP 2.299). Further, he stated elsewhere, "[A]n index is essentially an affair of here and now, its office being to bring the thought to a particular experience, or series of experiences connected by dynamical relations" (CP 4.56). The figurative suggestion that an indexical sign and its object are organically related is an important point to which I must return. However, at the moment it is important to recognize that the object to be interpreted, that is, the dynamical object, must be referred to indexically and thus experienced in a moment of reaction to brute resistance. This is the dynamic dimension of the object.

The idea that the dynamical object is one of the correlates in a dyadic relation is, it seems, a necessary condition of its functioning in triadic, or interpretive, relations. It is one of three ways it relates to signs; the other ways, of course, are iconically and symbolically. And symbols do not exclude indexical reference; nor do icons function as signs without at least a degenerate dyadic reference. The dynamical object, then, is the active aspect of its function in serving as a constraint on interpretation.

However, constraints consist of more than resistances; they also consist of compulsive nudges that have what I have called vectorial functions. The pressures of the dynamical object on interpretation have varying degrees of forcefulness and direction. The direction they have is no more than a heading of interpretation this way or that. But this is not the here and now as such that comes with pure seconds. The vectors provide more than the specificity of this, here, now, but add a hint of this way rather than that. However, that is the only clue to interpretation that they give. I will return to this idea of vectorial force in the pressures of seconds. It is important to note in the context of the third proposal, however, because dynamical objects do, after all, contribute to the direction interpretation takes within semeiotic systems.

VII

The fourth possibility, like the second and third, includes the idea of multiplicity so that the dynamical object is not, after all, thought to be simply one object or source—perhaps equivalent to a Kantian transcendental object. Since I take this fourth way of understanding the dynamical object, along with the fifth, which remains to be introduced, to be closest to the preferred proposals, I shall dwell on it at greatest length.

For this fourth option, the dynamical object is effective within particular experiences. On this view of its function, it is what Peirce sometimes calls the real object. For example, I may take the law of gravity, which has been interpreted differently in different scientific and philosophical systems. Or consider a physical, space-time plaque with a series of inscriptions on it. This is an object to be interpreted by linguists and archeologists. For a third example, consider a dot on the horizon that invites interpretation as a vehicle moving toward an observer or as a distant building. According to this fourth option, the plaque with inscriptions and the dot on the horizon are each dynamical or real objects that are subject to and that enter into semeiotic processes. In the case of the law of gravity, the real object may be the law itself, since, according to Peirce's scholastic realism, generals are real. However, supporting generals there are real objects consisting of instances of the law—most obvious are instances of falling objects.

The multiplicity of real objects consists in the diverse origins and conditions of interpretation—like percepts that are subject to perceptual judgments. It must be emphasized, however, that real objects are not independent as things-in-themselves. From the inception of the interpretive act, they are interdependent with the interpretant that is developed as an evolving sign. As Peirce said, interpretation—hypothesis or abduction—pervades all intelligible experience all the way to pre-conscious experience.

It will be helpful to consider several more examples. A hydrogen atom may be regarded as a dynamical object, a factor in constraining the form of a water molecule. A ball and the motion of the ball rolling from one point to another may be thought to be a dynamical object in relation to another ball that is struck and moved by the first ball. The reaction of the two balls is a case of secondness. But the interpretation of the event by a physicist studying velocity, mass, and force would concern the event as a dynamical object for interpretation. In these examples, the atom and the occasion of one ball striking another function as dynamical objects for interpretations.

Several of Peirce's own examples support this fourth option, and, in addition, these examples show the complexity and impossibility of giving a descriptive account of the nature of the dynamical object. In a passage in which he distinguishes immediate from dynamical objects, Peirce refers to the immediate object of the term *the sun* as the "occasion of sundry sensations," and he refers to the dynamical object as "our usual interpretation of such sensations in terms of place, of mass, etc." (CP 8.183). In another passage, when discussing the relation of immediate to dynamical objects, Peirce mentions as an example answering his wife's question, "What sort of day is it?" He says that the dynamical object of his report about the weather is "the impression which I have presumably derived from peeping between the window-curtains" (CP 8:314). In the case of the weather, Peirce seems to imply that the constraint and propulsion of an impression is a factor in constraining the interpretation of the object. However, soon after referring to his wife's impression as the dynamical object of the sign, Peirce adds that there is a dynamical object present both to his wife and to him. It is "the identity of the actual or Real meteorological conditions at the moment" (CP 8.314). And this statement clearly confirms the idea that dynamical and immediate objects are functionally related in a certain order.

Additional support for option four can be found in Peirce's insistence that collateral experience of the object to be interpreted is needed in order for an interpretation to be intelligible.

> All that part of the understanding of the Sign which the Interpreting Mind has needed collateral observation for is outside the Interpretant. I do not mean by "collateral observation" acquaintance with the system of signs. What is so gathered is not COLLATERAL. It is on the contrary the prerequisite for getting any idea signified by the sign. But by collateral observation, I mean previous acquaintance with what the sign denotes. (CP 8.179)

He goes on to say that one must have previous experience of the individual object of the sign. Denoting "calls for no particular Intelligence or Reason." What is required is acquaintance with the usual concomitants of appearances of the thing denoted (CP 8.181). The relation of the interpretive processes to their objects suggests again that dynamical objects must be understood functionally and relatively with respect to each interpretation. This may be clearer if I observe that those things called real or dynamical are, after all, interpreted objects. As such, they are immediate objects ready to be interpreted further. Consider the function of individual dynamical objects within a relation of atoms to molecules and molecules to water, or the relation of the impression of the weather to describing or reporting the weather. In each case, the object said to be dynamical is already interpreted, even though it is identified as a dynamical object for a sign. Thus, it functions as a constraining, dynamical object. In short, if dynamical objects are identified as conditions for signs playing roles within a system of signs, they are immediate objects. The atom, the molecule, the impression of the weather, which are singled out as examples, are immediate or dynamical objects, depending on their roles within interpretation. The relations of one to the other are at bottom between more fundamental or conditioning immediate objects and other immediate objects that are partially dependent on the initiating and conditioning or constraining immediate object within the system of signs and their immediate objects. Dynamical objects are caught up in an interpreted and interpreting network. Let us reiterate and elaborate briefly on the points I am trying to make.

Dynamical objects understood as referential conditions of interpretation function as those things that condition interpretation and through semeiosis are interpreted. These objects bring with them certain resistances and demands with respect to how they may be interpreted. At the same time, interpreters bring with them their own resistances or feelings of compulsion that are not (not yet) intelligible nodes but which are associated with the larger semeiotic system of meanings that frame interpretation. In any case, these restraining experiences of the surrounding system are, I believe, what Peirce refers to as what comes to interpreters as "acquaintance with the system of signs" (CP 8.179). On the other hand, collateral experience with dynamical objects, which is pre-interpretive within the context of an initiated semeiosis, is presupposed as the basis for the semeioses contributing to the system. Collateral experience must spring from some kind of acquaintance the interpreter has or presupposes as necessary to the object to be interpreted.

It is enlightening to turn to another way to explain how collateral experiences function in relation to interpretation. This other way is found in a discussion by Peirce of the relation of percepts and perceptual judgments to immediate objects and dynamical objects. Peirce says that "[t]he Immediate Object of all knowledge and all thought is, in the last analysis, the Percept" (CP 4.539). This placing of such importance on the percept, as I will discuss later, is consistent with what Peirce indicates elsewhere about percepts in relation to perceptual judgments, namely, that percepts are the beginning and the end of inquiry. What then, is the dynamical object in relation to the immediate object of all thought, that is, the percept? It must be something either pre-interpreted or finally interpreted as the final goal of thought. The notion of a Final Percept will appear again in connection with the fifth proposal. Pre-interpreted percepts initiate perceptual judgments, which are the interpretants that are necessary to all empirical knowledge. Peirce suggests an answer to this question with a puzzling statement: he says that immediate perceptions are not percepts, but "a Percept is a Seme, while a fact of Immediate Perception or rather the Perceptual Judgment of which such fact is the Immediate Interpretant, is a Pheme that is the direct Dynamical Interpretant of the Percept, and of which the Percept is the Dynamical Object, and is with some considerable difficulty . . . distinguished from the Immediate Object, though the distinction is highly significant" (CP 8.539). One way briefly to make this "highly significant" distinction is to note that Peirce defines the seme as that which is indexical:

> An Index or Seme (σῆμα) is a Representamen whose Representative character consists in its being an individual second. If the Secondness is an existential relation, the Index is genuine. If the Secondness is a reference, the Index is degenerate. A genuine Index and its Object must be existent individuals (whether things or facts), and its immediate Interpretant must be of the same character. (CP 2.283)

If a percept is a genuine index, then it and its object—presumably, its dynamical object—must be existent individuals. And this reinforces the interpretation of dynamical objects as objects that have some kind of constraining and active bodily effectiveness that is taken into account in an interpretation. I cannot try to untangle the complicated account Peirce offers in calling the percept both a dynamical object and a seme. However, for our purposes, what is important is the way the immediate and dynamical objects converge in percepts. This not only confirms the suggestion that the relation between them is relative to the functions of the objects involved, but it is also suggestive, at least in the case of the post-interpreted percept, that the final outcome of interpretation may lie in the unity of dynamical and immediate objects, or the unity of the final opinion and its object. And this would support the objective idealism that I have claimed is not Peirce's final word. The only hint that Peirce did not intend this to be found in the passages just quoted is that Peirce says that even though it is difficult to distinguish immediate and dynamical objects, the distinction is "highly significant."

The function of dynamical objects, then, is not exhausted by the relational and relative relations proposed in option four. Dynamical objects that function simply as more fundamental immediate objects for other immediate objects must themselves be interpretations, which have origins in a still more fundamental or more primordial constraining function. And the primordial object is not—not yet, at any rate—caught up in the network of immediate objects. In the example of the weather report, the state of the weather that Peirce is said to report to his wife is constrained by certain conditions, including wind direction, velocity, barometric pressure, fronts, jet streams, and so forth. These, of course, are identified as well as they can be by meteorologists. As such, they are interpreted objects. But still there is the inevitable function of the object, the original or most fundamental dynamical object, which is not internal to the system. We, as philosophically motivated inquirers, may push the inquiry to its limit. And if the continued inquiry supposedly leads to some primordial or a final dynamical object that constrains our immediate objects, we may be tempted to propose the fifth option, namely, that the dynamical object of all semeioses is what functions as the object of the final opinion. It is now appropriate, indeed necessary, to turn to an appraisal of this fifth proposal.

VIII

The fifth possibility construes the dynamical object as a teleological condition toward which all interpretation or inquiry is headed. I noted earlier that Peirce said that the dynamical object, related to truth as the object of inquiry, would be the object of unlimited and final study (CP 8.183). The dynamical object is "the Object of every true Proposition," and may be called "The Truth" (CP 4.539). This indicates that one way in which Peirce understood the function of the dynamical object was to view it as an end or goal of all inquiry and all interpretation. It lies at the ideal limit of evolutionary development. Further, this idea of a final end confirms the teleological function that the dynamical object has for interpretation. It offers a telos, although it is one that is not known at any specified or specifiable time in the future. However, does it follow that I should understand the dynamical object as a unity functioning in a final state of convergence?

Peirce's account of the evolutionary structure of the cosmos might seem to call for an answer in the affirmative. And his notion of agape, as I have proposed in other places, includes the idea of an open-ended evolutionary principle (conforming to a developmental teleology) yet which, as agapistic, is headed toward some end—an end that is not predetermined. Put in a crudely figurative way, the road of inquiry, or of semeiosis, does not end in a box. Or at least is doesn't unless the box is infinitely large. If that were the case, then semeiosis would end in an infinite mind—the final inquirer and the final opinion would be one with the mind of divinity. But this terminus, this convergence, is an ideal limit, not something realizable as an actuality. I believe that its status bears a resemblance to Kant's transcendental object.

If this account is accurate, then the fifth interpretation of the function of the dynamical object is to be accepted. However, the culminating function of the dynamical object, here regarded as the Final

Immediate Object, does not exhaust its function. For serving as Final does not preclude its also functioning at finite stages of interpretation, in the ongoing progress of semeioses. In so functioning, it is independent in part from immediate objects functioning as otherness from any finite context of interpretation. This is to say that it functions as a condition external to all influencing immediate objects. This point is supported by Peirce's account of collateral experience, some of which is based on acquaintance prior to any interpretation. This is consistent with the idea that pre-interpreted percepts may serve constraining functions. However, what is most important is that the inexhaustible apparent residue of pre-interpreted conditions is to be accounted for as the Final, inexhaustible, Dynamical Object. It is what the Final Immediate Object has as its Dynamical Object. The Final Immediate Object is not merged with the Dynamical Object. As Peirce says, any such actual merging would lie in the infinite future and is never actually reached.

The inclusion of finite functionings of the dynamical object supports resistances to alleged infallible conclusions, that is, knowledge of the state of things as given in the final opinion. At the same time, synechism implies that the individualization and local convergence of constraints in the here and now must be understood in the larger context of a continuum of ongoing development. Reality, then, may include spontaneity and moments of departures from established laws, which departures then contribute to the growth of laws that have as an ideal limit a would-be final true thought about reality as a whole, a whole that embraces all past diversification as well as individualized convergences.

IX

What my proposal comes to is the claim that the dynamical object is to be understood as an integration of options four and five. The integrating of these two options leads to many questions, one of which concerns how a multiplicity of dynamical objects or their manifestations function in relation to the one, final dynamical object.

How is the overall constraining of the one Final Dynamical Object effective with respect to the many? This, of course, is a version of one of the fundamental enduring questions of philosophy. I shall only hint at an answer in terms of a suggestion I made earlier about the way constraints coming from the object and experienced initially as seconds have vectorial functions. And I will take only a brief time to elaborate on this. In doing so, I will also reiterate my proposal for how this view of the dynamical object shows the uniqueness of both Peirce's idealism and realism—and, in my opinion, supports the claim that he leaned toward a unique metaphysical realism that did not violate what he seems to have taken as the insights of objective idealism. I hope to offer this last proposal within the context of an illustration, a hypothetical example. The illustration will be the occasion to return to our point about the presence of vectorial constraints.

Suppose two hikers see a dot on the horizon. The first, A, says, "There is our fellow hiker returning to report about what is ahead." The other, B, says, "No, I don't think so, that is a tree." Both hikers have offered interpretations, and their objects are immediate objects. The dynamical object is the dot on the horizon just prior to the interpretations. Hiker A's past collateral experiences suggest a human shape and information about a mission the third hiker was to accomplish. Here it seems that collateral experience, a percept (uninterpreted), and general semeiotic information about distances, light, and so forth that affect vision add to the constraints on A's interpretation. Hiker B also has collateral experiences, some shared with A and some distinct to himself.

At this point, I add a vectorial function in all these constraints. They are experienced in different ways, with different pressures. For instance, recollection of the third hiker's mission probably has a good deal of force, and the direction the force comes from depends on memory, trust in the friend's faithfulness, and so forth. These constraints seem obvious and relatively clear as to their strength and direction in influencing both hikers' interpretations. But for B, the vectors are different. They consist of the greater dominance or force the specific shape of the dot has on B's eyes.

What is at issue here, however, is the proposal that constraints function with respect to the percept, or the dot on the horizon, which is presumably the dynamical object—that is, the real object that prompts the two interpretations and will prompt more as the distance between the hikers and the object decreases. This real object, too, has vectorial functions. Its impact on vision is not particularly strong, and it has a particular location, so that what is seen comes from a certain direction. These constraints need not be attended to, unless later when refinement of interpretation is added. But once they are attended to, they are interpreted, and they begin to contribute explicitly to the immediate objects that are developing as the object of interpretation. Furthermore, and most importantly, the pressures of the real object, before it is interpreted, constrain at least negatively. They do so by appearing as resistances to interpreting one way rather than another. The most blatant example of this in the case of the hikers is that interpreting the dot on the horizon as a cloud would be strongly resisted, at least assuming the hikers have normal eyesight and thinking processes that are not subject to hallucinations. However, even supposing they were hallucinating, sooner or later constraints would bring resistance, for instance, if when they got to the spot on the horizon they bumped against a large rock, which was the object that had first appeared as a dot. Their immediate objects would then change. In any case, the force and direction of these constraints contribute to what the hikers bring with them in collateral experience and semeiotic contexts. And some of these constraints are pre-interpreted, that is, not prior immediate objects.

Now suppose that the hikers draw nearer while vectorial constraints change, including more specific direction and increased forcefulness of the impacts on the eyes of the hikers. Suppose, then, that hiker B says, "See, that is a tree, after all," and A concedes. What is the dynamical object now? Presumably, it is, finally, the real object. Is that the tree? But the tree is an interpreted object, which is an immediate object. This becomes obvious if when approaching closer, the hikers change their minds and one of them says, "We were both wrong; that is a strange rock formation." What then is the real object? The rock formation? The rock prior to being interpreted? But what is that? The tree? The third hiker? The dot? Each of these, even the dot insofar as it has been interpreted as such-and-such an item, called a dot, was on the horizon.

I might here interject that if this illustration shows that there is nothing more to what appears and is interpreted, and that all there is is thought alone, then I would be adopting a semeiotic idealism. This would be tantamount to insisting that there are no dynamical objects, after all. There are only immediate objects, that is, the products of theories and interpretations—the sort of position, as we saw, that Margolis and Rorty defend. What Peirce called real objects, then, would be pre-interpreted immediate objects. In response, I think that this conclusion suggests that Peirce's real objects stand in a correspondence relation to interpretation, and the semeiotic idealism has internal to it a correspondence notion of interpretive accuracy. This would deny Peirce's insistence on the importance and inevitability of vagueness in the universe.[3] Further, the conclusion would also conflict with Peirce's hypothesis that things in the world evolve in such a way that departures from regularities, or the growth of generals, occur. If all objects in the universe were determinate and waiting to be discovered, the universe could not evolve, but would be a fixed system waiting to be matched by thought.

What then is the real object in the case of the provisionally final interpretation that the dot is a rock formation? The functional approach implies that I could stop at this point and say that pragmatically, I have all I need. But pragmaticistically, I cannot stop with concluding that the real is the rock. As I indicated briefly earlier, philosophically, I am led to continue inquiry. I may then take the step of the idealist and insist that real objects are after all the products of interpretation, and I might do so while granting that there is evolution in the cosmos, but it is an evolution of mind. I need nothing more than mind as what constitutes the semeiotic system. This conclusion can also accommodate the idea of a convergence of all inquiry in the Final Object of the Final Opinion, which serves as the final end of evolutionary love. However, there are two overlapping reasons why I cannot help resisting this as the final word on Peirce's view of idealism and realism.

The first reason is that evolutionary love is not eros, understood as the notion of having a final goal sought for by the evolutionary dynamism. Peirce's evolutionary love is agapistic, which means that it is not driven to merge with a determined purpose. Instead, it is open to the emergence of new purposes. Thus, agape would have to cease to be agape on the conclusion of the idealist view of finality. Why shouldn't I admit this kind of finality so long as I also admit that this final end itself evolved? This consideration leads to the second reason for resisting the idealist conclusion. This second reason is that for Peirce, any such emergence and convergence in a Final Object that is the same as the Final Opinion—the merging of the final immediate object and the final dynamical object—lies in the infinite future to which no actual time or place is assignable. It is this inexhaustibility of the dynamical object that resists idealism. And the function of this inexhaustibility is manifest in all conditions of resistance within finite, individual contexts.[4]

Thus, I see no way to understand the integration of the fourth and fifth ways of understanding the dynamical object, except to say that what counts as a dynamical object is the way the object fits into or functions in relation to interpretation. It can be a prior immediate object for a developing interpretation, and as such, it functions dynamically. But underlying all these strands of interpretations, and all these related immediate objects, is externality, the inevitable function of the inexhaustible condition of thought in general.

X

I should like to conclude with a final brief and somewhat speculative idea about the kind of self-transcending idealism that is equated with the unique realism that, I believe, Peirce held, or at least meant to hold. If I think of the cosmos as evolutionary, as Peirce did, then there are grounds for supposing that the dynamical object is evolutionary. Thus, its constraining function, acting in part independently but also in interactions with the interpreting semeiosis, may vary too. Over long periods of time, and sometimes in short ones, so-called matter, or law itself, evolves. The universe changes, not only because new theories are developed, but because reality itself plays a role in the evolution of science and thought in general. Most theorists of cosmology now believe that the universe is in continuous expansion. This view of the cosmos, of course, appears to conflict with the generally accepted view that Peirce saw theory or inquiry in general as converging on a kind of closure, that is, on a final truth about a final object, reality. But the object of the final opinion, I have proposed, is still the Dynamical Object, which, as the label implies, is dynamic. And this understanding fits a description of the final object as the object of a system of theories concerning laws, that is, a system of generals or continuities. But if these as generals are themselves subject at least to infinitesimal departures, then even the final opinion, the final immediate object, is not, after all, final. That is one reason, I think, that Peirce said that any such closure of inquiry is a would-be and would be actualizable only in an infinite future. But an infinite future for actualization, which is to be actual temporally, is never actually forthcoming.

In the final analysis, Peirce's self-transcendent idealism is his unique realism. Both of these, or the combination of them, must be found in the infinite escape from closure on the part of interpretation. The dynamism and openness of this realism place it squarely in the tradition of what we have come to call process philosophy.

SIX

ANOTHER RADICAL EMPIRICISM: PEIRCE 1903

Doug Anderson

The discussion of Peircean realism led us to consider how, for Peirce, perception, which begins and ends inquiry, is related to the conditions that constrain semeiosis. Peirce had corresponded with William James on the nature of perception and concluded that he and James shared a version of the doctrine of immediate perception. In this chapter, I pursue some of the similarities in their respective outlooks.[1]

I n 1904 William James marked his "radical empiricism" by maintaining that I perceive not only individual things but also the relations of conjunction and disjunction in which they appear. "To be radical," he asserted, "an empiricism must neither admit into its construction any element that is not directly experienced, nor exclude from them any element that is directly experienced. For such a philosophy, the relations that connect experiences must themselves be experienced relations, and any kind of relation experienced must be accounted as 'real' as anything else in the system."[2] Peirce, as a fellow

pragmatist, though he never used the phrase *radical empiricism* to describe his own views, agreed in principle with James's assessment of
experience and perception. In a series of seven lectures delivered at
Harvard in the spring of 1903, Peirce described and illustrated his own
version of what James called radical empiricism. Because of their different styles and temperaments, it is occasionally difficult to see the
similarities in the work of James and Peirce. No doubt their motivations and underlying assumptions were often at odds, but the cash
values of their respective positions were often remarkably alike. In
Peirce's 1903 lectures I find not only a sophisticated defense of our
perceptions of relations and what Peirce called "Thirdness," but also
a consequent emphasis on the importance of individual experience
and perception in setting thought and reason in motion. And finally,
I find in Peirce's lectures evidence of his ongoing revision of scientific
inquiry away from Comtean positivism and the narrow nominalism
that dominated much thought in the nineteenth and twentieth centu-
ries.[3] In this revision I find the creativity and richness in human inquiry that James sought and tried to exemplify in texts such as *The
Varieties of Religious Experience.* My aim here is to exhibit, through a
brief examination of the 1903 lectures, some of the features in Peirce's
work that bear an affinity for the spirit of James's radical empiricism.

Peirce began his subtle assault on nineteenth-century scientism by
asserting that perception is a process, not a set of discrete, unrelated
mental events that need to be glued together. For Peirce, no description or theory of inquiry could justifiably arise—as Hume had seen—
under such a typical empiricist view of perception. Peirce rested his
case for the perceptual process on two bases: 1) his phenomenological
investigation of experience, in which generality and continuity appear; and 2) the experiential insistence that we are reasoning beings.
To reject these is, for Peirce, to deny the efficacy of reason and inquiry, a reduction Peirce believed most of us would reject in practice
if not in theory.

As Peirce saw it, the perceptual process begins with the percept,
the ongoing moment in which ego and non-ego jointly create the immediate content of experience. The percept, however, must be

brought "to mind" or "to consciousness," and this occurs directly through what Peirce called "perceptual judgment"—"a judgment asserting in propositional form what a character of a percept directly present to the mind is" (EP 2:155). What keeps this process perceptual, and thus distinct from other mental phenomena, is its absence of self-control and immediate criticizeability. "Even after the percept is formed," Peirce argued, "there is an operation which seems to me to be quite uncontrollable. It is that of judging what it is that the person perceives" (EP 2:191). The "what-it-is" indicates clearly Peirce's emphasis on the fact that thirdness or generality appears in perception itself. Thus, in Peirce's version of the perceptual process, there is an awareness (ego) and an undergoing (non-ego) that together generate an experience from which cognition, inquiry, criticism, and, ultimately, action can be launched.

Perceptual judgment brings the process of perception to the brink of self-control. "I do not see that it is possible," says Peirce, "to experience any control over that operation or to subject it to criticism" (EP 2:191). In the absence of control or criticism—at least of an immediate sort—we are left with the very commonsensical and empiricist result that all of our thinking must begin with perception. Our thinking sets out from the propositional beliefs that perception yields. Without perceptual judgment, for example, my percept of the table before me would remain inarticulate. "It follows," Peirce stated, "that our perceptual judgments are the first premises of all our reasonings and that they cannot be called into question" (EP 2:191). Thus, in his own peculiar way, Peirce adopted the empiricist dictum: "*Nihil est in intellectu quia prius fuerit in sensu*" (EP 2:226).

On the nether side of the perceptual process lies abductive inference, where control and criticism are initiated; here is where logic discovers the first stage of inference. "The third cotary proposition," Peirce argued, "is that abductive inference shades into perceptual judgment without any sharp line of demarcation between them; or in other words our first premises, the perceptual judgments, are to be regarded as an extreme case of abductive inferences, from which they differ in being absolutely beyond criticism" (EP 2:227). And as Peirce pointed out, because the modes of experience are continuous, it is often difficult to distinguish a perceptual judgment from an abductive inference. Reason, creative and experimental, emerges continuously out of perception. I will consider this continuity further in assessing the consequences of Peirce's outlook.

The shift in Peirce's "empiricism" occurs at the same juncture at which James's appears: in the description of the general contents of perception or experience. Traditional empiricists had settled on the claim that only particular or singular entities or qualia serve as the content of perception. As Hume put it, "all our distinct perceptions arc distinct existences."[4] Traditional empiricism in general consequently found itself with Hume's problems of trying to bind together the loose ends of perception and experience; it excluded relations and then was perplexed when it couldn't find any. James and Peirce asserted that there is more in experience and perception itself. Peirce, following the outlines of his own phenomenology, maintained that perception involves all three of his categories: firsts, seconds, and thirds, or qualities, reactions, and generals.

In focusing on the perception of firsts, or qualities, Peirce was intent on separating his view from that of traditional empiricism. The nominalistic bent of that tradition had led qualities for the most part to be reified, so that, in Peirce's terms, firsts and seconds were simply merged or conflated. Peirce prescinded qualities from the perceptual process and provided them their own status. Thus, qualities are experienced as felt immediacies that enrich experience. As Bernstein argues: "Peirce was sensitive to this dimension of felt immediacy and argued that an adequate theory of perception must give it its proper due."[5] Thus, whereas traditional empiricism reduced qualities to thinghood, Peirce saw them as the esthetic qualifiers of experience: "our perceptual judgments are the premises for us and these perceptual judgments have icons as their predicates, in which icons Qualities are immediately presented" (EP 2:194). This feature of perception underwrites Peirce's suggestion that an artistic dimension is requisite for successful inquiry, a suggestion to which I will return.

Peirce's prescinding of qualities from the reified impressions of traditional empiricism leaves a residue of secondness. In asserting the otherness, externality, or resistance of the percept, Peirce stood in agreement with traditional empiricism. As Bernstein puts it, for Peirce, a percept "simply forces itself upon my attention."[6] The difference is that Peirce did not hold a materialist conception of secondness; there are many forms of resistance or otherness in perception. Moreover, because otherness suggests relationality, the perception of seconds establishes the duality that calls forth the perception of thirdness or generality.

To get at the secondness of perception, Peirce again relied on his phenomenological investigation of experience. Focusing on "such perception as involves surprises," he maintained that we find ourselves in opposition to something other that forces the surprise on us and generates the experience of otherness: "I ask you whether at the instant of surprise there is not a double consciousness, on the one hand of an Ego, which is simply the expected idea suddenly broken off, on the other hand of the Non-Ego, which is the Strange Intruder, in his abrupt entrance" (EP 2:154).[7] From this experiential position, Peirce suggested, "it is downright nonsense to dispute the fact that in perception two objects really do react upon one another" (EP 2:154). Secondness or otherness thus is a feature of the perceptual process and, in this regard, Peirce seemed to agree with James that relations— especially, in this case, disjunctive relations—are experienced. Indeed, Peirce made the point in somewhat Jamesian fashion: "Every philosopher who denies the doctrine of Immediate Perception [two objects reacting],—including idealists of every stripe—by that denial cuts off all possibility of ever cognizing a relation" (EP 2:155). Perceiving secondness is a first step in cognizing relations. Peirce, however, moved a step further because, for him, otherness is, when taken in itself, a degenerate relation. Full relatedness appears only when thirdness and generality enter the picture; even disjunctions are in a comparative relationship and are therefore mediated. Thus, for Peirce, to fully meet James's claim that relations—especially conjunctive relations— are experienced, it is requisite that generality or continuity be found in the perceptual process. James appeared to agree in principle, since he argued at length that we experience continuity directly: "But continuous transition is one sort of a conjunctive relation; and to be a radical empiricist means to hold fast to this conjunctive relation of all others."[8] Indeed, it is worth noting that Peirce saw this direct perception of continuity as standing in the tradition of "immediate perception," a tradition he believed both he and James followed. In a 1905 letter regarding James's essay "La Notion de Conscience," he wrote: "I am quite sure the doctrine is not at all so novel as you say. . . . [I]t is nothing in the world but the well-known doctrine of immediate perception." Referring to his own 1903 lectures, Peirce then added, "I have myself preached immediate perception as you know" (CP 8.261; see also EP 2:195). It is this claim that continuity or generality is perceived that became the focus of many of Peirce's final lectures.

As is well known, Peirce conceived his philosophical system as a cable of mutually supportive strands of belief. In these lectures we see instances of this cable structure at work. In these pragmatism lectures, Peirce put his scholastic realism to work on behalf of his claim that generality is found in perception; "general principles," he asserted, "are really operative in nature. That is the doctrine of scholastic realism" (EP 2:183). Thus, inasmuch as the cosmos exhibits laws, principles, habits, and meanings, it offers realities for the interpreting inquirer to perceive. Although realism as a belief or philosophical doctrine is a result of inquiry, these examples of thirdness make their appearance in perceptual judgment where the percept is given its "what-it-is-ness." In the judgment there is thirdness—concept, meaning, generality, and continuity; but because it is uncontrolled and uncritical judgment, the thirdness is perceived as it is conceived. In his 1898 lectures in Cambridge Peirce used the Johnsonesque example of dropping a stone to demonstrate the "law" of gravity. Although the law requires inquiry for its full description and testing, it is nevertheless perceivable in the immediate event. The "gravitationalness" of the rock and its environment is perceived. For Peirce, then, "If you admit the principle that logic stops where self-control stops, you will find yourself obliged to admit that a perceptual fact, a logical origin, may involve generality. . . . Generality, Thirdness, pours in upon us in our very perceptual judgments, and all reasoning . . . turns upon perception of generality and continuity at every step" (EP 2:207; see also 211). Thus, for Peirce, perceptual judgment initiates the possibility of controlled reasoning: "our perceptual judgments are the first premises of all our reasonings" (EP 2:191; see also 204).[9]

Peirce was intent in these lectures on persuading logicians and scientific inquirers who, because of their nominalistic habits, have difficulty admitting the perception of generality. For Peirce, if inquiry develops out of a perception that involves three categorial features— quality, reaction, and continuity—then science must broaden its scope to keep these in view. Traditional empiricism's scope is much too narrow and, again because of its inherent nominalism, tends to overlook both quality and continuity as features of experience.

Peirce realized, I think, that his phenomenological approach to perception and its categories was unlikely to satisfy the scientistic nominalists of his day; nor does it appeal to contemporary constructivists. He was well aware, as I will show in more detail later, that thinkers such as Karl Pearson rejected the perception of generality and continuity. For Pearson and others, general ideas of natural laws and habits were fictional—"mere representations" concerning the only realities, singular facts. As Peirce saw it, for Pearson "the laws of nature are of human provenance" and "all pretended laws of nature [are] figments" so that "all natural science is a delusion" (CP 8.145). In short, if Peirce could not persuade through phenomenology, he could bring the aims of science to bear on its own practices and call into question the nominalist tendencies of traditional empiricism. In concert with his claim that we perceive generality and relations, Peirce asserted not only his realism but a set of arguments aimed directly at the exclusive focus of nominalism and traditional empiricism on the secondness of perception. If, as Pearson maintained, there are no real laws or generals in the cosmos, then there can be no scientific heading toward truth even as an ideal or regulative hope. There can also be no constraints on inquiry other than causal ones and, as Peirce repeatedly argued, causal connections are not reasonable—

that is, not lawful—but arbitrary. In short, without the perception of generality as the inception of cognition, no inquiry or reasoning can get off the ground. Even a localized or historically contingent logic requires a ground and telos of cognition. The upshot for Peirce is that science needs to be reconsidered in light of his version of perception, much as James believed it needed to be revised through his radical empiricism. Let us turn then to the consequences of his account.

The consequences I sketch here by no means constitute an exhaustive list. I simply mean to be suggestive of some affinities in the respective philosophical outlooks of Peirce and James—affinities that grow out of their respective revisions of traditional empiricism. The first consequence develops out of Peirce's emphasis on the perception of generality and is one that I think was foremost in Peirce's mind as he presented his lectures. It is a consequence that James shared in its basic outline. This first consequence is that scientific inquiry as the seeking of the general categories and laws of actuality is possible for the human community. The second consequence, which follows Peirce's insistence that we pay attention to qualitativeness in experience, is more strictly Jamesian in flavor. It is that science should be more inclusive and recognize the richness presented by experience; inquiry is not reducible to the quantification of perceived entities and qualities.

The first consequence of Peirce's version of perception is that a process of scientific inquiry is possible. Establishing this possibility was a task Peirce saw himself as inheriting from both Aristotle and Kant, and it played a role in his work as early as "On a New List of Categories." On the surface it may seem a bit anticlimactic to highlight the underwriting of science as an important consequence of Peirce's revised empiricism, and a bit ironic, since science seemed to dominate the intellectual climate of the late nineteenth century. But it is important precisely because Peirce believed that most theorists and practitioners of science of his time maintained a traditional empiricism that was inadequate to both the historical practices of the sciences and to the stated aims of science in general. In the first place, as I mentioned in noting Peirce's consideration of Pearson's work, scientism supposed it sought "the laws of nature," but at the same time held that such laws were nominal, not real. In Peirce's theory of inquiry and in the practice of science, laws were to be established by a community of inquirers over time. However, since traditional empiricism believed inquiry began with the perception of discrete, atomistic impressions, it had no means for seeing laws or any general ideas as reals. Thus it could not meet its own aim of describing laws as features of human experience. Under Peirce's version of perception, the reality of generals and of laws makes an appearance not only at the end of inquiry but in the very perceptions from which inquiry springs. Peirce's outlook makes laws possible at both the inception and the outcome of inquiry.

Second, but not less importantly for Peirce, his notion of perception as a continuous process makes sense of the possibility and importance of a history of inquiry that is capable of development and of self-correction. Again, the continuity of perception, perception's continuity with abduction, and abduction's development into experimentation constitute a history of inferencing. As Manley Thompson put it: "When the logic [of events] becomes normative, the gap between subject and object is bridged by identifying the reasoning of the individual with that of an unlimited community, so that the first premises [individual perceptual judgments] of such reasoning will eventually become identical with those of nature."[10] Because perception is not a mental replication of individual entities but a process involving uncontrolled judgment, it is, as Bernstein argues, compelled by reality but not, in itself, immediately authoritative as knowledge of reality. Therefore, perception, as fallible, moves into the process of inquiry and into a history of inquiry that tests its adequacy. Science, thus, is not a matter of present, original thought or of a set of conventional beliefs, but of the ongoing historical development of beliefs.

Finally, just as for Peirce his theories of perception and inquiry underwrite the reality of laws, they also make sense of the reality of truth as a regulative hope. This claim is a key element in his description of inquiry in "The Fixation of Belief." Again, the reality of thirds or generals, found in perception and corroborated by experience and the history of science, allows for us to conceive truth as a relation that is both real and general. For Peirce, "every scientific research goes upon the assumption, the hope, that, in reference to its particular question, there is some true answer. That which that truth represents is a reality. This reality being cognizable and comprehensible, is of the nature of thought" (CP 8.153). A theory of perception that involves continuity and generality makes room for the possibility of truth's reality, but from a Peircean perspective, it isn't clear how the correspondence truth of traditional empiricism could be a relation, since in it relations are discounted as unreal. Truth could only be a single fact—say, in God's mind, as for Berkeley. Ultimately, traditional empiricism must compromise its own basis and turn to some form of subjectivism that either gives up on truth in a Humean way, or turns to a form of sense certainty as in Scottish common-sensism. Truth is therefore either illusory or unable to develop historically. As a result, thinkers such as Pearson look for other aims that inquiry might have besides truth. Pearson states that its ultimate goal is to preserve the species, though as Peirce points out, he comes much closer to saying that it ought to preserve nineteenth-century British culture. Peirce instead conjoins his realism and his notion of perception: "[T]he saving truth is that there is a Thirdness in experience, an element of Reasonableness to which we can train our own reason to conform more and more. If this were not the case there could be no such thing as logical goodness or badness" (EP 2:212).

Although I believe James agreed in general with Peirce's version of perception and its ability to make sense of scientific practices, his own version of science focused less on the historical development of truth and more on the richness of human experience that is lost when science is too narrowly construed.

James's first concern was that traditional empiricism tended to reduce all phenomena to matter, a direct result of its notion that what we perceive—and therefore what is ultimately real—are independent, discrete physical entities. James presented his concern clearly: "I know of nothing more deplorable than this undiscriminating gulping down of everything materialistic as peculiarly scientific."[11] Peirce agreed with James's concern. If perception involves a judgment that discloses all three categories to us, there is no reason to move to the sort of materialistic reductionism that even now continues to dominate popular notions of science. This is precisely what makes the empiricisms of both James and Peirce radical. "To be a nominalist," Peirce said, "consists in the undeveloped state in one's mind of the apprehension of Thirdness as Thirdness. The remedy for it consists in allowing ideas of human life to play a greater role in one's philosophy" (EP 2:197). In allowing this greater role, we will find the richness to which James attends.

This richness indicated to James and Peirce that science itself involved artistic and creative features. As Charlene Seigfried points out, "James incisively undercuts the naivete of the presumption that the scientific method alone discloses the real world by situating science along a continuum of selective, creative activity. He dislodges scientific explanations as paradigmatic of all explanations by showing that such explanation is a subset of the creative imposition of form on an otherwise chaotic world."[12] Peirce's move in this direction may be more subtle and less apparent than James's. But it is nevertheless similar. Science, as inquiry, must be broader inasmuch as perception itself yields qualities, relations, and continuities. Science must deal with all the features of our experience and it must do so experimentally. Thus, science engages us in a creative process.

This creative dimension arises from the fallibility of Peircean perceptual judgment and inquiry. Though perception is not *immediately* criticizeable, it *is* criticizeable through inquiry. The task of inquiry thus becomes to determine, creatively, hypotheses that might make sense of present perception and the background "world" in which it takes place. Fallible perceptual judgment requires us to move from individual perception to a community of inquiry. And here we take up the "controllable" nether side of perceptual judgment—abduction or hypothesis development. At this juncture we can no longer operate just mechanically; we must awaken to the task of becoming creative inquirers. As Peirce suggested, a "scientific imagination" is required to bring hypotheses into play. On a larger scale, he maintained: "Since through reason he has the power of reflection and a high degree of self-control, man holds the unique and privileged position of co-creator" (CP 5.403, n. 3).

The other side of the Jamesian concern is that inquiry must pay attention to the qualitative richness that experience presents. Not only do we perceive qualitative variation, as in our experiences of red, green, or blue, but we feel the qualitative immediacy of art, as when I experience, the unique quality of King Lear, to borrow a Peircean example (CP 1.531). In Lecture 4, Peirce drove this point home at the cosmic level: "Now as to their [i.e., qualities'] function in the economy of the Universe,—the Universe as an argument is necessarily a great work of art, a great poem,—for every fine argument is a poem and a symphony,—just as every true poem is a sound argument" (EP 2:194). Peirce explicitly rejected Hegel's suggestion that "presentness" is empty and abstract; for Peirce, it is qualitatively loaded (EP 2:149–50). Thus, for inquiry to fulfill its task, it must come to grips with this qualitative, esthetically rich experience.

We have, under traditional empiricism and nominalism, absorbed a cultural tendency—still prevalent—to ignore or overlook these qualitative features. As Peirce stated, "the nominalistic Weltenschauung has become incorporated into what I will venture to call the very flesh and blood of the average modern mind" (EP 2:157). We have developed a kind of cultural blindness; "most of us," he said, "seem to find it difficult to recognize the greatness and wonder of things familiar to us" (EP 2:158). Thus, scientific inquiry requires a lesson in perception and judgment from art and esthetic criticism. Peirce returned to this theme throughout his lectures.

Inquirers need an attitude of openness that is too often lacking in traditional science. Although, again, we cannot control perception as it occurs, we can alter the way in which we approach perceiving. This alteration is one of the pragmatic meanings of Peirce's anti-nominalism. We can, for example, decide not to exclude some phenomena and experiences from our inquiry. Thus, we see that both Peirce and James, though with somewhat different consequences, countenance

the investigation of psychical phenomena such as telepathy and pre-
monitions of the deaths of relatives. These are features of individual
perception and, like any other perceptions, are fair game for inquiry.
On a wider scope, both Peirce and James took seriously the consideration of all varieties of religious experience. To model this attitude of
openness, Peirce turned to artistic experience.

In Lecture 2, introducing us to phenomenological practice, Peirce
made his first appeal to artists. To be effective phenomenologists—
and, therefore, perceivers—we require "that rare faculty, the faculty
of seeing what stares one in the face, just as it presents itself, unre-
placed by any interpretation, unsophisticated by any allowance for
this or for that supposed modifying circumstance. This is the faculty
of the artist who sees for example the apparent colors of nature as
they appear" (EP 2:147). Whereas traditional scientists have a tendency to ignore or downplay features of perception, artists tend to
see things just as they are presented. Nevertheless, it is not an unme-
diated seeing; for Peirce the presence of something has temporal
spread. What's key is the attitude or orientation of the artist as perceiver. "The poetic mood," Peirce said, "approaches the state in
which the present is present" (EP 2:149).

If the poetic or artistic mood is crucial for scientific observation
and phenomenology, it is also perhaps as important in making critical
judgments and in attempting to state truths. Although Peirce did not
go so far in this direction as did James, he did make two suggestive
claims. In the first, Peirce intimated that good criticism requires an
aesthetic temperament: "I venture to think that the esthetic state of
mind is purest when perfectly naïve without any critical pronounce-
ment, and that the esthetic critic finds his judgments upon the result
of throwing himself back into such a pure naïve state,—and the best
critic is the man who has trained himself to do this most perfectly"
(EP 2:189).

In short, for Peirce as for James, scientific inquirers should be
more than solvers of technical and quantitative puzzles. The following quotation is perhaps even more provocative in its suggestion that
art may be a legitimate—and in some cases a more legitimate—

vehicle of truth. After a brief discussion of the intersubjective sharing of qualitative experience, Peirce anticipated a complaint from his scientific brethren: "I hear you say: 'All that is not fact; it is poetry.' Nonsense! Bad poetry is false, I grant; but nothing is truer than true poetry. And let me tell the scientific men that the artists are much fairer and more accurate observers than they are" (EP 2:193).

Peirce's radical empiricism does not seem to match the intensity of James's concerning these issues. In *A Pluralistic Universe* James called on inquiry to include all "the wild beasts of the philosophical desert," including intuition, autobiography, and psychical events as tools of inquiry. James, I believe, came much closer to Bergson on this score than did Peirce. Nevertheless, Peirce's suggestions in this direction should not be discounted; they are consistent with his theory of perception and have had an important impact on the development of pragmatic notions of science and inquiry. John Dewey, for example, recognized the rich possibilities in Peirce's theory of perception:

> I am quite certain that he, above all modern philosophers, has opened the road which permits a truly experiential philosophy to be developed which does not, like traditional empirical philosophies, cut experience off from nature.[13]

Even more to the point, Dewey, under the influence of Peirce, argued that "scientific thought is, in its turn, a specialized form of art, with its own qualitative control."[14] In focusing on the perception of thirdness, Peirce met the basic criterion of James's radical empiricism. In focusing on the perception of firstness, he bequeathed to pragmatism an esthetically rich notion of science.

SEVEN

PEIRCE ON INTERPRETATION
Carl R. Hausman

Our conversations concerning Peirce's notions of perception and percep-
tual judgment led directly to considerations of judging and reasoning in
the process of inquiry. For Peirce all reasoning—including inferencing
and perceptually judging—involves interpreting, and it is this that is the
focus of the present chapter.

In an earlier chapter I examined the metaphysical implications of
Peirce's dynamical or dynamic object; in this chapter I will consider its import for Peirce's conception of interpretation. Interpretation, for whatever purpose, relates a referent or a dynamic object, that
which is to be interpreted, to the interpreter. What sort of relation is
this and what constraints contribute to the process of moving from
referent to interpretation? This question signals a topic that concerned Peirce not only in his semeiotic but also in his philosophy in
general. I would like to extend some of the claims I have made elsewhere about ways to answer the question. I will propose an interpretation of how a Peircean approach suggests a way to mediate between

two apparently opposing views. One view is the postmodern claim that interpretation creates its referent or object; the other view leans toward a kind of realism, that is, a qualified affirmation of a condition that constrains and thus limits the power or hegemony of interpretation over its object.

It seems incontrovertible that assumptions and funded experience influence interpretation. In science, these presupposed conditions include accepted theories, axioms, discussions with colleagues, and whole networks of thoughts about which scientists generally agree. In the arts, these conditions include accepted prior interpretations that inform art historians and art critics. I believe that the same claim can be made about literary interpretations and about interpretations of music. In addition, the presuppositions include acknowledged as well as tacit prejudices or biases about what is to be expected in a culture.

Frameworks of assumptions with which interpreters approach their objects, however, do not make up all that influences interpretations. Applying some of Peirce's insights, I will try to show how an aspect of the object to be interpreted functions as a condition that is partially independent of prior assumptions and the process of interpretation. There is objectivity attributable to this aspect of the object. Thus, an objective factor acts as a condition that interacts with the assumptions and that provides constraints on the interpreter.

Since I intend to get underway with the help of what I take to be Peirce's central semeiotic, I must mention some key ideas in his terminology. In doing so, however, I will also initiate a transition into my proposal concerning the way constraints are not reducible to the interpreter's imposition on the referent. What the interpreter brings to the semeiotic process is a complex or system of previous interpretations of referents. As I noted previously, Peirce called the referent that is interpreted a *dynamic* or *dynamical object*, and the dynamic object as interpreted is called the *immediate object*. Thus, the assumed system that is brought to interpretation by the interpreter consists of immediate objects, that is, previous knowledge and suppositions. I take it that the interpreter brings not only previously known immediate objects but also memories of previous acquaintance with similar experiences and also consciously recognized and even unconscious prejudices and persuasions that have resulted from previous interpretations.

Dynamic objects initiate interpretations. Let us return to a version of my earlier example: a spot appears on the horizon of the sea, catches an observer's attention, and causes the observer to wonder what it is and thus to begin to interpret it. In the context of this semeiosis, the spot serves as the dynamic object. Suppose that the developing interpretation determines that the shape of the spot is that of a ship. What develops, then, is an immediate object—the dynamic object as interpreted, or in this case as being interpreted. Continued observation might lead to a different interpretation as the tide brings the spot closer. It may then appear to be a log rather than a ship. And a bit later when brought even closer, it might be interpreted as an unusually large mass of seaweed. Thus, a series of immediate objects develops during the semeiosis. At each stage, the dynamic object as interpreted has changed. Yet has the "thing" that initiated the interpretation, apart from or prior to what interpretation decides, changed? One could answer "yes," and insist, assuming the most extreme view, that the only access we have to the object shows it to be nothing but the latest immediate object. If this conclusion stands, then one's epistemology, and in turn one's ontology, would affirm that we, the interpreters, construct or create what we interpret. On this view, there is no object independent of the interpretation, which *seems* consistent with some of Peirce's early rejections of the Kantian notion of a thing-in-itself. However, what I want to show is that he did not therefore reject entirely the view that dynamic objects are nothing but immediate objects. Nor did he say that dynamic objects do not undergo some modification through interaction with interpretive acts and thus with immediate objects.

The approach to Peirce's references to dynamic objects that, I believe, can be misleading tends to slip into conflating dynamical objects with immediate objects. This occurs in at least some accounts that make use of illustrations such as mine. The illustrations may refer to a presumed initial dynamic object. However, what follows conflates the dynamical objects with their interpretations. For instance, in a closely argued book about Peirce by Christopher Hookway, we are given an illustration of a misinterpretation of "a real object":[1]

> Looking at a distant hillside . . . I judge that the sheep next to the tree has not moved. . . . Suppose that in fact I am looking at a bush. . . . In spite of this error, there is a sense in which I know what I am thinking or talking about. . . . This is because my judgement is sensitive to further information about the object. . . . I might walk up to the "sheep" in order to see it better. . . .[2]

And at this point, the discovery that it is a bush would be made.

Hookway's account suggests that the final interpretation, the bush, is the dynamical object—as "what the object really is." However, the object interpreted as a bush is, after all, an immediate object: it is the dynamic object as interpreted. What then can be said about what the object really is? Suppose that on closer examination, the bush moves and is then seen as a bear. Is the bear the dynamic object? Presumably, on Peirce's view, the answer must be consistent with the point that we can only say what the dynamic object is in terms of an immediate object. Given Hookway's account, the dynamic object, then, could only be the most recent immediate object.

The force of this idea of the dynamic object has led me to the claim that any attempt to assign attributes to dynamic objects must assume a functional view—the view that we cannot say what the dynamic object "really" is, but only what most recent immediate object has functioned as a dynamic object. However, there is something that can be said about the dynamic object that does not ascribe specific attributes to it and does not reduce it to the most recent immediate object. It can be said that the dynamic object is that which initiates and to some extent constrains the development of the interpretation. This ascribes functions but not properties. Thus, the dynamic object is the condition of constraint that is not reducible to a semeiotic complex and the immediate object that is accepted at a juncture of inquiry.

The point is that since it is only by describing the immediate object that the dynamic object can be identified, what illustrations such as that offered by Hookway refer to as "real" objects must be immediate objects functioning as dynamic objects.

I

I do not consider it necessary to decide whether Peirce thought that every sign, including icons and symbols as well as indexes, refers to an object, and I think that, for our purposes, this issue can be side-stepped. But I believe it helpful to observe that one of the reasons Peirce scholars have dwelled on the question of whether such things as fictions or works of art have objects may be that the term *object* is assumed to refer to something with spatial-temporal properties. More generally, the referents in question are construed as publicly encountered individuals. Thus, I suspect that when the idea of the dynamic object arises, it is assumed that the dynamic object must be some individual thing or something that physically constrains immediate objects.[3]

This assumption about the reference of "object" might be avoided, or the issue sidestepped, if the word *referent* were substituted for *object*. I take it that the term *referent* is broader in comprehension than the term *object*. A fiction has a referent, whether one calls it an object in the sense of intentional object or fictional object. To avoid the complaint that what is fictional cannot be an object, I assume that a fictional expression does, however, have a referent. There is no centaur if centaurs are considered spatial-temporal things that can be photographed. But a referent need not be something capable of being photographed. A representational painting of a fantastic monster has a referent, something that can be described and that is a construction based on other existing things that can be described. In addition, an abstract or nonobjective painting may have a referent, at least insofar as it exhibits insights into society, individual experiences, life, or "reality." That into which the work exhibits insight functions as a referent, which is a condition of constraint. Much more needs to be developed to make my point, however; this discussion need not settle the issue. In any case, I will rely on Peirce's own use of the term *object* for referents of interpretations.

II

My hypothesis, as already suggested in discussing Hookway's illustration and my example of interpreting a spot appearing on the horizon, depends on recognizing that immediate objects can function as dynamic objects when those immediate objects are referents constraining interpretation. Their function is to constrain interpretation as conditions that are not themselves present prior to their construction. In the case of the spot on the horizon, continued observation may show it to be a boat, and still further observation may call for revision, so that the "boat" is then seen to be a gigantic log. Persuasions initially assumed by the interpreter and then imposed by the interpreter do not exhaust the constraints on interpretation. In the case of the spot on the horizon, the spot functioned as a dynamic referent, for it persisted, insisting to the interpreter that it was something intelligible and therefore in need of interpretation. Throughout the stages of interpretation, first the spot, then the boat functioned as dynamic objects, and later the log functioned dynamically in another revision, according to which the log was seen as a large mass of seaweed. However, along with each stage, what originally constrained the observer's seeing it as a dot is still present as a constraining condition pressing interpretations onward.

Thus, even to recognize what is called a spot as a spot is at least an incipient interpretation. Such initial interpretation is possible because the example being discussed is in a language and within a framework of assumed experience of sightings at sea and of recognizing spots. As suggested, whatever it was that initiated even the statement that there is a spot on the horizon is the dynamic condition that constrains perception to see it as a spot on the horizon rather than a floater in my eye, or an insect stopped momentarily in front of me. This condition does not vanish with each immediate object; otherwise revision would not occur. Consequently, the object first seen as a spot on the horizon and later seen as a log is interpreted as something else because of constraints that continue to impose themselves on interpretation and interact with the agency of interpretation. One might insist that these constraints have their source or their loci in the interpreter, in a subconscious dimension of mind, perhaps in a collective unconscious, in the universal structure of all minds, in Mind or an absolute intelligence, or in unrecognized physical changes in the body. Nevertheless, the function of the object as seen would be something independent of the deliberate and conscious activity of interpretation. I cannot here consider the suggested ontologically idealist question that is raised if someone claims that all constraints are fundamentally mental or are the responsibility of an absolute mind. What is of importance for what follows is the point that what seems to be present as a dynamical object is, when identified within interpretation, an immediate object viewed functionally as a dynamic object.

III

At what stage does the pre-interpreted begin to be interpreted, and how does the pre-interpreted function as a way in which interpretation is constrained? It should be helpful for answering these questions to turn to Peirce's analysis of perceptual judgment, which begins with a percept, evolves into the judgment through what Peirce calls the *percipuum*, and is terminated when the judgment refers to the interpreted percept insofar as it has been given provisional determination. I will attempt to apply Peirce's ideas first to the way perceptual judgments are formed. Peirce's analysis provides ideas that suggest that constraints for which dynamic objects are partially responsible are vectorial.

The analysis of perception exemplifies epistemologically Peirce's semeiotic account of interpretation. In particular, the semeiotic explanation is grounded on his distinction between immediate and dynamic objects.

> [A] Sign has an Object and an Interpretant, the latter being that
> which the Sign produces in the Quasi-mind that is the Interpreter

by determining the latter to a feeling, to an exertion, or to a Sign, which determination is the Interpretant. But it remains to point out that there are usually two Objects, and more than two Interpretants. Namely, we have to distinguish the Immediate Object, which is the Object as the Sign itself represents it, and whose Being is thus dependent upon the Representation of it in the Sign, from the Dynamical Object, which is the Reality which by some means contrives to determine the Sign to its Representation. (CP 4.536)

In the context of this account of immediate and dynamic objects, the question is: how is interpretation initiated and developed once the interpretation is in process?

It seems clear that our encounters with that which prompts interpretation—the referent to be interpreted—are, epistemologically speaking, percepts. There is confirmation of this in a passage from a few years earlier than the passage just shown. In the earlier writing, Peirce said, "Deceive yourself as you may, you have a direct experience of something reacting against you" (CP 2.139). The something, then, is not controlled or dependent on one's opinion: "The knowledge which you are compelled to admit is that knowledge which is directly forced upon you, and which there is no criticizing" (CP 2.141). What is important here is that in the same paragraph, Peirce added that his discussion is about "an imperfect description of the percept that is forced upon me" (CP 2.141). The experience of a percept, then, must be intimately related to, if not identical with, what Peirce believed to be an experience of a dynamic object.

Another way to view this experience is to observe that it falls under the category of secondness, which is dyadic, pre-cognitive, and therefore pre-interpreted. It should be noted, however, that Peirce said that what we are compelled to admit is knowledge that is directly forced on the interpreter. Given the pre-interpretive status of the compulsion, it may seem puzzling that Peirce refers to knowledge as being "directly forced upon you." The puzzle may be clarified if not resolved, however, if Peirce has in mind that the condition of compulsion incites and directs the interpreter toward the interpretation, which is knowledge. I think this is borne out in Peirce's explanation of the way perceptual judgments are initiated and developed. A series of passages from volume 7 of the *Collected Papers* contains his relatively detailed account of perceptual interpretation:

> Let us say that, as I sit here writing, I see on the other side of my table, a yellow chair with a green cushion. That will be what psychologists term a "percept" (*res percepta*). . . . The chair I appear to see makes no professions of any kind, essentially embodies no intentions of any kind, does not stand for anything. It obtrudes itself upon my gaze; but not as a deputy for anything else, not "as" anything. (CP 7.619)

Such is the percept. Now what is its logical bearing on knowledge and belief? This may be summed up in three items, as follows:

> 1st, it contributes something positive. (Thus, the chair has its four legs, seat, and back, its yellow color, its green cushion, etc. To learn this is a contribution to knowledge.)
> 2nd, it compels the perceiver to acknowledge it.
> 3rd, it neither offers any reason for such acknowledgment nor makes any pretension to reasonableness. This last point distinguishes the percept from an axiom. (CP 7.622)

The three items raise the crucial issue: how can something that is itself blind, unrepresentative, and without reasonableness contribute something positive to knowledge? On the one hand, we have the percept, and on the other hand, we have the perceptual judgment: "We know nothing about the percept otherwise than by testimony of the perceptual judgment, excepting that we feel the blow of it. . . . But the moment we fix our minds upon it and think the least thing about the percept, it is the perceptual judgment that tells us what we so 'perceive'" (CP 7.643). The originating percept does not initially appear with four legs, as chair, or "as anything." The percept is *transformed* as it is taken up into the interpretive process. However, Peirce suggested a way to account for the transformation. "For this and other reasons," he said, "I propose to consider the percept as it is immediately interpreted in the perceptual judgment, under the name

of the 'percipuum'" (CP 7.643). There is, then, a stage, the percipuum, mediating the initial percept and the judgment. Since Peirce
said that the percipuum is the percept as immediately interpreted, I
think it is reasonable to conclude that the percipuum is the epistemological version of the immediate object. I assume that an immediate
object per se, in abstraction from ensuing interpretive connections,
is not itself a judgment. A perceptual judgment "tells us what I so
'perceive.'" As Peirce added, "the percipuum is what forces itself
upon your acknowledgment, without any why or wherefore" (CP
7.643). We recognize it as something before predicating anything of
it. The percipuum is a stage that evolves in the perceptual experience
and thus is a kind of bridge to relating it to other perceptions and
perceptual judgments. The distinction here is fragile. But the force of
it depends on the view that immediate objects, before being related
to anything, are interpretations accepted without yet any mediation
further than interpretation to which the dynamic object had been
subjected.

   Thus, whether we are correct in saying this depends on how much
one expects of the interpretation required to bring about the immediate object; the immediate object is something that is an immediate
interpretation of the dynamic object. It may afterwards be caught up
in a semeiotic process, in a mediatedly interpreted system or web of
immediate objects. Then, like the percipuum, it would no longer be
something that simply "immediately forces itself" on one; it would
then be something over which there is some cognitive control. However, prior to this control, there is that which is immediately interpreted in the sense of being an "acknowledgment" of what is there, but
not why it is what it is. I am proposing that this is the status of the
immediate object rather than the mediated object. Thus, I claim that
the immediate object epistemologically is the percipuum.

   We still are faced with the issue raised earlier concerning the percept that initiates the process of evolving toward the judgment—now,
as pointed out, evolving through the percipuum. There must be
something about percepts, or there must be additional stages of semeiosis, that at least nudge the acknowledgment and interpretation

—something that gives a kind of impetus to the growth of the percipuum.

Peirce referred to two kinds of refinements of the perceptual process that are relevant to this issue. The first opens up the discussion to his broadest perspective, that is, his categorial description of all experience. This refinement can be seen in the following quotation:

> Let us say, then, that anything is, for the purposes of logic, to be classed under the species of perception wherein a positive qualitative content is forced upon one's acknowledgment without any reason or pretension to reason. There will be a wider genus of things partaking of the character of perception, if there be any matter of cognition which exerts a force upon us tending to make us acknowledge it without any adequate reason. (CP 7.623)

"Perception" here, I take it, refers to the total process from percept to perceptual judgment. Within this process, we are told that there is a "positive qualitative content," which is without reason, without cognitive character, but which is not so blind as to disclose nothing in the experience. Further, there is a force "tending" to make us acknowledge qualitative content. Quality and force, then, apparently are two aspects of percepts that, as Peirce remarked, two paragraphs later, can be separated in thought, presumably after interpretation has been initiated (CP 7.625). It seems obvious that these two aspects of percepts fall under Peirce's categories of firstness and secondness—of qualitative tone and resistance or force. This appeal to the two categories is confirmed explicitly:

> Thus, two utterly different kinds of elements go to compose any percept. In the first place, there are the qualities of feeling or sensation, each of which is something positive and *sui generis*, being such as it is quite regardless of how or what anything else is. On account of this self-sufficiency, it is convenient to call these the elements of "Firstness." In the percept, these elements of Firstness are perceived to be connected in definite ways. A visual percept of a chair has a definite shape. If it is yellow with a green cushion, that is quite different from being green with a yellow cushion. These connectives are directly perceived, and the perception of

each of them is a perception at once of two opposed objects,—a double awareness. In respect to each of these connections, one part of the percept appears as it does relatively to a second part. Hence, it is convenient to call them elements of "Secondness." The vividness with which a percept stands out is an element of secondness; because the percept is vivid in proportion to the intensity of its effect upon the perceiver. These elements of secondness bring with them the peculiar singleness of the percept. (CP 7.625)

Putting the categorial application in alternative terms, the interpretive process introduces monadic and dyadic relations that function in perception or interpretation in general as preliminary to triadic relation, which is reached when a cognitive aspect has raised percept to judgment, or dynamic objects to immediate objects known through mediation. These observations about the relevance of the categories do not advance the consideration of how the percept nudges a process toward a percipuum. But they do show that the different kinds of problems and topics Peirce addressed are interlinked. Furthermore, the suggestion that there is an intrusion of dyadic relations in percepts shows that percepts have functions that are not restricted simply to being singulars isolated and wholly self-contained.

Peirce probed further in discussing the ways percepts may initiate interpretation. He suggested that given with the percept there is "near anticipation," or "the antecept" and "the recent memory," or "the ponecept." He also raised the question whether such distinctions should be permitted in view of his insistence on the principle of continuity, which is affirmed in metaphysical proposals as synechism. Here, he referred not to the basic generalization of continuity as the heart of synechism, but to "the serial principle":

It is a difficult question whether the serial principle permits us to draw sharp lines of demarcation between the percept and the near anticipation, or say the antecept, and between the percept and the recent memory (may I be permitted to call this the ponecept, a distant and dubious memory being perhaps quite another thing?), or whether the percept is at once but an extreme case of an antecept and an extreme case of a ponecept. (CP 7.648)

This passage adds two additional stages that Peirce claimed are relevant to connecting percepts to perceptual judgments, and it makes clear that although there may be tones that show how percepts link to oncoming interpretations, the entire process is a continuum, which will be recognized as central to Peirce's synechism. The identification of the stages of interpretation is what Peirce, even early in his career, called a kind of abstraction, that is, a prescinding of what is a logically supposed condition for a more complex experience. The abstraction is not to be equated with the richer experience to which the mind has attended. In the present context, the idea of prescinding indicates that for Peirce, the process initiated by the percept and an interaction with it can be an object of reflection, no matter how powerful its brute forcefulness. The agent of interpretation is compelled to interpret it.

The problem here, of course, is common to all attempts to analyze or describe what is felt, what is sheer presence, not as a datum, which is an abstraction, and not as a series of data, but as a vague but qualitative experience. To describe it is to turn on it and try to capture something that was here but is gone as an immediate experience. Peirce emphasized this problem when he described firstness.

As just mentioned, the problem is common outside Peircean thought. It is interesting to note that a philosopher who was working some twenty years after Peirce died offered a resolution, if not a solution, to the same kind of issue. R. G. Collingwood attempted to account for how artists focus on the expression, which is a clarification, of an initiating feeling of perturbation, which is taken to be a feeling that is not identified or as yet brought under the control of the artist's attention.[4] Collingwood spoke to the issue by arguing that we must propose that there is something there to be determined by conscious attention and then to be taken as approximated by the outcome of this attention.

The issue of concern here, of course, is the way Peirce addresses the relation between pre-cognitive percepts and the transitional development to cognitive interpretation. Our focus, then, must be on the two added stages, antecept and ponecept, that are directly related to the percept. Peirce made it clear that the antecept and the ponecept are not internal to the percept. They seem to appear in interaction with the percept. The antecept and the ponecept have to do with anticipation and memory. These might be regarded from an objective perspective so that they could be attributed to the percept itself. This would be consistent with some of Peirce's accounts of the phenomenologically approached category of firstness as qualitative presence. Thus, the anticipation of the antecept would be recognition of a quality of predictability. However, Peirce referred to one origin of the term *percept* in psychology. He attributed the term *percept* to a concern psychologists had. And Peirce did, after all, refer to the antecept and ponecept in terms of mental processes of anticipation and memory.

Peirce added the two terms while cautioning against "drawing a sharp line" between the percept and the antecept and ponecept, and he suggested that the percept may be an extreme case of each. It is clear, then, that he regarded the entire passage from percept to judgment as an instance of a continuum, so that the answer to his implied question of whether the percept is an extreme case of antecept and ponecept must be "yes." It does not, however, follow that the percept is not a distinct objective presence. It does not lose its status of externality as a constraining condition that presses on interpreters a force and a resistance. At the same time, the percept is not taken up as an independent condition the characteristics of which are discovered in interpretation. Instead, the percept acquires an interacting relationship with the agency of judgment, the interpreter. This interaction does not deliver immediate contact with the interpreter, for there are intervening stages that translate what the percept presents. Peirce identified these as the percipuum and in turn the antecept, which he refined by calling it, as it serves as a vehicle to the percipuum, *antecipuum*, and similarly, he introduced the ponecept, which he refined as *ponecipuum*. These are "the direct and uncontrollable interpretations of percept, antecept, and ponecept" (CP 7.648). Notice that he did not say they are "immediate" interpretations, which would assign them status as firsts, or instances of firstness, which would not have the constraining force of the percept. They are direct interpretations. A relation of directness opens up the relation to initiating mediation. Some degree of interpretation must be entering the reaction of the interpreter to the interpreted.

My intention from the beginning was to suggest how the dynamic object or percept acts with vectorial constraints on the interpreter. I believe these are accounted for by the function of antecipuum and ponecipuum. In what follows, then, let us consider this hypothesis.

IV

If I am correct about Peirce's appeal to antecipuum and ponecipuum, then there is reason to make the claim, as I have, that the percept, or the epistemological manifestation of the dynamic object, can nudge interpretation from the external side of semeiotic processes. Vague memories and vague anticipations are mobilized when the percept is encountered. The percept prompts the interaction, and once interpretation begins, the intervening stages begin. In reaction with the constraints of the percept, the ensuing interpretation is given direction. Thus, the immediate object is in process until the process reaches the provisionally determinate pause in semeiosis. I will conclude this discussion by trying to apply my claim about the constraining force of the dynamic object on the immediate object. The injection of anticipation and memory are crucial components of what Peirce called collateral experience.

> The person who interprets that sentence (or any other Sign whatsoever) must be determined by the Object of it through collateral observation quite independently of the action of the Sign. Otherwise he will not be determined to thought of that object. (CP 8.178)

And in another place, Peirce said,

> We must distinguish between the Immediate Object,—i.e. the Object as represented in the sign,—and the Real (no, because perhaps the Object is altogether fictive, I must choose a different

term, therefore), say rather the Dynamical Object, which, from the nature of things, the Sign cannot express, which it can only indicate and leave the interpreter to find out by collateral experience. (CP 8.314)

Collateral experience consists of awareness of past acquaintance with things associated with the object being interpreted. An explicit explanation of collateral experience may be seen in the following passage.

> Two men are standing on the seashore looking out to sea. One of them says to the other, "That vessel there carries no freight at all, but only passengers." Now, if the other, himself, sees no vessel, the first information he derives from the remark has for its Object the part of the sea that he does see, and informs him that a person with sharper eyes than his, or more trained in looking for such things, can see a vessel there; and then, that vessel having been thus introduced to his acquaintance, he is prepared to receive the information about it that it carries passengers exclusively. But the sentence as a whole has, for the person supposed, no other Object than that with which it finds him already acquainted. (CP 2.232)

The ponecipuum is present in the acquaintance of the person who did not see the ship but understood where to look and what to look for. The antecipuum is that person's being prepared to receive information about the ship. What is relevant here is that these factors are the outcomes of interaction between interpreter and percept. In this interaction, the percept constrained the interpretation in certain ways, in certain respects, and these ways or respects, I propose, work vectorially, because they have the force of the percept that is directed toward an evolving interpretation. Similar illustration may be provided by a return to the first example mentioned in this discussion.

It seems proper to say that the dot on the horizon mobilized the observers in certain respects. That is, it constrained them from its own presence but with a force that acted on each observer in different ways, although there must have been more common aspects than difference in the force for each observer; otherwise, they could not have converged as they continued interpreting. The first observer presumably had previous acquaintance with seeing ships at sea. The second observer had previous acquaintance, perhaps, with driftwood or, perhaps, had little or no experience looking at horizons of the sea. The two observers, however, also shared past experiences with ships, water, seaweed, logs, and so forth. These ponecipuua were affected by the constraints of the percept or series of percepts such that the provisionally final convergence of agreement could be an object or referent consented to by both, rather than, say, a referent they agreed to call a whale or an illusion.

V

Let us conclude the discussion with two questions with suggested answers. First, what conceptual (or nonconceptual) application can this proposal about Peirce's view of constraints on interpretation have? I think there are two ways it may be helpful. The account of how dynamic objects and thus percepts manage to act so that they are effective in interpretations extends what Peirce provided only in hints. I have tried to bring together several aspects and key ideas in Peirce's semeiotic and his theory of perception. This, I hope, shows the way in which Peirce's thought as a whole had fundamental interconnections. If his thought was not fully architectonic, it was at least a network.

The second consequence or application of the hypothesis I propose is its relevance for interpretation theory in general. I think that interpreters of artworks or historical evidence might be helped if they were alert to the complexity of their own enterprises with respect to the authority of both their objects and their own contributions. To take an extreme case as illustration, a historian who assumes that the interpreter does nothing but create the object of interpretation could legitimately write "historical" novels and submit them as accurate accounts of the past. Or a historian who assumes that the past is independently real and that the job of the historian is to blindly dig into past "facts" would not recognize the substantive role of his or her own collateral experiences in interpretation. He or she would not recognize the legitimacy or at least the positive contribution of another historian's account of the past they both had studied. The Peircean ideas of dynamic objects, percepts, immediate objects, and perceptual judgments provide a way to understand the crucial place of both sides of the interpretation—the objective and the intersubjective.

EIGHT

PEIRCE AND PEARSON
The Aims of Inquiry

Doug Anderson and Michael J. Rovine

Our discussions regarding perception and inquiry naturally led to conversations on how Peirce's method of inquiry operated in both science and practical affairs. Karl Pearson's account was the more standard account for the time, and Peirce used this fact to highlight important features of his own understanding of science.

Peirce and Karl Pearson, his contemporary and British counterpart in the study of statistics and the logic of inquiry, lived radically different lives. Peirce, having alienated himself from the university communities in which he might have found work, lost his full-time job when the Coast and Geodetic Survey was overhauled in 1891 in the wake of accusations of financial improprieties. Pearson, on the other hand, held a major university appointment in England and was a member of the British Academy. Both were practicing scientists, mathematicians, and philosophers of science. During his lifetime Pearson was honored for his contributions to statistics and the development of the social sciences. Subsequently his name has figured prominently in histories of statistics and the social sciences. Peirce, on the other hand, lived the last twenty years of his life in poverty and relative obscurity. Legend has it that though his manuscripts made their way to the Harvard Library, they nearly disappeared by being used as notepaper for students to record call numbers of books in the library. The papers were saved by Josiah Royce, who had them moved to the Department of Philosophy at Harvard.[1] Peirce made what little income he could by writing journal articles, encyclopedia entries, and book reviews. One such review was of the second edition of Pearson's *The Grammar of Science*; it appeared in *The Nation* in 1901.[2]

In the review we find evidence of Peirce's respect for Pearson's intellectual abilities:

> If any follower of Dr. Pearson thinks that in the observations I am about to make I am not sufficiently respectful to his master, I can assure him that without a high opinion of his powers I should not have taken the trouble to make these annotations, and without a higher opinion still, I should not have used the bluntness which becomes the impersonal discussions of mathematics. (CP 8.132)

But we also find an articulation of important differences concerning the theory and practice of scientific inquiry—differences that seem to have underwritten some of the directions the social sciences took in the early twentieth century. Some of these differences were so important to Peirce that segments of the review were cast in an extremely polemical fashion. Though Peirce was often extreme and polemical in his manuscripts, he more often than not toned things down in print. The fact that he did not do so in this instance is not, we think, a mere oversight on his part. Rather, we believe it is a function of the importance he attached to the difference in outlooks that he and Pearson presented and of a genuine concern regarding the consequences of Pearson's notion of scientific practice.

As Peirce saw it, the most fundamental difference between Pearson's outlook and his own was, as noted in earlier chapters, the difference between nominalism and realism. Pearson's thought was thoroughly governed by the nominalism of the tradition of British empiricism. This meant that for Pearson laws and truths were not real but were a function of an inquirer's perspective. For Pearson, the "outside world" was "a construct":[3] "Without the mental conceptions the law [of gravity] could not be, and it only comes into existence when these mental conceptions are first associated with the phenomena."[4] A natural law is thus created, not discovered, and it is, for Pearson, "essentially a product of the human mind and has no meaning apart from man."[5] For Peirce, on the other hand, natural laws were discoverable reals:

> The very being of law, general truth, reason—call it what you will—consists in its expressing itself in a cosmos and in intellects which reflect it, and in doing this progressively; and that which makes progressive creation worth doing—so the researcher comes to feel—is precisely the reason, the law, the general truth for the sake of which it takes place. (EP 2:58–59)

In his 1892 review of the first edition of *The Grammar,* Peirce stated his view more succinctly: "[G]enerality is essentially involved in that whereon the reality of a thing is said to depend; and that consideration is fatal to nominalism" (W 8:352). Thus, from Peirce's perspective, Pearson's nominalism was deeply ironic when used to develop a "grammar of science," for it undermined the very practice of disclosing natural laws in which most inquirers believed themselves to be engaged. In short, it implicitly denied science's identity and importance. In his review, Peirce asked Pearson rhetorically:

> In other words, is there anything that is really and truly a law of nature, or are all pretended laws of nature figments, in which latter case, all natural science is a delusion, and the writing of a grammar of science a very idle pastime? (CP 8.145)

Pearson, as Peirce saw it, could not sustain what Peirce took to be the primary aim of science: the indefinite and ongoing pursuit of the truth. Thus, depending on how one looks at it, Pearson was either "free to" or "forced to" pursue a new aim for scientific inquiry and the everyday practice of science. This, as we noted earlier, he did.

"The sole reason that can be given for any social institution or form of human activity," he maintained, "lies in this: their existence tends to promote the welfare of human society, to increase social happiness, or to strengthen social stability."[6] It is easy to see here a relaxed melding of utilitarian goals and Darwinian description. Pearson had in mind here two outcomes. The first had to do with the actual benefits produced by scientific studies—improved medicine and technology, for example. The second involved the political enhancement of one's citizenry, inasmuch as "Modern Science, as training the mind to an exact and impartial analysis of facts, is an education specially fitted to promote sound citizenry."[7] Ironically, Peirce, who was unwilling to trust politics to scientific practice on its own, maintained impartiality to a much larger degree than did Pearson. Pearson's political prejudices—both classist and racist in nature—ensured that he used science as a tool for social manipulation, not as a model of fallible inquiry. He was, after all, among the initial leaders of the British eugenics movement.

At first glance, the difference between Peirce's and Pearson's versions of scientific inquiry might seem merely verbal and innocuous. After all is said and done, they appear to be talking about the same sort of practice. However, from a pragmatic perspective, the difference is not innocuous but is a difference that makes a difference. For Peirce, belief in Pearson's version of science leads practitioners of science in quite a different direction than does his own account of inquiry. Peirce's responses to Pearson's instrumentalizing of science were several, and insofar as Pearson's work influenced twentieth-century practices in the social sciences, we can project these lines of criticism in the direction of our own current practices. Against "the doctrine that social stability is the sole justification of scientific research" Peirce had three complaints, "first, that it is historically false, in that it does not accord with the predominant sentiment of scientific men; second, that it is bad ethics; and, third, that its propagation would retard science" (CP 8.135). It is historically false insofar as thinkers such as Galen, Galileo, and Kepler were interested in solving problems or overcoming doubts, not in manipulating social events.

Indeed, Galileo clearly would have served the status quo better had he remained aligned with an Aristotelian outlook. Moreover, Peirce believed that the aim of "social welfare" was, on the whole, bad ethics because it made the *summum bonum* the mere "perpetuation of the biological stock." The sheer survival of the human race did not strike Peirce as the highest possibility of the cosmos, despite our own obvious interest in it. Moreover, mere survival did not speak to the quality of life humanity might sustain. "Is there nothing in the world or *in posse*," Peirce asked, "that would be admirable *per se* except copulating and swarming?" (CP 5.36).

In his review and elsewhere in his work Peirce worried about the actual consequences of Pearson's misguided ethics of inquiry. His most immediate concern was that the focus on "social stability" and "social welfare" in Pearson's hands led directly to seeing science as a "nationalist" and "classist" undertaking. Peirce wanted to know just whose welfare and stability were at stake for Pearson. "Professor Pearson's aim," Peirce argued, "'the stability of society,' which is nothing but a narrow British patriotism, prompts the *cui bono* at once" (CP 8.141). In some notes that he prepared for the writing of the review Peirce stated his concern even more directly: "Professor Pearson . . . 'in the foremost and first place,' values science as leading 'to increased social stability,'—that is, I suppose, to support the House of Lords" (MS S-76, 0004–05). Peirce's worry was pretty well confirmed by Pearson's stated commitments in *The Grammar of Science*:

> From a bad stock can come only bad offspring, and if a member of such a stock is, owing to special training and education, an exception to his family, his offspring will still be born with the old taint. Now this conclusion of Weissmann's—if it be valid . . . radically affects our judgment on the moral conduct of the state and society toward their degenerate members.[8]

Thus, what initially looks like an altruistic aim for science becomes a commitment to preserve and endorse a particular mode of living for a narrow group of persons. Peirce resisted Pearson's classism in his insistence that the genuinely altruistic aim for science is to keep open every avenue toward the truth for the community of inquirers in the long run. Pearson's initial classism is not, however, as bad as it gets. He moved quickly from his agreement with August Weissmann to a full-blown eugenicism. Not only was his aim to have science sustain British aristocratic culture, but his understanding of how this could be accomplished was linked to his belief that the degenerate and destabilizing elements of British culture were identifiable not only by social class but by genetic inheritance. In *National Life from the Standpoint of Science* Pearson made the point emphatically:

> You will see that my view—and I think it may be called the scientific view of a nation—is that of an organized whole, kept up to a high pitch of internal efficiency by insuring that its members are substantially recruited from the better stocks, and kept to a high pitch of external efficiency by contest, chiefly by way of war with inferior races, and with equal races by the struggle for trade-routes and for the sources of raw material and of food supply.[9]

For Pearson science was to be our instrument for genetic purification, a theme that has underwritten much of the history of the twentieth century and that remains an issue on the current scene. This is what he meant by "the improvement of society" and "seeking social stability." It is certainly not an innocuous stance:

> Class, poverty, localization do much to approximately isolate stock, to aggregate the unfit even in modern civilization. . . . What we need is a check to the fertility of the inferior stocks, and this can only arise with new social habits and new conceptions of the social and the anti-social in conduct.[10]

If Peirce was bothered by Pearson's overall rejection of truth as the aim of inquiry, he would have been even more deeply provoked by passages such as this because of the fact that he himself had been living on the edge of poverty for a number of years. The implications of Pearson's *Grammar* were borne out by Pearson's role in the eugenics movement in England in the early part of the twentieth century. Peirce clearly saw the upshot of Pearsonian science: "A family in

which the standards of that society [British aristocracy] are not traditional will go under and die out, and thus 'social stability' tends to be
maintained" (CP 8.134).

On Peirce's outlook, any version of "social welfare" as the aim of
science was problematic, because, whatever its other consequences, it
would lead to poor practices in science. We have already noted the
most fundamental issue, which is that visions of "social welfare" will
inevitably be used to close certain avenues of inquiry and this may
preclude a pursuit of the truth. For example, Pearson's assumption of
genetic determinism in matters of intelligence, industry, and physical
ability precludes any inquiry into the efficacy of education as a tool
of social transformation. To see the full scope of Peirce's concern,
however, we need to examine other ethical dimensions of his conception of inquiry.

The first is that a community of genuine inquirers needs to be established. Since no single, finite individual can possibly carry out the
indefinite inquiry necessary for the pursuit of truth, it is only through
a community in history whose aim is truth that the project could be
carried out. The community's inquirers must share both an aim and
a method, thus placing them in historical and social relationships.
The social nature of these inquirers requires of them moral features
that allow them to constitute a community rather than a mere aggregate. Science is not merely "accumulation" of knowledge; it constitutes a living history with dialectical transitions in a variety of
directions, not all of which hang together perfectly at any given time.

The members of such a community will be most effective if they
are pursuers of truth: "Science is to mean for us a mode of life whose
single, animating purpose is to find out the real truth" (CP 7.54–55;
see also 7.87). This animating purpose, however, places further constraints on the community's participants. They may not, for example,
be full-blown skeptics, since skepticism or cynicism denies the hope
for truth. Yet they must have traces of skepticism, since they must
also avoid the tenacious and authoritative features of dogmatism. In
short, in Kantian fashion they must work the middle ground between
skepticism and dogmatism. As pursuers of truth, genuine inquirers

must also be open to all ideas that meet abduction's mark of validity—plausibility.[11] An idea need not be immediately relevant or
"practical" in the narrow sense of immediately useful. To modify the
way William James put it, truths will eventually "work" because they
are true, but they are not final truths *because* they work. For Peirce,
the history of science is littered with ideas that, in their day, seemed
to have little relevance. Indeed, many scientific "truths" have met
with initial ridicule. Galileo's is perhaps the best-known case of ideas
being closed out for nonscientific reasons, but it is certainly not the
only case. Peirce saw this feature of intolerance at the heart of Pearson's work: "In section 10 [of chapter 3] we are told that we must not
believe a certain purely theoretical proposition because it is 'anti-social'
to do so, and because to do so is opposed to the interests of society"
(CP 8.143). Thus, Pearson's position is analogous to that of medieval
Christianity just insofar as ideas are to be measured by a present
moral outlook rather than by their plausibility in answering questions
generated by experience.

Being animated by openness and the quest for truth, Peircean inquirers must also be non-egoistic. They must be fundamentally un-
selfish and willing to engage in self-aversive thinking and self-
sacrifice. Interestingly, this consideration may have been underwritten by the New England transcendentalism with which Peirce grew
up; such self-aversive thinking was a hallmark in particular of the
work of Emerson, who believed that individual and community
growth was like ascending to higher platforms from which one could
see the limitations of one's previous self. These features of the inquirer's will are crucial because the truth is *in futuro*, and the findings of
any given generation will often find their "uses" in the future. On the
immediate scene they may be useful in developing knowledge further
and, down the road, they may find applications that help ameliorate
human existence. Madame Curie died from prolonged exposure to
radiation. Two generations later, what she discovered has found uses
in improving human existence. "Given a body of men devoting the
sum of their energies to refuting their present errors, doing away with
their ignorance," said Peirce, "and that not so much for themselves

as for future generations, and all other requisites for the ascertainment of truth are insured by that one" (CP 7.50). In this spirit, Peircean inquirers should not be driven by money, fame, or status, all of which are real temptations for scientists in an age in which science is honored and information can be widely and easily distributed, and in which professional success is measured by both income and reputation.

The inquirer's self-sacrifice involves a specific kind of social structure. As Delaney argues, for Peirce "the life of science demands the transcendence of both selfishness and skepticism through the active hope that rational cooperative effort will, in the end, prevail."[12] As we noted, Peirce maintained that inquiry was not an individualistic affair but the work of a community of inquirers. To constitute a community, however, requires certain conditions. Most importantly, members of the community must work co-operatively, sharing findings and ideas, and learning from others. In short, being in the community involves taking what Peirce called in "The Fixation of Belief" the "social impulse" (the fact that others have different beliefs from one's own) seriously. In several accounts of scientific method, Peirce described this cooperative nature of community at length. In one, he described the cooperative nature of inquiry:

> The scientific world is like a colony of insects, in that the individual strives to produce that which he himself cannot hope to enjoy. One generation collects premises in order that a distant generation may discover what they mean. When a problem comes before the scientific world, a hundred men immediately set all their energies to work upon it. One contributes this, another that. Another company, standing upon the shoulders of the first, strike a little higher, until at last the parapet is attained. (CP 7.87)

The cooperation is both cross-cultural and transhistorical. Lured by the common aim of truth, scientists together produce the history of science, which is at least a part of the cosmos's development toward truth.

In a second description, Peirce not only portrayed the cooperative mood of science but introduced a key feature of the inquirer's self-sacrifice—the possibility of failure:

The considerable numbers of the workers, and the singleness of
heart with which . . . they cast their whole being into the service
of science lead, of course, to their unreserved discussions with one
another, to each being fully informed about the work of his neighbor, and availing himself of that neighbor's results; and thus in
storming the stronghold of truth one mounts upon the shoulders
of another who has to ordinary apprehension failed, but has in
truth succeeded by virtue of the lessons of his failure. This is the
veritable essence of science. (CP 7.51)

The community of scientists thus sees what nonscientists do not: the
importance of failure on the road to truth. A rightly animated inquirer, as Peirce saw it, should not only expect some failure because
we are fallible, but should also recognize its importance to the general
progress of inquiry. In short, scientists who fail in particular surmises,
predictions, or experimental practices are by no means "failures" in
a pejorative sense. They are, on the contrary, legitimate and contributing members of the community of inquirers. It is unfortunate that
in our current practices, especially where funding is concerned, we
take failure in science to be utter failure rather than an integral part
of the history of inquiry. To the extent we do this, from a Peircean
perspective we establish barriers to successful inquiry in the long run.

Peirce clearly recognized the ideality of his descriptions of science.
Nevertheless, as a pragmatist, he took them seriously precisely because one's ideals govern self-controlled conduct. That is, the practice
of science is, both tacitly and openly, guided by what one thinks the
aims of science are. His resistance to Pearson, then, was not merely
an intellectual dispute over the nature or essence of science; it was
also about how inquirers should conduct themselves. It was about the
actual consequences of belief. Pearson's choice of "social stability and
welfare" as the aim of science not only entailed the "bad ethics" we
noted above; it determined all the necessary conditions for "good"
science. And ultimately, it found its upshot in determining the modes
of scientific practice.

Again, Peirce's largest complaint was that the demand for social
relevance too easily closed the doors on inquiry. We noted earlier that

it led to social censoring of hypotheses. But at the level of intellectual development, it also entailed an inherent resistance to any ideas that show no immediate promise for the welfare of society. Thus, ideas need not be socially dangerous to be excluded; they need only to be indifferent to someone's account of social welfare. In his 1898 Cambridge lectures Peirce made this concern explicit. What he feared was that "practical or applied" science would supplant theoretical science. In his own work, Peirce encountered this phenomenon when his studies in logic were rejected as nonscientific in large part because they seemed to hold no immediate value for society—they did not save lives, cure diseases, or make money. Peirce did acknowledge the importance of practical and theoretical sciences working together and inspiring one another. "The mechanical theory of heat," he pointed out, "grew out of the difficulties of steam navigation" (CP 7.52). But the relationship needed to be dialectically ordered. Given Pearson's aim of social welfare, there was a genuine—and historically actual— temptation to displace and ignore theoretical inquiries that seemed irrelevant to current affairs. This constituted for Peirce bad science precisely because it closed avenues of inquiry for illegitimate or irrelevant reasons.

We also noted earlier that Pearson's notion of social welfare was guided by his own social status and the interests that accompanied it. Peirce saw that there was a slippery slope—not of necessity but of possibility—to egoism in science. One's social interests can easily become simply a blown-up version of one's personal interests; this is not an uncommon phenomenon. At the very least, Pearson's aim of science did not preclude egoism in the practice of inquiry. In his review of *The Grammar of Science* Peirce commented on this worry in a way that may speak to Pearson's own practices as a scientist:

> The worst feature of the present state of things is that the great majority of the members of many scientific societies, and a large part of others, are men whose chief interest in science is as a means of gaining money, and who have a contempt, or half-contempt, for pure science. Now, to declare that the sole reason for scientific research is the good of society is to encourage those

pseudo-scientists to claim, and the general public to admit, that they, who deal with applications of knowledge, are the true men of science, and that the theoreticians are little better than idlers. (CP 8.142)

These claims may reflect resentment not only of Pearson but of others such as Simon Newcomb who stood in the way of Peirce's receiving funds from the Carnegie Institute for his study of logic.[13] But Peirce was also genuinely concerned about how this state of affairs—especially over a long time—would stifle the development of science, especially if it became a cultural habit and the "accepted" understanding of science. We might ask about our own practices of seeking funding for scientific research; funding often hinges on showing how one's research "improves" society in the short run.

Pearson's version of inquiry also has a social structure, but it is not one of cooperation. Rather, the egoist impulse that it enables leads to a competitive, entrepreneurial social structure. In a rough sense, his model is Darwinian; it is competitive rather than cooperative at its root. While Peirce's agapastic, cooperative community leaves room for what we might call "friendly" competition, it does not advocate the sort of cutthroat interaction inspired by the rough notion of "the survival of the fittest." Pearson's egoism not only permits the pursuit of money and fame as central motives for inquiry, but it engenders a competitive mood that leads to a number of practical consequences in scientific endeavors.

Most noticeably, Pearson's science does not encourage the sharing of ideas, and it openly practices the theft of ideas. It is a thoroughly entrepreneurial—or social Darwinist—model. In Pearson's own life this was exemplified in his routine failure to give credit to those whose work influenced his own and his extremely arrogant responses to those who worked the same fields of inquiry as he. Pearson's competitive attitude led to longstanding and bitter wars with colleagues and students. His student R. A. Fisher, for example, became a lifelong enemy. Some called Pearson a liar, and evidence suggests that, at the very least, he was never generous in acknowledging previous work in statistics that influenced his own.

Some of the petty practices generated by this competitive model run directly against the grain of what Peirce took to be good science. First, it generates an environment in which the pursuit of fame underwrites a "scoop" mentality. One needs to be the first to propose or verify a hypothesis, or the first to bring some useful conclusions into the public realm. In recent years we have had such extreme examples as the presentation of "cold fusion" and the cancer-preventing claims for oat bran and other substances. From Peirce's perspective, Pearsonian inquiry is made too hasty and incautious in its experimentation. Such haste not only leads to some foolish claims, but along the way creates a culture of blindness to the "social impulse." Inquirers fail to take seriously or examine closely the views and beliefs of other investigators. In a Pearsonian ethos, it is more expedient to defend one's initial position dogmatically.

Competition for fame and money also leads to a thoroughgoing politicization of scientific practice. Professionals will find ways not only to "scoop" others, but, when necessary, to downplay, denigrate, or dismiss the work of others *not* on the basis of evidence but on dogmatic grounds in an attempt to sustain their own research agendas. Such politicization was indeed evident in Pearson's work with the Royal Academy—his differences with Fisher were political as well as intellectual. Moreover, as we noted, personal politics conspired to prevent Peirce from pursuing some lines of study. Recently, the race to map the human genetic structure has led to some less-than-generous relations among the competing groups of inquirers.

Competition may, as in the case of the genome projects, intensify inquiry and produce results in shorter periods of time. However, the potential costs to science over the long run made such a model impractical for Peirce. It encouraged the selling and marketing of ideas for their usefulness and not for their truth. In this way wrong roads could be too easily created. Dead ends could be dogmatically defended. The lack of cooperation might increase tenacity and create blindness to the social impulse. And, perhaps most importantly for Peirce, the competitive, entrepreneurial model cannot countenance failures in science. That is, because inquirers are led to fight for funds, professional reputation, and payoffs, they do not willingly acknowledge the importance of some failures in moving knowledge forward, even as these failures continue to play a role in the development of truth. In short, Pearson's aim of social stability and welfare has led, as Peirce predicted it might, to a scientific culture whose interest in truth seems to be almost a secondary affair.

There is, no doubt, much cooperation in the sciences, and our practices have not altogether forgone an interest in truth-seeking as a motivation for inquirers. Nevertheless, it seems clear that today's businesslike entrepreneurial structure in university life is governed much more by Pearson's ideals than by those Peirce championed. Competition for funding, for jobs, and for fame has led to a culture of exclusion and manipulation; we ask inquirers to "referee" work of those who may be competing with them for limited research funds. It has also led to a situation in which highly speculative and theoretical work is marginalized in favor of applied-science projects that can show an immediate payoff. Respect for the importance of failure in inquiry has virtually disappeared. It is very difficult to re-enlist money for one's projects if in fact what was predicted in some specific project does not pan out. In short, we have developed a peculiar, and perhaps not the most effective, economy of research.

To be sure, we are not faced with the end of science. But we are, from a Peircean outlook, faced with a degenerate science—one that is nominalistically inclined, that speaks the language of "truth" but at bottom is not at all certain of nor interested in the reality of truth. Ours is a scientific culture that on one hand appeals to "the evidence," but on the other hand argues opponents out of the competition on dogmatic political, not evidentiary grounds. It exemplifies, perhaps, pragmatism gone astray and acting with an ill will—so interested in accomplishing short-run goals that it jettisons concern with the ideal aim of truth. This was perhaps the sort of pragmatism Peirce envisioned when he renamed his own "pragmaticism." Ideas are indeed to be understood through the habits they engender and, as

Peirce predicted, we have reaped many of the negative fruits of Pearson's grammar of science. Now may be a good time to revisit the issue of the aims of science.

Because the differences between Peirce and Pearson in part grew out of their respective realist and nominalist tendencies, we thought it worth pursuing the bearing of these tendencies on their mathematical work. Thus, we offer an addendum to our text that explores some of Peirce's work in statistics and suggests some of its differences from Pearson's work—work that had a significant influence on twentieth-century research in the social sciences. Those interested in such connections may want to turn directly to the addendum before proceeding.

For other readers, we now shift our focus toward another, and less often explored, feature of Peirce's philosophy—his treatment of other cultural features such as our outlooks on religion, cosmology, and nature.

CONVERSATION III

CULTURAL CONSIDERATIONS

NINE

THE PRAGMATIC IMPORTANCE OF PEIRCE'S RELIGIOUS WRITINGS

Doug Anderson

Carl and I have both written on the import of Peirce's thought for aesthetics, creativity, ethics, and politics. Our conversations have often turned towards discussing the relevance of Peircean ideas for a variety of cultural issues and practices, including education, cosmological speculation, history, and religion. In the following chapters we focus on a few of these themes. One of the seemingly peculiar aspects of Peirce's philosophy was his commitment to a belief in a vague idea of God. Because nineteenth-century idealism was often limited to theisms, Carl and I have often tried to sort out what it was to which Peirce was committed when he made such claims.

Many scholars come to Peirce's work from backgrounds in which matters of religion are of little or no interest, and when they encounter Peirce's religious writings, they see them as an aberration. These writings are interesting or off-putting according to one's inclinations and aversions. For some scholars, these writings stand out as a blemish on an otherwise elegant and technically compelling philosophical architectonic. But, as Michael Raposa[1] and Hermann Deuser[2] have shown, Peirce's interest in religion was manifest at every stage of his career. If then these writings constitute an aberration, the aberration is not a momentary madness but a deeply habitual feature of Peirce's outlook on life. Given the pervasiveness and consistent presence of religious matters in Peirce's work, it seems at best arbitrary to suggest that they do not belong. Seeking their role and import in Peirce's thought seems a more relevant endeavor than does seeking ways to excommunicate them, even if one is not fond of their presence. Judging their importance is a pragmatic task; we can ask what consequences these religious interests have for Peirce's work.

Such consequences are to be found both within and without the structure of Peirce's philosophy. I begin with a few remarks about the outward influence of Peirce's ideas concerning religion, about their usefulness in addressing some traditional questions in the philosophy of religion and natural theology. The bulk of what I have to say will, however, look inward to the heart of Peirce's philosophical architectonic and practice, and by implication to the heart of the origins of pragmatism.

I read Peirce first and foremost as an American scholar. This is not to say that he might not be the most cosmopolitan of the pragmatists, but rather that his work nevertheless emerged in an American intellectual context. Specifically, Peirce and James were the immediate successors to New England transcendentalism. Late in his career Peirce acknowledged this:

> I may mention, for the benefit of those who are curious in studying mental biographies, that I was born and reared in the neighborhood of Concord—I mean in Cambridge—at the time when Emerson, Hedge, and their friends were disseminating the ideas that they had caught from Schelling, and Schelling from Plotinus, from Boehm, or from God knows what minds stricken with the monstrous mysticism of the East. But the atmosphere of Cambridge held many an antiseptic against Concord transcendentalism; and I am not conscious of having contracted any of that

virus. Nevertheless, it is probable that some cultured bacilli, some benignant form of the disease was implanted in my soul, modified by mathematical conceptions and by training in physical investigations. (CP 6.102)[3]

I take this description not as an off-hand remark, but as a reasonably sound self-assessment. I will follow it to focus not only on the transcendentalist environment out of which Peirce's thought developed, but on the transformations his other experiences brought to this environment. My hope is that in so doing, we can catch a glimpse of the importance of his religious writings within the confines of his own developing system.

The outward influence of Peirce's religious writings was generated by his transformation of transcendentalist ideas. In the trajectory of American philosophy of religion and theology in the twentieth century, Peirce's work played some interesting mediating roles. Early on, for example, it served as a way to stand between James's pluralistic individualism and Royce's aggregational monism. As I discussed in chapter 2, Peirce warned Royce of too much closure, and Royce responded with *The Problem of Christianity*, in which he developed his notion of the beloved community in light of Peirce's semiotic descriptions of communication and his idea of a community of inquirers that could develop historically without closure. After the appearance of James's *Varieties of Religious Experience*, Peirce corresponded with James and cajoled him to explore the church as a site of communal religious experiences. If we look in another direction, we see that the richness of Peirce's realist categorial scheme and his willingness to apply it both to human practices and to metaphysical descriptions allows this scheme to serve as a medium for holding together James's focus on religious experience and practice and A. N. Whitehead's interest in a cosmogony, cosmology, and metaphysics of process. In short, Peirce's religious ideas had an immediate impact on pragmatic, idealist, and process philosophies of religion.

Beyond specific historical consequences such as these, Peirce's ideas have had an impact in religious thought in a number of general ways. His notion of a developmental teleology has allowed theologians to consider the possibility of a universe that is ordered but ever-developing. His semeiotic has been appropriated as a tool for interpreting religious texts, religious rituals, and religious doctrines. His conception of agapastic evolution has suggested to others the possibilities both of bringing science and religion into a working relationship and of consciously adopting religious belief as a political ground. And his theory of inquiry has caused some thinkers to rethink and revise the traditional arguments for God.

Peirce's religious writings have thus produced some consequences for twentieth- and twenty-first-century thought, despite the fact that they have not been widely available to scholars. I have no doubt that this external influence will continue to develop—religious belief, after all, has not yet met its oft-predicted death. The depth of this impact, however, will be affected by how we Peirce scholars, with or without religious inclinations, pay attention to the roles these writings play within Peirce's work. And this brings me to my present task—to examine the continuities and the discontinuities between Peirce's thoughts on religious matters and the ideas of American transcendentalism.

What, then, are some of the consequences of Peirce's engagements with religious issues in his own work? Two things come to mind. One, Peirce's general outlook and attitude in approaching inquiry seem to square with his descriptions of the religious life. And two, these engagements give articulation to some of the key elements of Peirce's architectonic. In other essays and books, for example, I have tried to show how his notions of developmental teleology, instinct, love, vagueness, fallibility, and community are given clear presentation in his discussions of religious topics. So, at the very least, the religious writings are instrumental as vehicles of presentation. In his late essay "A Neglected Argument for the Reality of God" one can see both of these consequences clearly at work. Now, however, I want to ask if the religious talk that Peirce undertakes is not even more integral to his dynamic philosophical system—if it is not more than a vehicle of presentation. To do this, I do not want to look only at the end of his career, for one may be tempted to say of something like the "Neglected Argument" that in it Peirce was merely using the religious talk to find a venue for selling his philosophical project. Instead, I want to begin with a review he wrote somewhat earlier in his career—a review that, both overtly and by way of implication, established Peirce's Janus-faced relationship with American transcendentalism. It is his review of Henry James Sr.'s *The Secret of Swedenborg*, published in the *North American Review*. It provides a vantage point from which to see how and in what ways Peirce wished to transform the transcendentalist take on religious affairs. This piece provides an angle of vision that allows a reader to see Peirce setting his own philosophical course, a course not dominated by dogmas of religion or science.

Though the review serves well to foreshadow much of Peirce's later philosophical work, I will here focus on only two related themes: 1) the way in which Peirce handles the relationship between matters of the "heart" and matters of the "head," and 2) the primacy of love in Peirce's thought. It is love, as a *real*, that underwrites the attitude of openness that, for Peirce, describes the practice of inquiry, and it is love that conditions the possibility of real community. I do not offer these themes as some sort of exhaustive menu of important religious ideas in Peirce's work. Rather, my aim is to suggest that some of Peirce's religious thought is pragmatically fundamental and integral to his overall architectonic. This thought presents ideas not easily exorcised from Peirce's philosophical outlook, regardless of one's inclinations toward or aversions from religious belief.

Peirce's review appeared in 1870. The full title of James's book speaks for its transcendentalist lineage: *The Secret of Swedenborg: Being an Elucidation of His Doctrine of Divine Natural Humanity*. In the opening line Peirce placed some distance between himself and James: "Though this book presents some very interesting and impressive religious views, and the spiritual tone of it is in general eminently healthy, it is altogether out of harmony with the spirit of the age" (W 2:433). Transcendentalism was indeed waning, and the presence of evolutionary theory marked the ascension of science and scientism. Six years earlier Peirce had written that "the most striking tendency of our age is our materialistic tendency" (W 1:111). Peirce himself, though certainly attuned to the science of the day, was not altogether in harmony with the spirit of his age either—this is evidenced by his very willingness to review James's book without dismissing it out of hand.

The majority of the review is a restatement of the general themes that James presented in his book. This description is interspersed with side-remarks by Peirce and rhetorical inflections that give away his leanings. Peirce opened his description by asserting that for James, "Philosophy and religion are one. The matter of deepest moment to the heart is the matter of deepest moment to the head" (W 2:435). This opening identification was problematic for Peirce, and he returned to it later in the review to argue against what he took to be James's confusion. James's claims, Peirce argued, "are not scientifically established" (W 2:435). This is not surprising from a transcendentalist perspective, since inductive reasoning from sense perception was not thought capable of providing any sort of important knowledge. Indeed, as Peirce pointed out, James believed that "no cordial lover of truth can long endure to reason about" God, creation, and redemption. In this respect, Peirce wryly remarked, James is "a very cordial lover of truth" (W 2:435). The upshot is that, for James, "Religion must be supreme or it is nothing" (W 2:435). Transcendentalism presents us with an either/or, and concludes that because reasoning does not yield certainty, we must make matters of the head ancillary to matters of the heart. Peirce responded that James's religion, a matter of the heart, "fails to be philosophy while it appeals not to the head, but only to the heart" (W 2:436).

The relationship between matters of the head and matters of the heart was a concern of Peirce's thought throughout much of his career. In 1911 he returned to it to again point to the difference between the two, stating that "no two spirits (tendencies) not downright conflicting can well be more opposed than the spirit of science and the spirit of religion" (MS 851:1). This is a view he shared with the spirit of the times and with many thinkers who believed it was time to supplant religious belief altogether with scientific belief. However, we should attend to the note of hesitation in this 1911 remark. Although science and religion place their emphases and develop their tendencies in different directions, they are "not downright conflicting." Thus, the historical conflicts are in principle mendable—the opposing spirits should be able to live together. This hesitation is foreshadowed in the 1870 review by Peirce's unwillingness to reject or abandon the "heart" dimension in James's book. Instead, he tried to locate its proper sphere: "The reasoning of natural science is valid because it proceeds from outward appearances only to outward appearances. If religion could, in a parallel way, restrict its conclusions to spiritual experiences, it might find a scientific foundation in spiritual experiences" (W 2:435). In short, Peirce left the door open for matters of the heart to play a role in personal and cultural life.

The nature of this role is hinted at in Peirce's review. As I noted, he admitted that the "spiritual tone" is "eminently healthy." Later he suggested that if James's "sanction of the heart" would simply rest with the fact that a proposition or belief is "one altogether delightful and comforting," it would remain within its proper sphere. These hints were openly developed in Peirce's later work. The spirit of religion, which for Peirce is driven by instinct, feeling, and the heart, aims directly at guiding the conduct of life and is inherently conservative. The spirit of science, on the other hand, is theoretically minded and remains open to change. We see science's natural inclination to freedom, change, and liberality when we understand it not as a static body of beliefs but as "a living and growing body of truth" (CP 6.428). The upshot is that religion and science, instead of excluding each other, stand in a relation of reciprocal dependence. They stand in a continuum in which each pole tempers the other in different ways. This continuity and relatedness is cashed out in several ways in Peirce's subsequent work, and I attend to two of them here: the relationship between practice and theory, and the relationship between instinctive or common-sensical belief and reasoning.

As is well known, the first of these is treated extensively in Peirce's 1898 Cambridge lectures. There he began with what seems like an ineradicable break between the two, confessing that he is "an Aristotelian and a scientific man, condemning with the whole strength of conviction the Hellenic tendency to mingle philosophy and practice" (CP 1.618). However, as many commentators have pointed out, the starkness of the contrast is in part a function of Peirce's reaction to James's request that he speak about "vitally important topics" when he wanted to discuss logic, mathematical theory, and their relation to a philosophy of synechism. Ironically, it is just this synechism that brings theory and practice back into relation. He maintained that morality and religiosity are practically oriented and are crucial to human existence as guides to conduct; philosophy and science, on the other hand, are theoretically oriented and are dangerous if taken as immediate guides to action precisely because the beliefs they establish are tenuous. Nevertheless, insofar as theoretical inquiry must itself be practiced, it will be influenced by religion and morality. In the transactional relationship Peirce established between theory and practice, the lines of influence run the other direction as well: "I do not say that philosophical science should not ultimately influence religion and morality; I only say that it should do so only with secular slowness and the most conservative caution" (CP 1.620). Thus, matters of the heart are important as guides to conduct, but they nevertheless can become too dogmatic, entrenched, and inflexible. They need to remain open to gradual transformation. At the same time, however, they should not be merely overcome by every new theory that comes down the road.

Peirce's position set him at odds with the transcendentalists. As has already been noted, James tried to reduce philosophy to religion. But such a move, because it bases *all* judgments on the heart, disallows orderly and ongoing criticism of whatever beliefs are established on religious grounds. As Peirce complained, James's book is "deficient in argumentation" (W 2:436). In short, transcendentalists were as likely to fall into uncritical and dogmatic belief as were the Calvinists and Unitarians against whose worlds they were reacting. This is the standard concern Peirce and others have about the essentially conservative nature of religious and practical beliefs. By making theory and practice continuous, Peirce tried to negotiate a middle ground between a dogmatic transcendentalism and, as we will see, the developing nominalistic scientism of the late nineteenth century. Religion is important as a guide to our practical existence—this he shared with the transcendentalists. This middle ground receives further illumination if we turn to the relationship between common sense and reasoning.

In this pairing, religion is aligned with instinct or common sense and reasoning with science and philosophy. If we return to Peirce's review we see that he left the door open for common sense to work on behalf of matters of the heart:

> [W]e do not in the least oppose the Scotch philosophy which makes all knowledge finally to repose on what are sometimes called ultimate beliefs; because these beliefs are the common sense of mankind which belongs to all men and which no man can resist. If religion can be traced to such premises, it becomes truly philosophical. (W 2:436)[4]

Embedded here is another moment of separation between Peirce and the transcendentalists—even as he aimed to make room for religious belief. As students at Harvard, the transcendentalists had been routinely exposed to Scottish common-sensism through the works of Thomas Brown that Levi Hedge had introduced to the curriculum. For them, it was related to the sensualism of Locke and to the Unitarianism they were confronting. Peirce's introduction of common sense as a way of making religion reasonable thus would have struck Henry James as ironic at best. And yet, it is precisely this move that Peirce made in systematic fashion in his own later work. He identified religious beliefs—such as a belief in the reality (not existence) of God—as instinctive or commonsensical. This marks them as useful for guiding conduct.

At the same time, in his 1903 pragmatism lectures, in his 1905 discussions of pragmaticism, and in the "Neglected Argument for the Reality of God," Peirce identified instinctive and common-sense belief as the "bedrock" of reasoning. Reasoning—scientific and philosophical inquiry—are then launched from these common-sense and instinctive beliefs in such a way as to test over time not only their efficacy in practice but their truth. In considering the instinctive belief in a vague conception of God, Peirce says, we must take a stand in pragmaticism, "which implies faith in common sense and in instinct, though only as they issue from the cupelfurnace of measured criticism" (CP 6.480). In adopting common sense and instinct, which for Peirce were matters of the heart and do generate religious beliefs, Peirce remained open to the healthfulness of James's "spiritual tone" in *The Secret of Swedenborg*. In making his common-sensism critical, he made religion answerable to scientific inquiry. He thus made religious talk philosophical, as he suggested in his review, by making instinctive religious beliefs guides to practice on the one hand and the initial stage of inquiry on the other. Richard Trammel sees this point made manifest in Peirce's discussion of musement in the "Neglected Argument": "This argument shows that the same course of meditation which, for practical purposes, produces a living belief in God, from another point of view is the first stage of a theoretical inquiry."[5]

In both of these cashings out of the reciprocal relationship between the head and the heart, Peirce developed the suggestions he made in his 1870 review. But another undercurrent of the review and of the relationships just noted is less apparent. In making room for matters of the heart, Peirce implicitly resisted scientism and those philosophers of science who were intent on replacing the functions of the heart with reasoning and scientific inquiry. It was just this issue that provoked William James to write "The Will to Believe" in response to W. K. Clifford's "The Ethics of Belief." Clifford's take was that all of our beliefs, theoretical and practical, must await the certainty to be yielded by the final evidence of scientific inquiry. In this way, matters of religion could be quickly dispensed with since no scientific inquiry, as Clifford saw it, seemed to lead toward religious beliefs. Peirce, though he worried about the arbitrariness of William James's "will to believe," just as he worried about the elder James's "sanctions of the heart," agreed with both father and son that losing the heart dimension altogether might bear serious negative consequences for the practice of inquiry and the conduct of life. In a similar vein, we have already seen a corresponding response from Peirce to the work of Clifford's student Karl Pearson. As detailed in chapter 8, Peirce vehemently attacked Pearson's claims that the essential aim of science was to ensure the stability of society. Like Clifford, Pearson had committed the second sin of discontinuity, reducing matters of the heart to matters of the head. On the whole, Peirce's aversion to the dogmatic religionism of the transcendentalists is well matched by his resistance to the dogmatically nominalistic scientism of Pearson, T. H. Huxley, and the like.

The upshot of pointing to these themes in Peirce's work is that he gives clear articulation to the structural dialectic of the heart and the head in establishing the continuity between theory and practice and between common sense and reasoning. Thus, even if one is disinclined toward Peirce's religious talk, one must acknowledge its central role in illuminating and maintaining these relationships. From Peirce's perspective, even if one gives up his religious talk, one will still be left with something analogous, something that, pragmatically speaking, functions very much like religious belief. If the dialectical role maintained by matters of the heart is not filled, the structure of Peirce's architectonic will become distorted. Thus, one internal value of Peirce's religious writings is to bring meaning and stability to the practical dimensions of human existence. In terms of the outward influence this internal structure might have had, it is worth considering whether John Dewey was sensitive to something like this pragmatic necessity of matters of the heart when he wrote *A Common Faith*.

This brings me to my second theme, the primacy of love in Peirce's work. Here the case I want to make is perhaps less evident. What I want to suggest is that at the heart of all of Peirce's religious writings and, by implication, at the heart of his descriptions of ordinary human life, is his belief that love, especially agapistic love, constitutes the motive force of a well-lived life. Specifically, however, I will focus on the roles Peirce seems to give to love in constituting both a genuine inquiry and a genuine community. Let me sketch some suggestive outlines to support these claims.

In his review of *The Secret of Swedenborg*, Peirce elaborated on the role love played in James's world view. For James, he said, "the essence of God is love" and "the creature's being also lies in another, namely, in God; and, therefore, his life too is love" (W 2:434). Love thus pervaded James's world—it is the principle force of creation and creativity, it is other-directed such that the lover loses herself or himself in allowing another to develop and grow, and it is the bonding principle for a "brotherhood" of persons who can live well together without the intrusions of governmental force. As we might expect, James produced a highly romantic, transcendentalist picture of the efficacy of love.

For anyone well acquainted with Peirce's work, this description of James's consideration of love brings to mind the cosmological essay "Evolutionary Love." It is not accidental that in that essay Peirce explicitly drew on James's conception of love—"the creative Love, all whose tenderness *ex vi termini* must be reserved only for what intrinsically is most bitterly hostile and negative to itself" (CP 6.287, W 8.185). It is a theme that persisted in Peirce's writing from his youth. In a journal entry in 1853, for example, Peirce wrote that "Love is the foundation of everything desirable or good" (W 1:4). Though "Evolutionary Love" reveals Peirce's transcendentalist roots, it also, I think, makes *us* recall Peirce's concern about having contracted some of the transcendentalist virus. Instead of focusing on the worrisome nature of cosmological agapasm, therefore, I will try to see if there isn't a more benign form of Peirce's commitment to love in his explorations of inquiry and the development of communities.

Here, then, are my suggestions: first, that love underwrites the attitude of openness and receptivity that Peirce believed to be essential to genuine inquiry. And second, that Peirce's conception of community is shot through with agapistic features. I again take Peirce at his word in supposing that he took seriously James's notion of love but that he also transformed it, that it might be more in harmony with the spirit of his age. For both inquiry and community, Peirce's scholastic realism underwrote the efficacy of love as a real general, not an existent individual cause.

As is well known, one of Peirce's primal fears was that inquiry would be closed and that the adventure toward truth would be abandoned. Thus, as noted earlier in the discussion of reciprocity between theory and practice, he even-handedly resisted both an uncritical transcendentalism in which common sense and heartfelt beliefs were not left open to criticism, and the dogmatic scientism of the late nineteenth century that, at its outset, excluded an array of hypotheses from consideration. Peirce's fear of closure was coupled with his belief that inquiry is properly directed not toward ourselves, but instead should be directed outward toward an ideal of truth: "He who would not sacrifice his own soul to save the whole world, is illogical in all his inferences, collectively" (CP 2.653–54, W 2:270–71; see also W 3:284).

This other-directedness is an agapistic trait of Peircean inquiry. Thus, while eros, as a drive to inquire, is useful, it is not sufficient for inquiry precisely because it runs the risk of becoming egoistic— captured by what Peirce called "the gospel of greed." Inquiry is not *for me*, nor even *for us*; it is *for achieving the ideal of truth*. Indeed, in many instances, Peirce pointed to the loss of the individual in the history of inquiry. Whether through success or failure, as inquirers we are always relegated to the role of supporting cast. In part for this reason, as we noted, Peirce aggressively assaulted Pearson's suggestion that inquiry's true purpose was to produce local social improvements. In his review of *The Grammar of Science* he said, "I must confess that I belong to that class of scallawags who purpose, with God's help, to look the truth in the face, whether doing so be conducive to the interests of society or not" (CP 8.143). To pursue Pearson's line of thought, a popular line at the time, meant making inquiry a mercenary activity. As noted in chapter 8, Peirce also commented, "The worst feature of the present state of things is that the great majority of the members of many scientific societies, and a large part of others, are men whose chief interest in science is a means of gaining money, and who have a contempt, or half-contempt for pure science" (CP 8.142). For Peirce, scientific and philosophical investigations undertaken without an agapistic attitude run the risk of foreclosing on genuine inquiry.

The other-directedness of inquiry has two corollaries in Peirce's thought. On the one hand, because inquiry should not be an eros-driven process, we should not become dominators of our ideas. This is the attitudinal key to the efficacy of abduction. As Peirce put it, we must be receptive to the force of the ideas themselves; a "hypothesis ought, at first, to be entertained interrogatively" (CP 6.524). More-over, once we begin to explore an idea or a hypothesis, we must re-main open to its growth and development. "It is not," Peirce argued, "by dealing out cold justice to the circle of my ideas that I can make them grow, but by cherishing and tending them as I would the flow-ers in my garden" (CP 6.289). On the other hand, this agapistic open-ness to ideas also means that we should not too quickly dismiss ideas to which we may be culturally disinclined, since "any hypothesis . . . may be admissible, in the absence of any special reasons to the con-trary" (CP 5.197). This was precisely William James's point in his at-tacks on "medical materialism" in the *Varieties*. The materialists excluded the very possibility of religious experience's causal efficacy before considering it. Analogously, Peirce's persistent anti-nominal-ism was an attempt to keep open an avenue to an entire class of ideas that were dismissed uncritically by way of cultural habit.

These, then, are the ways in which agapism may inform Peirce's theory and practice of inquiry. We must remain receptive to all possi-ble ideas and we must remain open to the development of any partic-ular idea. If we simply dominate our ideas, as for example through tenacity or authority, we will always risk losing inquiry altogether.

My second and final sketch has to do with Peirce's conception of community. What is best known is his conception of a community of inquirers who, throughout history, work cooperatively in an ongoing historical dialogue to move inquiry in the direction of truth. For this community, all of the agapistic features of inquiry just described ob-tain. This establishes one link between community and love. If we look more closely at Peirce's corpus, however, we will find a second model of community—the community of a nontheological church of love. This community puts us in mind of Henry James Sr.'s "brotherhood" of love described in Peirce's review. "Man's highest developments,"

Peirce argued, "are social; and religion, though it begins in a seminal individual inspiration, only comes to full flower in a great church coextensive with civilization. This is true of every religion, but supereminently so of the religion of love" (CP 6.493).

Such a church or community remains down-to-earth and not overly transcendentalist just insofar as it attends to its agapistic work and insofar as it remains open to all. In short, this community must be ameliorative and inclusive. The principle of love expressed commonsensically in the Golden Rule, Peirce maintained, "does not . . . say, Do everything possible to gratify the egoistic impulses of others, but it says, sacrifice your own perfection to the perfectionment of your neighbor" (CP 6.288). The loving community's general task, then, is to employ agape to resist the degenerative consequences of self-love and self-seeking (see CP 6.448). "The *raison d'etre* of a church," Peirce believed, "is to confer upon men a life broader than their narrow personalities, a life rooted in the very truth of being" (CP 6.451). Just as inquiry is directed outward toward the ideal of truth, the practical community aims to liberate and thus to ameliorate. Indeed, one feature of the world that such an ameliorative stance would have to sustain is the openness of inquiry.

The other-directedness of such a community also entails inclusivity in its membership. Peirce's fundamental rejection of theology arises from his concern that its primary aim is to create rules of exclusion—it is a tool for destroying a community of love. As he put it, "the principal business of theologians is to make men feel the enormity of the slightest departure from the metaphysics they assume to be connected with the standard faith" (CP 6.3). Such exclusivity was anathema for Peirce. In the opening of the "Neglected Argument," for example, he insisted that if the truths of religion are a good, then there ought to be some argument for God's reality that is "obvious to all minds, high and low alike, that should earnestly strive to find the truth of the matter" (CP 6.457). This, in part, is why the instinctiveness of a belief in God's reality is central to Peirce's argument. Peirce seems to have inherited something of the transcendentalists' democratic outlook.

The inclusivity of his universal community is twofold. Not only must the community be open to all, it must also attend to all. It must be such that, "recognizing germs of loveliness in the hateful, [it] gradually warms it into life and makes it lovely" (CP 6.289). The ameliorative function should not be limited to a particular privileged class or society, but on the basis of agape should extend to those out of favor in the universe. In a letter to Francis Russell in October 1896 Peirce brought some surprising particularity to this notion: "My natural sympathies are with the poor rather than the rich; and I favor what will educate the masses" (MS L387a, 00258). No doubt, the transcendentalists would have been pleased by such an admission.

I close this final sketch by noting that the loving community and the community of inquirers are not at odds. Both are underwritten by Peirce's conception of agape and both aim at truth. Thus, the reciprocity between common sense and reasoning reappears in this context. The religious community must be careful not to move toward closure—it must be a community that "will gladly go forward, sure that truth is not split into two warring doctrines, and that any change that knowledge can work in [its] faith can only affect its expression, not the deep mystery expressed" (CP 6.432).

Through Peirce's responses to transcendentalism and specifically to the thought of Henry James Sr., we can see the middle ground he tried to mark out between its blind romanticism and the equally blind scientism of those who believed that a nominalistically driven practice of science was a panacea for the world's ills. I am willing to admit that one could move Peirce's view even further from its transcendentalist inheritance without destroying its integrity. However, my aim is simply to show that matters of the heart, matters of religious interest, are so thoroughly woven into the fabric of Peirce's thought that eliminating them without replacing them with something strongly analogous *would* undo the Peircean outlook. These religious ideas—God, love, hope, and inclusivity—must be seen to constitute a difference that makes a difference in Peirce's architectonic. They are integral, not additive, and they are enabled by Peirce's scholastic realism. This goes a long way toward measuring their importance for those who wish to take full advantage of Peirce's pragmatic transformation of philosophy. In the following three chapters we will explore some of the specific implications of Peirce's religious ideas for some theoretical and practical issues.

TEN

REALISM AND IDEALISM IN PEIRCE'S COSMOGONY

Doug Anderson

Our exploration of Peirce's cosmological writings initially developed out of our shared interest in artistic creativity. We suspected that Peirce's speculative story of creative evolution might offer some insights into how humans create. In Peirce's conceptions of metaphor, firstness, spontaneity, agape, and developmental teleology we believe we have found a few such insights. The chapter at hand simply traces the radicalness of Peirce's cosmological speculation.

As we have noted several times, Peirce often described his metaphysics as a kind of "objective idealism" (CP 6.24, 6.163); he believed matter to be "a specialization of the mind" (CP 6.268). Peirce's testimony is borne out by a number of similarities his writings share with the work of Hegel, Schelling, and Royce. Yet he resisted Hegel's tendency to reduce all being to thirdness; "in the Hegelian system," Peirce said, "the other two [categories] are only introduced to be *aufgehoben*" (CP 5.79). And as suggested in chapter

6, he shied from Royce's tendency to introduce closure into his idealistic system. The only idealism he consistently aligned with his own was that of Schelling and the New England transcendentalists. In response to Paul Carus's critique of his essay "The Doctrine of Necessity Examined," Peirce said, "I frankly pigeon-hole myself as a modified Schellingian, or New England transcendentalist" (MS 958, 202–03).

On the face of it, the combination of realism (as opposed to nominalism) and idealism (as opposed to materialism) seems unproblematic. Peirce's scholastic realism asserts the reality of general ideas (continua of feeling; see CP 6.151), and these ideas play a central role in the growth of reasonableness that marks his objective idealism. But if we look closely at Peirce's cosmogony and cosmology with which these ideas are associated, another kind of idealism emerges as potentially in conflict.

This potential problem arises, on the one hand, from the fact that Peirce's realism demands the independence of real ideas from any particular mind: realities are those things "which have an existence independent of your mind or mine or that of any number of persons" (CP 8.12; see also 5.311). On the other hand, Peirce's objective idealism was tied directly to his theism—his belief in a God who is creator of all. Peirce freely acknowledged that he conceived God to be mind in a vague sense, or at least an "analogue of mind" (CP 6.502). These two points raise the question, then, whether the real ideas that are found at the origin of the universe—and out of which the universe evolves—are independent of God, such that God is a mere "friend of the forms," or whether God is in full control of the ideas, such that, as Donna Orange suggests, they are "God's ideas."[1] In short, is Peirce an extreme Platonic realist, or is he a neo-scholastic idealist? The relation between these outlooks is not unproblematic, since it is a historical fact that many, if not most, idealists take themselves in some sense to be realists. That is, ideas are not held to be unreal because they are God's or the Absolute's. On the contrary, idealism is often viewed as a way to account for the reality of ideas. Two points, however, are in order here. First, Peirce defined the real as that which is, irrespective of what anyone thinks. Now, Peirce did not say whether God is included among these "thinkers," but it remains a possibility that in certain respects God is among them. Second, though idealists say that ideas are real as God's or the Absolute's ideas, they (e.g., Spinoza and Berkeley) often make the ideas so completely dependent on God that it is really God's reality, not that of the ideas, that is at stake. Such a pantheism of ideas was unacceptable to Peirce insofar as it makes God's love a self-love, a point he made clear in "Evolutionary Love." It is for these reasons that I want to set out by taking the relation of cosmogonical realism and idealism in its most dichotomous form; the opposition allows us to see why Peirce wanted to maintain both in certain respects, and thus to carve out a third way that could mediate between the realism and idealism I have outlined.

I

Before establishing any kind of answer to the question I have posed, I need to present a variety of difficulties facing the inquirer. Most important is the fact that with regard to the specific question at hand—whether Peirce is a cosmogonical realist or idealist—Peirce's writings are to some degree indifferent. That is, Peirce did not raise the question precisely as I have raised it, and therefore of course never answered it in direct fashion. This indifference stems in part from Peirce's belief that the notions of ultimate origin and God are inherently vague and therefore cannot be adequately articulated from any finite perspective. Thus, for example, he maintained that cosmology is "decidedly a difficult subject on which to break ground for oneself" (MS 948, p. 1). Moreover, the inherent vagueness of the notions opens discussion of them to the possibility of confusion since, for Peirce, "[e]very concept that is vague is liable to be self-contradictory in those respects in which it is vague" (CP 6.496). This means that Peirce had little fear of contradicting himself in his discussions of God and creation. He argued, for example, that it seemed not to make sense to say that God grows, but that it was unavoidable to think so in light of evolutionary theory. Any exegesis of texts whose author is not concerned about self-contradiction is, needless to say, potentially problematic.

Such difficulties, however, once acknowledged, need not preclude inquiry. Vagueness is a warning for caution; it is not a dead end for inquiry. Peirce himself, admitting the difficulties he faced, did not refrain from speculating at length concerning both God and the creative origin of the universe. And it is from these speculations, as well as from other central features of Peirce's philosophy, that I hope to draw some preliminary conclusions concerning the question I have posed. My hope, as the chapter title might suggest, is to show that Peirce sketched an account of God and of aboriginal ideas that makes him both a realist and an idealist—that he sought to mediate the dichotomy I present, or better, that he was neither in the sense generally assumed within his tradition, but that he held a unique realist/idealist position.

II

In asking whether Peirce is an idealist or a realist in his cosmogony, it is tempting to frame the question in temporal terms. Which came first, God or ideas? The question put thus becomes an unanswerable question of historical fact. But if anything is clear in Peirce's cosmological writings, it is that he recognized the inadequacy, and indeed the impossibility, of using only a temporal framework. The problem is the timing of time. While Peirce tentatively asserted that time was prior to existence (MS 944), he was set in his belief that it followed from both God and the firsts that were the aboriginal ideas: "In short, if we are going to regard the universe as a result of evolution at all, we must think that not merely the existing universe, that locus in the cosmos to which our reactions are limited, but the whole Platonic world, which in itself is equally real, is evolutionary in its origin, too. And among the things so resulting are time and logic" (CP 6.200).[2] Thus, for Peirce, time was a creation, and a creation of the "latter" stages of creative act.

To get a sense of time's place, let us try to outline some of the features of Peirce's conception of creation. First, he seemed to propose that creation involved at least three stages.[3] The first stage of creation Peirce variously described as "the bare Nothing of Possibility" (MS 942, p.1), "the utter vagueness of completely undetermined and dimensionless potentiality" (CP 6.193), and "the general vague nothing-in-particular-ness" (CP 6.200). This was perhaps a world of Platonic worlds, a continuum of pure and undifferentiated firsts. As Peirce put it in a description of hyperbolic cosmology (c. 1905): "Feeling, then is assumed as the starting point; but feeling uncoordinated, having its manifoldness implicit" (MS 878, p. 12). Out of this real possibility or potentiality developed a particular chaos or world of firsts: the Platonic world that lies behind our own specific universe (CP 6.200 and 6.208). As we proceed, we must keep in mind that Peirce held both of these initial worlds to be "conscious" in some form, because they were constituted by firsts. For "whatever is First is *ispo facto* sentient," and feeling is a vague form of consciousness (CP 6.201; see also 6.221). The spontaneous relationships—what Peirce thought of as developing habits—of these firsts, or ideas, then yielded the third stage of creation—the evolution of our real and existent universe in which time comes into play. Thus, for Peirce, "we must suppose that the existing universe, with all its arbitrary secondness, is an offshoot from, or an arbitrary determination of, a world of ideas, a Platonic world" (CP 6.192). It is here of course that the importance of secondness and habit become apparent. Insofar as time appears here in the third stage, Peirce believed that to try to use time to understand orders or relations between God and aboriginal ideas was fundamentally impossible.

A consequent problem, however, was that in discussing the issue of creation Peirce saw no alternative to using temporal terms in a nontemporal fashion:

> We have therefore to suppose a state of things before time was organized. Accordingly, when we speak of the universe as arising we do not mean that literally. We mean to speak of some kind of sequence, say an objective logical sequence; but we do not mean

in speaking of the first stages of creation before time was organized, to use "before," "after," "rising," and such words in the
temporal sense. But for the sake of the commodity of speech we
may avail ourselves of these words. (CP 6.214)

Peirce was aware of the confusion this could lead to—especially
among those who were not accustomed to thinking mathematically—
and occasionally apologized for his usage (MS 944). This constitutes,
then, another result of the vagueness of the conceptions of God, creation, and origin that we must keep in mind as we proceed.

III

Peirce's 1891–92 *Monist* essays may seem an odd place to look for his
mature view concerning the nature of creation. On numerous occasions in his later writings, however, he referred the reader back to
these essays and indicated that his understanding of the evolution of
the cosmos had not changed in any significant fashion. Moreover, the
many later writings that focus on God's role in creation seem to be
in large part quite consistent with the earlier cosmology. These considerations, together with the fact that Peirce's most extensive cosmological writings are to be found in these *Monist* essays and in several
essays from the late 1890s, suggest that it is reasonable to begin here
in looking for an answer to our question. In particular, then, I will
build my case around the essay "Evolutionary Love," though I will
also pay close attention to its companion pieces and the later essays
mentioned above.

In "Evolutionary Love" Peirce addressed what he believed to be
the three possible theories to account for the evolution of the universe: tychasticism, anancasticism, and agapasticism. Peirce's explicit
self-identification as an agapasticist provided an inroad into assessing
his view of the aboriginal relation of God and ideas. Moreover, his
corollary rejection of the other two possibilities gives us a fairly clear
sense of how he might mediate the conflict of cosmogonical realism
and idealism as presented here.

Agapasticism is the view that agapasm or a love-driven evolution is effective in the universe—that the development of the universe has been governed by agape or cherishing love: "In genuine agapasm . . . advance takes place by virtue of a positive sympathy among the created springing from continuity of mind" (CP 6.304). Moreover, Peirce freely associated this agapasm with theism. Borrowing from the Gospel of John, he proceeded on the assumption that "God is love" (CP 6.287ff). But if God is love, and if, as we saw earlier, God is mind in some sense, and the evolution of the world proceeds by love's efficacy, it seems reasonable to conclude that Peirce must come down on the side of idealism. God would seem to be that which determines and discovers ideas; or conversely, we might say, the ideas are God's ideas. Indeed, what we see here is that agapasticism involves some elements of anancasticism, the claim that necessity determines the evolution of the cosmos. Insofar as ideas are under the sway of God's mind, their development is ordered by God's reason; this is why Peirce often described evolution as the growth of reasonableness.[4] But while it may be true that Peirce was an idealist, it is not true in an unqualified way. We must examine agapasm more closely.

Although Peirce willingly rejected tychasticism (the claim that chance governs evolution), he never rejected—and in fact he went to great lengths to make it clear that he did not reject—the more modest assertion of tychism. Tychism is the claim that *some* element of chance is operative in the universe. Thus, while agapasticism adopted an element of anancasticism, it also maintained a link with tychasticism. This is of particular importance for the question at hand, for Peirce argued that it was chance alone that could account for the initial development of ideas in the cosmos. "The very first and most fundamental element that we have to assume," he maintained, "is a Freedom or Chance, or Spontaneity, by virtue of which the general vague nothing-in-particular-ness that preceded the chaos took a thousand definite qualities" (CP 6.200). Chance, however, was not to be considered some external power; rather, it reflected the autonomy of the original ideas in as much as they were feelings and firsts. As

Peirce put it: "Thus, when I speak of chance, I only employ a mathematical term to express with accuracy the characteristics of freedom and spontaneity" (CP 6.201). Or again, with respect to the efficacy of evolution, he argued that we can think of "the ideas as springing into a preliminary stage of being by their own inherent firstness" (CP 6.199).

This assertion of the autonomy of the initial firsts, however vaguely conceived, precludes agapasticism from falling into necessitarianism. That is, Peirce used tychism effectively to block God's full control of the development of ideas, and these initial ideas, then, by virtue of chance, maintain an element of independence from God. Such independence suggests not cosmological idealism—at least not in the strict sense—but a realism of ideas. Such a realism qualifies the idealism inherent in agapasticism.

As Peirce developed "Evolutionary Love," he was well aware of the tension between idealism and realism that he was creating. He took it to be a virtue, not a weakness, of his position. This is nowhere better illustrated than in his claim that anancasm and tychasm represent degenerate versions of agapasm (CP 6.303). Tychasm lacks any element of order, and anancasm, any element of chance. To make the point affirmatively, Peirce still viewed creation as an *act*—an act in some sense of a God-like agency. It was not an act of dominance, however, but rather one of empowerment. Insofar as God is love, for Peirce, God's creativity involved, as I have argued elsewhere, allowing attractive ideas (qualities) to begin to develop themselves.[5] Agapasm thus asserts both God's priority and the ideas' autonomy; as Peirce put it, "The movement of love is circular, at one and the same impulse projecting creations into interdependency and drawing them into harmony" (CP 6.288).[6] This dual Peircean answer to the question with which we began can be seen from another angle if we turn to Peirce's later description of God as *Ens necessarium*.

IV

In "A Neglected Argument for the Reality of God," Peirce identified God in scholastic fashion: "The word 'God' so 'capitalized' (as we

Americans say), is the definable proper name, signifying *Ens necessarium*; in my belief Really creator of all three Universes of Experience" (CP 6.452). Once again, in view of Peirce's attribution of mindlikeness to God, we are led immediately to suppose a kind of strict idealist interpretation in which God is in complete command of ideas or aboriginal firsts. This is especially so if we are led to consider not only the argument from contingency, but all five of Aquinas' arguments taken together. But if we follow Peirce through the "Neglected Argument" and examine his other later descriptions of God, we see that such an interpretation is too strong.

Once again, it is tychism that plays the central role in checking the completeness of God's control of ideas, and thus of evolution in general: "It is not that such phenomena [growth and relations in nature] might not be capable of being accounted for, in one sense, by the action of chance with the smallest conceivable dose of a higher element; for if by god be meant the *Ens necessarium*, that very hypothesis requires that such should be the case" (CP 6.465). In this way, God, *Ens necessarium*, as Peirce saw it, creates the presence of chance. This is consistent with his earlier (1891) argument that the world proceeded by a developmental teleology. Such a teleology requires an intentional or self-imposed ignorance on the part of the "mind" whose telos is effective in the world. In other words, the initial autonomy of ideas—their spontaneity—loosens God's control of his own account of the outcome in the infinite future. Peirce put the point succinctly in his response to the question of God's omniscience: "I do not see why we may not assume that He refrains from knowing much. For this thought is creative" (CP 6.508).

Again, the ideas retain some element of independence from God, and this independence constitutes a partial realism. This limiting of idealism is a direct denial that God—and consequently the universe—is "pure act" in the traditional sense. Peirce had encountered this issue with both Hegel and Royce, and in a 1902 review of Royce's work he wrote the following: "This makes an apparent difficulty for idealism. For if all reality is of the nature of an actual idea, there seems to be no room for possibility or any lower mode than actuality, among the categories of being" (CP 8.126). The question here, then, as with the earlier cosmological writings, is what is the role of God? If God is *Ens necessarium*, in what sense is his being necessary?

The most obvious possibility, if God is not the complete determinant of all, is that God's being is a necessary condition of the initial ideas. This parallels in part what was meant in the scholastic tradition. And if we remember that the dependence we are discussing is not temporal, and therefore not causal, such an interpretation makes good sense. Creation, as we saw in "Evolutionary Love," is not so much a "molding" as it is an "enabling" or "empowering." God does not so much "make" the ideas as he "allows" them or, as Hausman has argued, "permits" them.[7] Nevertheless, if we consider the earlier cosmology of "Evolutionary Love" and "The Logic of the Universe," we can make some sense of this more limited understanding of God's necessity.

In "The Logic of the Universe" Peirce emphasized his notion that cosmology is equivalent to "mathematical metaphysics" (CP 6.213 and MS 948). Whatever else was behind this description, it was surely in part a corollary to Peirce's belief in the inherent vagueness of creation as well as its implicit atemporality, for mathematical reasoning is precisely that kind of reasoning that allows us to think beyond the limits of both time and an existent universe. Pursuing this understanding of cosmology, Peirce was led to offer a kind of mathematical "clue" to guide us through the maze of "the beginnings of creation" (CP 6.203–204). The essence of his clue was that the originary potentiality was "general" and therefore inherently continuous (CP 6.204).

The initial vague potentiality—the residence of the ideas—is thus a continuum out of which all else develops. When Peirce asserted that "all the evolution we know of proceeds from the vague to the definite," he took this to entail "that as a rule the continuum [in this case, our synthetic universe] has been derived from a more general continuum, a continuum of higher generality" (CP 6.191). This led directly to his oft-referenced analogy of a chalk line on a blackboard. The chalk line constitutes a spontaneous development, but itself displays "a certain element of continuity" (CP 6.203). But the line's continuity, Peirce argued, "is nothing but the original continuity of the blackboard which makes everything upon it continuous" (CP 6.203). The upshot is that the initial vague potentiality, as a continuum, with its spontaneity, is that which enables all evolution and growth. But the analogy is suggestive of a further step.

Insofar as God is *Ens Necessarium*, really creator of all, his being must in some analogical sense constitute the continuum of all continua; God, vaguely understood, is that which permits evolution to occur (CP 6.185). While I would not want to insist on the appropriateness of the claim, this does provide us with an interesting way of understanding God as agape or cherishing love. Insofar as God creates agapastically by drawing creatures into harmony and setting them into interdependency, we might construe agape as one way of naming the continuum that God is. It is the continuity—or generality—of love that constitutes Peirce's melding of idealism and realism. The continuum of agape grounds all other continua, but it does not specify them.

Let us try to draw these thoughts together by way of Peirce's 1898 attempt to distinguish his idealism from that of Hegel:

> Now the question arises, what necessarily resulted from that state [the initial potentiality] of things? But the only sane answer is that where freedom was boundless nothing in particular necessarily resulted.
>
> In this proposition lies the prime difference between my objective logic and that of Hegel. He says, if there is any sense in philosophy at all, the whole universe and every feature of it, however minute, is rational, and was constrained to be as it is by the logic of events, so that there is no principle of action in the universe but reason. But, I reply, this line of thought, though it begins rightly, is not exact. A logical slip is committed; and the conclusion reached is manifestly at variance with observation. It is true that the whole universe and every feature of it must be regarded as rational, that is as brought about by the logic of events. But it does not follow that it is constrained to be as it is by the logic of events; for the logic of evolution and of life need not be supposed to be out of that wooden kind that absolutely constrains a given conclusion. (CP 6.218)

If the development of the universe is not "constrained to be as it is by the logic of events," then *a fortiori* it is not so constrained by God. The initial Platonic realm or realm of realms, and consequently all that derives from it, remains in some part free in its spontaneity. Therefore, whereas Hegel—at least as Peirce read him—was a thoroughgoing absolute idealist in having absolute spirit constrain all that is, Peirce tempered his idealism by yielding to the firsts their firstness, thus making them real in precisely that degree to which they are unconstrained. This follows Schelling's emphasis on the reality and independence of freedom. At the same time, Peirce's realism in this respect is intended not so much as a limitation on God's will, but, given the world in which we find ourselves, as its only possible natural expression.

ELEVEN

LOVE OF NATURE
The Generality of Peircean Concern

Doug Anderson

Peirce used his notion of agape to guide his speculative cosmology, ulti-
mately giving it the name of "evolutionary love." Carl and I both found
this a useful tool for considering how artists create their works of art
without dominating them. This led to a reflection on how agape might
be deployed in recent environmental debates.

Peirce's realistic conception of God and, especially, of the love
that God is, holds consequences for issues that lie beyond the
boundaries of religious discourses. One such consequence has to do
with what we have come to call environmentalism. Although he did
not speak directly to what we today call environmental questions,
Peirce developed strands of thought that suggest responses to some
of these questions. Some connections between Peirce and environmentalism arise in considering Peirce's life. He claimed to be, for example, instinctively opposed to the hunting of wild animals, and, as
I have argued elsewhere, he claimed a strong affinity with domestic

animals.[1] And he often remarked, in a somewhat transcendentalist vein, that philosophy was best done in natural settings. Peirce was also a close friend of the parents of Gifford Pinchot, who were, like Peirce and his wife, residents of Milford, Pennsylvania. His biographer Joseph Brent suggests that Peirce directly influenced Pinchot's decision to pursue forestry.[2] Moreover, after Pinchot took control of the U.S. Forest Service, Peirce continued to correspond with him, occasionally suggesting mathematical practices to make the Service's work more efficient. It is possible even to see in Pinchot's conservationist approach to the environment something like Peirce's critical common-sensism (see CP 5.438ff). Tracing Peirce's modest influence on Pinchot's practices might be one fruitful way of exploring his relationship to environmental questions. There is another avenue of exploration, however, through considering Peirce's critical common-sensism together with his speculative cosmology. It is an avenue that is perhaps less congenial to the antimetaphysical spirit of the early twenty-first century, but one that will tell us more, I believe, about how Peirce might have approach the kinds of environmental questions that have arisen in the last eighty to one hundred years.

I

Peirce shared with Aristotle the belief that practice and theory ought to be distinguished, even if they were ultimately to be understood as continuous. This meant, for Peirce, that most immediate political questions—and thus some questions concerning the environment—should be handled by the common sense of the day. In this much, Peirce was decidedly un-Deweyan. However, he believed that common sense was only useful if issued "from the cupelfurnace of measured criticism" (CP 6.480). Thus in his view, there seems to have been a route, though only an indirect one, through which theory might influence the politics of the environment. Through his critical common-sensism Peirce suggested a spirit or an attitude appropriate to inquiry. It is this attitude whose character was informed by his speculative cosmology.

Peirce's cosmology had several different though not opposed manifestations in the 1890s. In the first version, he emphasized the role of
agape or creative love and the continuity or generality of ideas. In the
second version, he continued to emphasize the role of continuity but
also introduced his quasi-Aristotelian realism of possibles. Here I will
draw on both versions to make my case for a kind of Peircean attitude
toward the environment and environmental questions. Unfortu-
nately, this attitude will not answer practical environmental questions
in a clear and direct fashion. But that is, again, consistent with
Peirce's belief that theory should not, except in unusual circumstances, try to control practice directly. I will try to show that under
Peirce's agapasticism—the theory that the universe evolves through a
teleology the development of which reflects the character of agapastic
love—our concern for the environment must address nature's generality—that is, its lawfulness and consequently its possibilities—and
must avoid the pleading of special cases for individual environments
as ends in themselves.

We should recall at the outset that Peirce's approach to agape falls
outside of the theological tradition. He did not trust theology's judgment and was suspicious of the theologians of his own time for their
failure to pay attention to the role of love in the cosmos:

> I once bought and read through Dr. Schaff's three volumes upon
> the Creeds of Christendom for the purpose of ascertaining
> whether the theologians, who composed them, had ever once,
> from the first to the last, inserted a single clause in one of them
> by way of recognition of the principle of love; and I found that
> such a thing had never been done. (CP 6.3)

Peirce's treatment of agape is nevertheless related to traditional ren-
derings of it as cherishing or nurturing love.

Following the gospelist John, Peirce identified God with love. In
this identification God gained a pragmaticistic role for humanity—
that is, God, as Peirce argued in his "A Neglected Argument for the
Reality of God," becomes a guide for human conduct.

> If a pragmaticist is asked what he means by the word "God," he
> can only say that just as long acquaintance with a man of great

character may deeply influence one's whole manner of conduct, so that a glance at his portrait may make a difference, just as almost living with Dr. Johnson enabled poor Boswell to write an immortal book and a really sublime book, just as long study of the works of Aristotle may make him an acquaintance, so if contemplation and study of the physico-psychical universe can imbue a man with principles of conduct analogous to the influence of a great man's works or conversation, then that analogue of mind . . . is what he means by "God." (CP 6.502)

How is our manner of conduct in dealing with our natural environment, then, to be influenced by God? To John's assertion that "God is Love," Peirce added, "There is no logic in this, unless it means that God loves all men" (CP 6.287). I might further add, "and all that is created." This seems an easy, Augustine-like move: love all creation. This *is* one upshot of Peirce's agapasticism; however, it is not an easy achievement, nor is it simply obvious what "love" in this context means. Some loving, as for Peirce some believing, requires hard work to be brought to fruition. And some forms of love would not serve to emulate God's loving.

For persons, Peirce argued, true agape is "not directed to abstractions but to persons; not to persons I do not know, nor to numbers of people, but to our own dear ones, our family and neighbors. 'Our neighbor,' we remember, is one whom we live near, not locally perhaps but in life and feeling" (CP 6.288). This seems to land us in a peculiar place *vis a vis* Peirce's God. However vaguely we construe his God, this God has the advantage of a natural familiarity with and filiation for all that is created. It is for this reason that God may love all persons and all things. Such a universality is not however immediately open to us; this is something we must work to achieve. We find experientially that our agape is most easily and naturally directed toward those we know; our task then is to convert, where we can, the unfamiliar into neighbors or kin of some order (see W 1:124–45 and CP 6.288). Given his fallibilism, it is unlikely that Peirce believed any of us could become fully godlike, but he did believe we could work toward and develop an agapastic generality of concern under the influence of God's own agape.

Peirce distinguished agape from eros in a somewhat traditional fashion. Eros is passionate and ultimately self-directed, insofar as its end is the satisfaction or gratification of the lover. Eros is driven to fulfill itself rather than to give to others. Agape, on the other hand, is other-directed. Its telos is not an immediate self-satisfaction but the ongoing well-being of another. For Peirce, as noted, agape is a love in which you "[s]acrifice your own perfection to the perfectionment of your neighbor" (CP 6.288). Agape does not function through domination. To repeat: "It is not by dealing out cold justice to the circle of my ideas that I can make them grow, but by cherishing and tending them as I would the flowers of my garden" (CP 6.289). Agape, unlike eros, is a permissive love.[3] At the same time, this permissiveness is not wanton; growth, and the love that engenders it, must take place within general constraints or under the regulative guidance of emerging ideals.

At first blush, the project of adapting agape to environmental questions seems dead-ended: agape is directed only toward persons, toward neighbors or kindred spirits. However, if we look closely at Peirce's conception of persons, we find a more or less direct route from persons to nature. Peirce did not take persons to be simply concrete, physical beings or "animals," at least not in an unqualified sense. Persons were for him systems of living habits, loci of purposes that potentially constitute unified purposes, and whose task is "to embody general ideas in art-creations, in utilities, and above all in theoretical cognition" (CP 6.476). In short, while persons are concrete in part, they are characterized by their thirdness—that is, by their open-ended generality. The "character of man," Peirce argued, "consists in the ideas that he will conceive and in the efforts he will make, and which only develops as the occasions actually arise. Yet in all his life long no son of Adam has ever fully manifested what there was in him" (CP 1.615). This is the central point of Peirce's essay "The Law of Mind"; his notion was that a

> personality is some kind of coordination or connection between ideas [and] is itself a general idea, and that a general idea is a living feeling. . . . This personality, like any general idea, is not a

thing to be apprehended in an instant. It has to be lived in time; nor can any finite time embrace it in all its fullness. (CP 6.155)

Through this description of personality Peirce drew an analogy between persons and nature. Both involve the concrete development of generals. In short, the natural cosmos is itself a kind of person: "[A]s for the cosmos, only so far as it yet is mind, and so has life, is it capable of further evolution" (CP 6.289). The upshot is that agape can reasonably be directed toward the environment, not as a static collection of material items, but as a concretization or manifestation of nature's generality. Indeed, Peirce often described the esthetic ideal—what is in itself admirable and loveable—of the cosmos itself as the growth of concrete reasonableness. This is what he had in mind in suggesting that true scientists have a reverence for nature. For science, he maintained, "Nature is something great, and beautiful, and sacred, and eternal, and real—the object of its worship and its aspiration" (CP 5.589; see also CP 6.503). In a moment I will consider the Peircean scientist's agapastic approach to truth and nature as a model for considering environmental questions. First, however, let me make a brief sketch of the practical upshot of adopting this model.

II

In describing nature, Peirce put his scholastic realism to work. Nature is personlike in its development; it is intelligible, and natural laws are expressions of habits. When a stone falls to the earth when dropped, "there was," Peirce says, "a *real reason*, that is, a real general" that governed its falling (CP 6.99). However, for nature to become an object of agape's attention, it must, in Peirce's view, become like a neighbor, friend, or family member—it must not be treated in the abstract. In one sense, since we are always environed, nature is always a neighbor; this is experientially normal insofar as we have special places, for example, where we feel at home. However, physical proximity, as we saw, is not enough; we must attend to nature and become familiar—in the richest sense of that term—with it. There is here a

Thoreau-like moment reflected in Peirce's agapasm as applied to nature. It is a moment revealing the work necessary to establishing familiarity, one we find articulated, for example, in "A Neglected Argument for the Reality of God," where Peirce asked his readers to become musers on the three universes of experience and their interactions. We must seek, as does the artist or phenomenologist, to see nature as it reveals itself. In musing, Peirce maintained, the connections and relations found in nature will attract us; they are capable of drawing us into a relationship of love or caring (CP 6.464). As Peirce repeatedly stated, science as practice hinges on the regulative hope of an affinity between nature and the inquirer, on the belief "that man's mind must have been attuned to the truth of things in order to discover what he has discovered" (CP 6.476). This affinity must be "realized" or brought to life through experience and inquiry for the neighborliness appropriate to agape to arise.

In attending to nature as neighbor, we must, as we do with persons, emphasize its generality. However cynical we become, we must realize that we do not love others agapastically by attending to them merely as bodies or as momentary events. Bodies effect the concretization of certain habits or dimensions of personality, but they do not constitute the person. Likewise, however much we are enamored of a view or a photograph of Yosemite, Yellowstone, or the Grand Canyon, it is not the freeze frame we finally admire in nature. Rather, such instances are embodiments of a developing generality; they express the habits of an unfolding cosmos and suggest a range of future possibilities. They are loveable in their exemplariness, but not in themselves alone. The Grand Canyon has a history and provides different "looks" under different circumstances—these constitute its personality. In Peirce's somewhat obscure terminology, nature is neither an empty thirdness nor a blind secondness—it is a thirdness realizing itself in seconds through a variety of firsts, or possibles. If we can manage to begin to love nature in its generality and not merely in its individuality—that is, realistically instead of nominalistically—we enter a path toward emulating the universality of God's love.

We imitate God by expanding our realm of neighbors, thus in one sense generalizing our concern. By focusing on nature's generality— its habits and lawfulness—we enable ourselves to effect this expansion by moving continuously from one individual setting to others. At risk of losing our emphasis on generality, let us consider a simple example. If we know Adirondack forests well, if we know how they live and develop, either theoretically, or by experience, or both, in certain ways we can generalize our concern for them to include other similar forests with which we are not experientially familiar. With certain adjustments we can even begin to attend to other types of forests, such as alpine forests and tropical rainforests, with a similar affection and interest, since they will exemplify some habits like those of the Adirondack forests and may subsequently exhibit some interaction with such forests. This is not a simple mechanical process, but one in which lived feeling, in this case love, grows outwardly by its edges. For Peirce, this growth of familiarity is requisite for a genuine attention to the needs—the "perfectionment"—of the evolving whole of which foreign forests, for example, are a dimension. To love them as abstractions is an unhelpful enterprise, except perhaps for rhetorical advantage. First, although there might be an emotional outpouring, there would be no experiential bite to such love; the result is likely to be that of the attention of fair-weather fans. Second, even if one could obtain and sustain the proper loving attitude toward abstractions, without familiarity with its object this attention would be so poorly informed as to lose control of the seeking of its own end, the "perfectionment" of the rainforest and its environment. To conclude our practical sketch, then, to emulate God we begin to generalize our concern by familiarizing ourselves with nature's own generality through experience and knowledge.

III

Let us return now to the background consideration of the Peircean scientist as exemplifying the attitude or spirit of the critical commonsensist. Establishing familiarity or neighborliness requires knowing and/or experiencing the object of our concern. Since Peirce's theory of inquiry holds knowledge to involve experiencing in both its abductive and inductive stages, the Peircean scientist is in position to establish familiarity. Moreover, Peirce, as I noted, explicitly maintained that well-done science requires a cherishing concern for its object and the truth of its object. It is reasonable therefore to employ the ideal Peircean scientist as a model for those who seek to assist the growth of the cosmos as fulfilling their "appropriate offices in the work of creation" (CP 8.138). Two notes of caution, however, are in order.

First, it is a mistake to equate the Peircean scientist or inquirer with common nineteenth- and twentieth-century notions of a scientist. Despite all the similarities that might be found, the Peircean scientist is not a nominalist and does not understand verification to be the mere establishment of individual facts (CP 5.198f). For Peirce, a scientist is a scholastic realist. He made the point somewhat dramatically in a letter to Lady Welby:

> So if you believe that modern science has made any general discovery at all, you believe that general so discovered to be real, and so you *are a scholastic realist* whether you are aware of it or not. Not only does all *science* hang upon the decision but so do Truth and Righteousness! Nominalism and all its ways are devices of the Devil if devil there be. And in particular it is the disease which almost drove poor John Mill mad,—the dreary outlook upon a world in which all that can be loved, or admired, or understood is figment. (SS, pp. 117–18)

It is this realism that underwrites the practice of familiarizing noted above. The second caution is that neither Peirce nor I mean to suggest that everyone must become a scientist in a narrow sense. Peirce routinely argued that there are three general types of persons necessary to the world, one of which is the heuretic scientist (CP 1.43). Our point is rather that the genuine scientist exhibits a loving attitude that is important in dealing with questions concerning the environment, though I do not pretend that it can directly answer all such questions. It is rather an attitude that puts us in a position to begin to answer such questions. It is this attitude that I want to flesh out through the model of the Peircean scientist.

The dominant feature of the Peircean scientist's agapastic approach to nature is a recognition of a fundamental tension. As lovers of nature we are committed to the possibility of truth concerning it—a truth that might be employed in allowing the continued growth of nature, or in Deweyan terms, permitting such growth by ameliorating the present conditions. At the same time, the scientist admits our fallibility in the pursuit of truth. We must always be at work with revisable habits of belief, habits instituted through the cooperation of instinct (or common sense) and theory. In short, for Peirce, our hope of serving the perfectionment of nature is built on the regulative hope that we can be fallible knowers of nature in both its spontaneous development and its lawfulness.

This knowing itself forces a second order of humility on us. Peirce's cosmology, again, casts the character of nature as secondness displaying thirdness through firstness. That is, although the cosmos develops under laws, these laws do not specify particular events; nature's laws may be fulfilled—and perfected—in a variety of possible ways. As Emerson often claimed, there are many ways for nature to be beautiful. Moreover, Peirce entertained the possibility of divergence from laws—living habits—such that nature could develop new habits or laws; in both ways Peirce defended a realism of possibles. Thus, the attitude of the knower must include not only a belief in generals but an openness to these two elements of firstness, to what Peirce called the *real possibilities* that nature involves. This inclusion precludes, in principle, our knowing the future in its detail.

Both levels of humility—general fallibility and the acknowledgment of real possibles—suggest that the Peircean must not retreat to skepticism but rather must come to grips with her or his place in the growth of knowledge itself, and consequently in caring for the environment. Science involves agape and not eros:

> He who would not sacrifice his own soul to save the whole world,
> is, as it seems to me, illogical in all his inferences, collectively. . . .

> To be logical men should not be selfish. . . . Neither the Old nor
> New Testament is a textbook of science, but the latter is certainly
> the highest existing authority in regard to the dispositions of heart
> which a man ought to have. (CP 2.654–55; see also 6.503)

In this agapastic submissiveness—this willingness to listen to nature—I find an inherent resistance to two tendencies found in some
humanistic and traditional responses to environmental questions. On
the one hand, Peirce's scientist would have to avoid special preserva-
tionisms, including one that would make preservation of the human
species the ultimate end of the development of the cosmos. In contemporary terms, he was not a "speciesist." Peirce argued "that the
human race is ephemeral" (MS 1334, pp. 20–21). Not only would such
preservationism seem an unreasonably narrow view of things given
our present experience and our understanding of evolution, it would
be nonagapastic. For Peirce, a species egoism is no better than an individual one—both are consumed by eros. Moreover, Peirce would
generally oppose preservationism insofar as it involves an attempt to
maintain fixed or static situations or systems. If we are to preserve
anything, he would have us preserve the possibility of nature's growth
toward its own end. Roughly speaking, Peirce might, for example,
consider the guy-wiring of elm branches to prevent their falling in a
wind as somewhat short-sighted. On the other hand, as knowledge
now stands, the preservation of wetlands seems a reasonable step
toward the maintenance of nature's possibilities.

However, Peirce also resisted flirtations with self-righteousness. In
particular, it was this dimension of the humanism of F. C. S. Schiller
to which he was averse. There is in some cases a humanistic (or pragmatic) assumption that humans, armed simply with their theoretical
intelligence, can easily solve the here-and-now problems that society
and nature present. This can engender a kind of dogmatic, short-term
political correctness alien to the spirit of the Peircean inquirer. Indeed, such an inflated confidence in the *immediate* power of human
reason and theorizing can have precisely the unscientific effect of
closing avenues of inquiry. Peirce did not deny the need for practical
persons and present actions, but he denied that these could conduct

us rightly in the short run strictly by individual theorizing; he urged, as I pointed out earlier, a return to the guidance of *common* sense. Like Emerson, he was opposed to reform exercised in a narrow spirit. The fallibilistic attitude of the Peircean scientist tempers reform, including environmental reform, by identifying "one's interests with those of an unlimited community" and not merely with the present human community (CP 2.654).

While Peirce resisted the self-sufficiency of theorizing and thus encouraged attention to common sense in practice, he also resisted *its* unrestricted dominance. The scientist's attitude also places constraints on both the unbridled exercise of and the traditional entrenchment of instinctive or commonsensical moral claims. In short, although Peirce remained committed to the importance of instinct, common sense, and tradition as guides to practice, especially when living doubts did not arise, he also recognized their fallible nature. When doubts concerning them arise, the scientist takes those doubts seriously and his or her method, under the sway of agape, begins to suggest alternative approaches. Sexist traditions, for example, become more difficult to defend when the so-called evidences on which they are based are thrown into real doubt. The upshot in social terms is that Peirce's philosopher-scientist plays the role of *gradually* shifting the beliefs of practice over time and of keeping an eye open for the insurgence of real doubts concerning current habits of belief and practice. In individual terms, if we can each preserve a dimension of the scientist's agapastic attitude toward nature's development, we will each be in a position to work toward correcting our own habits and practices. Agape does not resist environmental reform but guides it, resisting *both* its absence and its excesses.

The agapastic attitude that develops through the exercise of these features thus encourages a generality of concern in two ways. An agapastic environmentalist will first be concerned with nature's real generality and real possibility: its lawfulness, spontaneity, and growth. She or he will not address only specific situations in their individuality, nor will she or he suppose that any present situation has only one possible outcome. Second, in seeing the general and the possible in the specific, individual case, the attitude encourages, as I suggested earlier, the expansion of one's concern and care to a wider realm—perhaps to what is meant by *global concern*, if we take *global* to mean universal or cosmic and if we understand the *concern* to involve agapastic familiarity. Again, Peirce saw this second generalizing of concern as an important feature of agapasticism:

> [L]ogicality inexorably requires that our interests shall *not* be limited. They must not stop at our own fate, but must embrace the whole community. This community, again, must not be limited, but must extend to all races of beings with whom we can come into immediate or mediate intellectual relation. It must reach, however vaguely, beyond this geological epoch, beyond all bounds. (CP 2.654)

The generality of concern reaches synechistically to attend to the perfectionment not of the inquirer but of knowing and its own cherished dynamical object, nature or the cosmos in its development.

Peirce was adamant in arguing for the unavoidability and importance of metaphysical speculation as a human art. Science, he maintained, always functions in the company of metaphysical beliefs. It is in this spirit that he offered his agapastic cosmology, and it is in this spirit that I appropriate his agapasticism in considering questions concerning the environment. The cash value I offer is not a direct answer to specific environmental questions, but the provision of a vague ideal and an attitude or dimension of character for moving in the direction of that ideal. No doubt some will want a more precise figure for the denomination of this cash value, but this is precisely the kind of certainty that we are not fit to command. We must recognize, as did Peirce, that battles over our relationships with our environment must and will be waged. For Peirce, the hope is that these battles will be waged in an agapastic spirit so that they will be open to the possibility of our own failures, large or small, in a cherishing concern for the growth of truth and nature. If waged only in order to win political ground—left, right, or in between—these battles, guided by self-interest, will impede both the development of knowledge and, subsequently, our ability to attend to nature's interests.

TWELVE

DEVELOPMENTAL THEISM
A Peircean Response to Fundamentalism

Doug Anderson

*In discussing Peirce's overall method of inquiry, we routinely used Chris-
tian fundamentalism as a marker of tenacious belief and as exemplary of
blocking the road of inquiry. This essay resulted from considering what is
so problematic about fundamentalism.*

Having brought matters of heart and mind into relation in chapter 10, I turn here to apply this relation to an issue that that
has important political import for contemporary culture. The specific
issue I wish to explore—religious fundamentalism—is a complex
one, open to several avenues of investigation. Though the term *fundamentalism* was not available to Peirce, he was concerned with its
pragmatic meaning in several ways. My purpose here, therefore, is
not to propose any radically new interpretations of Peirce's thought,
but simply to examine some of the ways Peirce might have responded
to fundamentalism. I also make no attempt at completeness; Peirce's
response not only to fundamentalism but to theologism in general

{ 191 }

cuts deeper than at first appears, and will not be fully captured in the confines of a single chapter.

The Peircean response I have in mind is double-edged. On the one hand, I will argue that Peirce would reject fundamentalism on the ground that it is unscientific. While this appears to be a rather standard attack on fundamentalism, given the Scopes Monkey Trial and like cases, I will try to show, following our discussions in the preceding chapters, that a Peircean version of this argument involves an approach sometimes neglected by other critics of fundamentalism. On the other hand, I will argue that Peirce would also reject fundamentalism on the ground that it is nonreligious or, at least, is insufficiently religious. This rejection involves the establishment, for Peirce, of religion proper as a sentiment, as well as the establishment of science as an avenue for further critical articulation of the concepts that arise in religion proper. I take this Peircean marriage of science and religion to constitute a developmental theism that attempts to avoid the dogmatic overdetermination of religious ideas found in fundamentalism. In all of this my purpose is neither to demonstrate the truth of Peirce's view nor to identify Peirce as something of a contemporary liberal. On the contrary, I mean simply to develop the central Peircean feature of scientific-mindedness—his Aristotelian-like commitment to the pursuit of truth—as a way, and perhaps an important way, of addressing the intellectual position of Christian fundamentalism.[1]

The coining of the term *fundamentalism* seems to have occurred some six years after Peirce's death in 1914. Yet, as historian of religion George Marsden points out, the general intellectual or theological view ascribed to Christian fundamentalism as we know it today had been extant in America for some time prior to 1920.[2] Thus, while Peirce was not familiar with the term, he was certainly familiar with New England Calvinism and with the reality of fundamentalist Christianity. As we might well expect, the theory and practice of fundamentalism in America has been, and is, no more univocal than the practice and theory of pragmatism. Nevertheless, in examining the series of essays in pamphlet form called *The Fundamentals*, from which fundamentalism acquired its name, we can find at least two tenets that appear central to most forms of Christian fundamentalism: 1) that the Bible ought to be the final measure of all claims to knowledge; and 2) that the Bible is without error.[3] In offering a Peircean response, therefore, I will focus on these two beliefs and some of the considerations they seem to involve. To set the stage a bit more fully, let us examine some claims made in *The Fundamentals*.

Fundamentalists, not unlike Peirce, tend to place a heavy emphasis on the importance of religious experience, so that religion is not reduced to a cold intellectualism. This emphasis is evident in the very style of much contemporary television evangelism, a good part of which is fundamentalist in nature. At the same time, and as we shall see with some difficulty, fundamentalism requires of a "true" religious experience that it be tied to Christian doctrine, that is, to the Bible. For the fundamentalist this is no minor restriction, for as James M. Gray put it in his contribution to *The Fundamentals*, with an almost pathetic appeal to the authority of the General Assembly of the Presbyterian Church in America:

THE BIBLE AS WE NOW HAVE IT, IN ITS VARIOUS TRANSLATIONS AND REVISIONS, WHEN FREED FROM ALL ERRORS AND MISTAKE OF TRANSLATORS, COPYISTS AND PRINTERS, [IS] THE VERY WORD OF GOD, AND CONSEQUENTLY WHOLLY WITHOUT ERROR.[4]

An important upshot of this Biblical foundationalism is that fundamentalism, contrary to some popular characterizations, is essentially both intellectual and theological. It places a premium on the reading and interpreting of the Bible.[5] Moreover, not only is most fundamentalism not anti-intellectual, it is not, as it sees itself, antiscientific. Rather, fundamentalists are prone to suggest compatibility between "true science" and "true religion"—a point with which Peirce might agree, but for significantly different reasons.[6] The question is: how might Peirce have responded to an intellectual and religious movement maintaining such claims? Let us turn to the first half of our answer.

I

Marsden has argued that "it is a mistake . . . to regard the fundamentalist controversies as at bottom a conflict between science and religion."[7] For reasons in part other than those he has in mind, from a Peircean perspective this seems correct. Some fundamentalists have, after all, accepted a Newtonian world order as evidence of God's rational creation.[8] Indeed, some have gone so far as to adopt elements of evolutionary theory; James Orr, for example, argued in *The Fundamentals* that " 'Evolution' . . . is coming to be recognized as but a new name for 'creation,' only that the creative power now works from within, instead of, as in the old conception, in an external, plastic fashion."[9] Nevertheless, there are instances in which fundamentalism does oppose specific scientific hypotheses; for example, any full theory of natural selection is rejected for being anticreationist. Such instances of course give rise to public debate and therefore to the perception that fundamentalism is essentially antiscientific. Thus, in *A Common Faith*, John Dewey maintained that "the fundamentalist in religion is one whose beliefs in intellectual content have hardly been touched by scientific developments."[10] As Peirce would have seen it, such a perception not only ignores some of the evidence, but insofar as it is a criticism of fundamentalism, misdirects us from a deeper problem of which the instances of antiscientific behavior are a result.

On the one hand, the charge of being essentially antiscientific both presupposes and fosters the assumption that some body of knowledge called *science* is correct and some body of knowledge called *religion* is wrong. This inevitably leads to a reverse dogmatism, such as that of evolutionism, as a response to fundamentalism. In such a case the so-called scientific response is as bad as the problematic outlook to which it is responding. Peirce was constantly on the alert to warn us against this trap of "scientism" (MS 856, 857, 863, 866). On the other hand, in fostering the notion that science and religion are simply two competing bodies of knowledge, the charge of being antiscientific essentially authorizes the method fundamentalists employ to undermine the charge. That is, as Marsden points out, fundamentalists become "scientific" by integrating scientific findings into their world order. Thus, they marry science and religion and are only antiscientific in cases where scientific hypotheses do not make this union a happy one. The so-called intelligent design theory, for example, incorporates contemporary theories of physics and chemistry, but its proponents dismiss Darwinian evolution as incompatible with their account of creative design. In a general way, then, fundamentalism is no different from any other world view that takes issue with some element or aspect of contemporary scientific thought. It is at this point, however, that Peirce would have begun his response to fundamentalism, for it is not the cases of being antiscientific that are fundamentally problematic, but the fact that these arise in the context of the attempt to integrate science and religion. This fact, from a Peircean outlook, points to the deeper problem on the part of fundamentalism: a misunderstanding of the nature of science itself that leads fundamentalists to be, not antiscientific, but unscientific.

Fundamentalists universally, so far as I can tell—though to be sure they do not spend much time with philosophy of science—maintain the traditional notion of science suggested above. That is, they take science to be an aggregate of facts or beliefs or, more simply, a "body of knowledge." William Jennings Bryan expressed this understanding of science when he wrote, in preparation for the Scopes case, "[T]rue science is classified knowledge and nothing can be scientific unless it is true."[11] Since the Bible is considered by fundamentalists to be revealed truth, it likewise constitutes a "body of knowledge." Within this view, the trick to marrying science and religion therefore is simply to bring the two bodies of knowledge into line with each other; and of course the fundamentalist addendum is that the knowledge offered by the Bible is the preferred partner.

Peirce would have rejected fundamentalism's integration of science and religion because he took the notion that science was a fixed body of knowledge to be a false one. "Science," he argued, "is defined as a body of knowledge. But it is not half so much knowledge as inquiry—the active wanting to know which implies we don't already,—that makes the scientific man" (MS 866: 4). Elsewhere, Peirce maintained that "[t]hat which constitutes science, then, is not so much correct conclusions, as it is correct method" (CP 6:428). When fundamentalists embrace the "body of knowledge" notion of science together with its implicit Newtonian suspicion of hypotheses, they are, as Peirce would see it, misunderstanding the nature of science. Consequently, in focusing on the integration of "bodies of knowledge," fundamentalism addresses the *effects* of science, not science itself; any marriage effected in such a fashion must end in annulment, if not in a series of annulments.

This misconception of science coupled with Biblical foundationalism has led fundamentalists not only to find instances in which they resist scientific hypotheses, but also to attempt to integrate "science" and religion in ways that push the limits of credibility. Marsden mentions, for example, William B. Riley, who "claimed that when in Job XXVII it says 'To make weight for the wind,' that the Bible was predicting air pressure."[12] These extremes of denying and accepting scientific claims suggest that something is awry in the method of fundamentalist thinkers who at once intend to be both religious and scientific. Peirce's response to this would not be an unusual one; he would likely point out that what is wrong is simply that compatibility or incompatibility with the Bible is not a good reason either for accepting or for rejecting a scientific hypothesis or claim. Peirce would answer the hubris of the fundamentalists in the same way that in 1893 he answered Paul Carus's attempts at the "conciliation of religion and science": "This pragmatical and unneeded absoluteness [of religious assertion] it is which is most deeply contrary to the method, the results, and the whole spirit of science" (CP 6.604). In short, fundamentalists are not even in the game; they are essentially unscientific.

The unscientificness of fundamentalism, from a Peircean outlook, becomes clearer if we examine Peirce's categorial structure of human activity and locate fundamentalism within it. Peirce often distinguished scientific persons from both practical and artistic persons (CP 1.43, 7.604–606; MSS 439, 604). In 1898 he measured the difference between science and practice as follows:

The practical man has a definite job which he sets himself to accomplish. For that purpose he has to adopt some consistent plan which must be based upon a theory, and to that theory he must be wedded before the work begins. . . . But a scientific man, who has any such immovable beliefs to which he regards himself as religiously bound to be loyal, cannot at the same time desire to have his beliefs altered. In other words he cannot wish to learn the truth. (CP 6.3)

In light of this distinction—one Peirce employed in attacking theologism—it is apparent that in Peirce's view fundamentalism is practical, not scientific, and fundamentalist thinkers are engaged in a practice. They are wedded to their tenets of Biblical foundationalism and inerrancy, and they set out to interpret every aspect of the conduct of life in light of these. Indeed, Peirce's somewhat bitter description of theology in general fits the extreme theology of fundamentalism: "the principle business of theologians is to make men feel the enormity of the slightest departure from the metaphysics they assume to be connected with the standard faith" (CP 6.3).

This perhaps seems a long way to go to arrive at what appears to be an obvious fault of fundamentalism: its dogmatic nature and correlate ignorance of scientific inquiry. As James Barr has pointed out, a central feature of fundamentalism "is its quite total complacency and lack of self-criticism."[13] However, Peirce's categorial distinction between science and practice, which shifts the response from antiscientificness to unscientificness, is not trivial. In setting science and religion in opposition to each other, the charge of being antiscientific presupposes the false notion of science that grants fundamentalism a competitor status in the scientific endeavor of pursuing the truth. Science becomes one more voice in the wilderness. Thus, interpreters such as Marsden are led to assert that the "issue [between fundamentalism and a "scientific" world view] was a classic instance of what Thomas Kuhn . . . describes as a 'paradigm conflict' of the two scientific worldviews."[14] On Peirce's view fundamentalism would not be granted competitor status precisely because it is not engaged in science in the first place. It does not seek truth, but endeavors to maintain and disseminate that which is already accepted as truth. As Peirce remarked with respect to theology's stifling of the development of metaphysics, the confusion of the categories of practice and science can lead to serious—and sometimes socially devastating—inhibitions to the development of thought. Giving vent to his own frustration with a theologism not unlike contemporary fundamentalism, Peirce wrote with irony—and a sharpness reminiscent of Aristotle's unwillingness to argue with vegetables—that "it is quite impossible for a practical man to comprehend what science is about unless he becomes as a little child and is born again" (CP 6.3).

Moreover, in not employing the "body of knowledge" notion of science, a Peircean response to fundamentalism would not be compelled to attack fundamentalism for its religiosity. That is, to attack fundamentalism for being unscientific is not to attack it for being religious. The necessity of a fundamental opposition between religion and science is thus avoided, and the way is opened for an alternative proposal for the marriage of science and religion that would replace the fundamentalist approach. This alternative approach, in reassessing the nature of religion, leads to the second way in which Peirce might have responded to fundamentalism.

II

Having suggested above that Peirce would tolerate fundamentalism insofar as it is religious, we must now ask from a Peircean perspective just how "religious" fundamentalism is. The answer is, at once, "not very" and "too much so." That is, fundamentalism turns out not to be very religious as Peirce understood religiosity precisely because it is too "religious" in the sense that it forces all of life into the confines of a so-called religious doctrine. Peirce not only denied that science was a body of knowledge, he denied that religion was as well. Rather than construing religion as assent to the propositions of a specific text, Peirce saw it as a roughly articulated sentiment concerning the "circumambient all" that could be associated with a fallible speculative cosmology (CP 6.429).

From a Peircean point of view, fundamentalism's marriage of science and religion is grounded in a misunderstanding of both science and religion, because Peirce believed that religion did not properly rest on special revelation or inspiration. Christian fundamentalists, for example, insofar as they maintain both foundationalism and Biblical inerrancy, rely entirely on the assumption that the Bible is a revealed—or, more properly, an inspired—text of wisdom. As Philip Mauro stated the case in one of his contributions to *The Fundamentals*, "the moment one receives an explanation of the universe as coming from God who made it, he can have no further use for philosophy."[15] Now, Peirce did "not think it is philosophical to reject the possibility of revelation," but he also argued that "revelation, far from affording us any certainty, gives results far less certain than other sources of information" (CP 1.143). In light of this, Peirce did not believe that revelation was the proper source of religious belief. Thus, in building "religion" on an uncritically held special revelation, fundamentalism brooks the possibility of effecting a nonreligious religion and encourages a specification of religious belief not warranted by religious experience.

In his "Neglected Argument for the Reality of God" as well as in a number of manuscripts, Peirce maintained that religious belief—in particular belief in God's reality—begins in feeling: "religion, in the proper sense of the term," he asserted, "can arise from nothing but the religious sensibility" (CP 6.433). And in this broad sense, Peirce understood religion to be universal as an element of human experience. He went so far, for example, as to speculate that belief in God's reality, vaguely considered, is "not unknown to anybody" (CP 6.457). Such universality, which Peirce believed revelation lacked, suggested that religious belief was instinctive or commonsensical. Moreover, insofar as instincts were for Peirce the "bedrock" of all reason, the instinctiveness of religion "vindicated" it as a belief. Indeed, it is precisely this "argument" for God's reality that Peirce, in his "Neglected Argument," charged theologians with neglecting (CP 6.484). Theologians, he argued, become so involved in theology that they forget religion:

They [theologians] swamp religion in fallacious logical disputa-
tions. Thus, the natural tendency is the drawing tighter and
tighter of the narrowing bounds of doctrine, with less and less attention to the living essence of religion, until, after some *sym-
bolum quodcumque* has declared that the salvation of each
individual absolutely and almost exclusively depends upon his en-
tertaining a correct metaphysics of the godhead, the vital spark of
inspiration becomes finally quite extinct. (CP 6.438)

Ironically, Peirce's emphasis on feeling and religious experience
sounds almost fundamentalist in nature. As *Fundamentals* author
David James Burrell put it: "Not to those who deem themselves wise,
but rather to the simple whose hearts are open Godward, comes the
great revelation."[16] However, this emphasis also points to what Peirce
saw as a central weakness of theologism—and therefore *a fortiori* of
fundamentalism. While Christian fundamentalists emphasize religious experience, they are interested only in religious experience that
accepts the inerrancy of the Bible. The upshot is that "being religious" for fundamentalists involves adopting a vastly and unwarrant-
edly overdetermined doctrine as one's guide to life. This of course is
what leads to the perpetual divisiveness within all religions of doctrine—overdetermined doctrines are used as measures of inclusion
and exclusion.

The irony can be demonstrated in examining an argument from
F. Bettex's essay in *The Fundamentals* titled "The Bible and Modern
Criticism." Here Bettex proposed a version of the cosmological argument as a common-sense demonstration of the necessity of a "cause
of all causes" or a "Supreme Intelligence."[17] From the argument Bettex concluded that finite minds cannot place limitations on the nature of God:

Hence what the Intelligence does is both illimitable and unfath-
omable, and it can at any time either change this world or make
a new one. It is therefore prima facie silly for us, with our prodi-
giously narrow experience, to set any kinds of bounds to the Supreme Being.[18]

To this point—that is, that our limited experience makes our conception indeterminate—Peirce would have agreed. But Bettex's next

move, as a fundamentalist, was precisely to specify the nature of God by endorsing the revelatory character of the Bible.[19] Such specification is itself a way of limiting our notion of God as the God who "speaks to the prophets," who "communicated the law to Moses on Mt. Sinai," and "who numbers the very hairs of our heads."[20]

The same irony appears in Burrell's essay "The Knowledge of God." In it Burrell distinguished "intuition" (akin to Peirce's "instinct") and "faith" (Christian intuition) as two experiential approaches to knowing God. He described each as an "indwelling sense of God."[21] However, intuition fails insofar as it leads the "vast multitude" into "idolatry"; "faith," on the other hand, because it is faith in "revelation," allows us to know God. And the God it allows us to know is the God of the Bible, "the written Word of God" which "makes us acquainted with His being, personality and moral attributes."[22] It is precisely upon this internal distinction within religious experience that fundamentalism and Peircean instinctivism come to blows. While fundamentalist revelationism cannot, from a Peircean perspective, be absolutely refuted, it certainly is *not* the *necessary* result of religious experience, instinct, or feeling; if it were, one would expect a vastly different account in the history of world religions.

In pursuing religion as determined by the inerrant Bible, Bettex, Burrell, and other fundamentalists—quite ironically, it would have seemed to Peirce—fail in several ways. First, by limiting religious feeling to the Christian experience, they go beyond the warrant of lived religious feeling or experience. Second, in doing so, they overspecify religious belief so that: 1) they close off the real possibility of scientific inquiry, as we saw above; and 2) they reduce religion to a tawdry exercise of "out-Christianizing" all other Christians. As soon as fundamentalists become embroiled in the problem of "who the true Christians are" (and what defines them) by employing Biblical foundationalism, they lose sight of Christian love. The rather bitter tone of "Evolutionism in the Pulpit," an essay in *The Fundamentals* written by "An Occupant of the Pew," is indicative of this tendency, which is still popular among contemporary fundamentalists.[23] Moreover, such a focus inevitably produces the kind of militant doctrinal disputes that seemed to Peirce both unchristian and generally untrue to the spirit of religion.[24] As Donna Orange points out, "A conception of God that sets people to fighting with each other Peirce would have called self-deception."[25]

Religion, according to Peirce, is essentially neither theological nor intellectual, as his response to philosophy of religion in his day indicated:

> And yet when you open the next new book on the philosophy of religion that comes out, the chances are that it will be written by an intellectualist who in his preface offers you his metaphysics as a guide for the soul, talking as if philosophy were one of our deepest concerns. (CP 6.654)

Religion proper Peirce considered to be a feeling, a sentiment about the world. Moreover, he did not take the religious beliefs that evolve out of religious feeling to be tied to any specific text, inspired or otherwise. On the contrary, precisely because religious beliefs arise from religious feelings that are instinctive, they are not specific but inherently vague. As Peirce put it: "All the instinctive beliefs, I notice, are vague" (CP 6.499). Therefore, so far as Peirce was concerned, any overly specific doctrines such as one finds among the varieties of Christian fundamentalism must be regarded as nonreligious in a crucial sense. While they may have begun with an element of religious feeling, they are bound ultimately to exclude it: "Like a plucked flower, its [religion proper's] destiny is to wilt and fade. The vital sentiment that gave it birth loses gradually its pristine purity and strength, till some new creed treads it down" (CP 6.430). Ironically, then, fundamentalism, insofar as it focuses on the specification of correct Biblical doctrine, is itself too intellectualistic to suit Peirce's account of religion.

This is not to say, however, that for Peirce there could not be an intellectual side to religious belief. On the contrary, he took seriously the notion that the conceptions of religious belief could be developed. However, he did not believe such development occurred in religion proper. Rather, the intellectual specification of religious concepts occurred properly in the realm of science. In his "Neglected Argument," for example, Peirce argued that the vague notion of God that arises in religion proper can come to serve as a scientific hypothesis (CP 6.466).[26] It is at this point that specification of the concept of God can begin to occur; as Pfeifer argues, the "hypothesis [of God] is vague, but it continually becomes more definite."[27] However, such specification is fallible and must cohere with other developments in science—that is, in the pursuits of truth. Herein lies Peirce's developmental theism, in which religion proper is allowed to prosper while the specific attributes of God are allowed to grow. It is this view that Peirce would offer as an antidote to the closure of fundamentalism.

On the one hand, religion proper, as a religious belief in a vague God, remains relatively immune to criticism precisely because of its vagueness. As Potter maintains, "Doubts about God's reality or about the attributes which most aptly describe Him arise from attempts at precision."[28] Moreover, Peirce believed that the vague conception of God could "answer the principle purposes" of religion proper; that is, that a person could reach "the point of earnestly loving and adoring his strictly hypothetical God, and to that of desiring above all things to shape the whole conduct of life and all the springs of action into conformity with that hypothesis" (CP 6.467).

On the other hand, insofar as scientific or philosophical inquiry adopts God as a hypothesis, the notion of God can begin to be specified. Peirce went some way in this direction himself, arguing that through science we can "catch a fragment" (CP 6.502) of God's thought and that the concept of God tends "to define itself more and more" (CP 6.466). Orange, having examined Peirce's conception of God at length, suggests Peirce's central identification of God and Reason. The point is that Peirce offered a theistic world view that he believed avoided both the unscientific and nonreligious aspects of fundamentalism. The upshot of Peirce's developmental theme is that it marries religion and science in a new way, as co-conspirators in the human attempt to grasp the world. Religion, as a sentiment about the world, provides some vaguely conceived beliefs that are worshipable and that can guide conduct. Science functions not just as a test of religion but also as a way of allowing religious concepts to be developed intellectually, without jeopardizing in any fundamental way the religious belief itself. This is precisely the point Josiah Royce, under the influence of Peirce, made central to his work in *The Problem of Christianity*. In short, science, and its corollary interpretive function, allows our religious beliefs to grow with the development of our knowledge of the world.

Thus a Peircean response to fundamentalism accomplishes several things, though clearly fundamentalists would view the price paid as tragically high. Peirce accomplished the fundamentalist goal of unifying science and religion, not by making the beliefs of the two bodies of knowledge isomorphic, but by introducing science and religion as related features of human experience, one picking up where the other leaves off in constructing one's developing world view. This in turn precluded Peirce from positing an account of religion that is forced to close the doors prematurely on numerous avenues of inquiry, thus making its followers practitioners only. And finally, in perhaps a more Christian manner than Christian fundamentalism, Peirce's developmental theism allows religious feeling to dominate religion, so that the "truth" of one's belief does not hinge on strict adherence to some rigid interpretation of a text, and thus does not allow religion to devolve into a war of doctrinal identification.

ADDENDUM

PEIRCE'S COEFFICIENT OF THE SCIENCE OF THE METHOD

An Early Form of the Correlation Coefficient

Michael J. Rovine and Doug Anderson

My interest in the relationship between Peirce and Pearson led me to seek the assistance of my colleague Michael Rovine in assessing Peirce's understanding of statistics in its relation to Pearson's work. After several years of reading Peirce's published work and manuscripts dealing with statistics and after many coffee shop conversations, we managed to produce chapter 8 and the present addendum. We have placed it at the end of book because it is not, strictly speaking, a philosophical essay. Nevertheless, it may be the most provocative essay in suggesting Peirce's foreshadowing of important developments in statistics in the twentieth century.

Introduction

The history of the correlation coefficient is often thought to have begun with Sir Francis Galton. His contribution was notably his realization of the importance of the relationship between two variables for the purpose of describing or predicting some phenomenon. Research in statistics prior to Galton involved a set of components that if ordered differently could have resulted in the enumeration of correlation. However, scientists seemed to stop short of explicitly stating the principles that represented Galton's contribution. The strain of research that led to Galton's synthesis or discovery involved modeling errors of measurement and eventually led to the description of the normal distribution. Galton's definitions of *reversion* (later *regression*) and *correlation* were steeped in the notion that the variables considered were normally distributed. Karl Pearson followed Galton and defined the correlation between two variables more formally in terms of the bivariate normal distribution. Pearson admitted into his model variables that deviated from normality by being skewed. Such variables could be re-normalized through transformation. Pearson thought that *normality* was an intrinsic property of measured characteristics of humans, and his notions of correlation and regression reflected that view. To put it another way, in terms of what Peirce described as Pearson's nominalism, there were no real habits in nature, so nature could be made to fit the inquirer's description—in this case, Pearson's normality. The idea that an empirical distribution of an attribute that was neither normal nor skewed normal could accurately describe a population characteristic had no place in Pearson's theory of correlation. It is somewhat ironic that the formulas derived by Pearson would ultimately prove to be correct for a wide variety of distributions, many of which Pearson would reject. It is also ironic that one form of the correlation coefficient, the N-coefficient for two dichotomous variables, resembled a coefficient derived by Peirce some twenty years earlier. Peirce's coefficient was derived with no assumptions regarding the distribution underlying the measures considered. The distribution could only be determined by the real habits of nature. This agreed with Peirce's *tychism*, the notion that chance elements contributed to the development of the cosmos. In Peirce's cosmos, one could expect a tychistic or chance distribution of observable phenomena as a real possibility.

Peirce developed his coefficient to demonstrate what he termed *the science of the method*, in modern terms referred to as *rater reliability*. His work anticipated Charles Spearman's extensions of Pearson, Galton, and G. Udny Yule's work on the reliability of measures.

Peirce's work in the area of variable association was apparently unknown to and certainly not referenced by Galton, Pearson, Yule, or Spearman. This is particularly surprising in light of Peirce's direct confrontations with Pearson and his indirect connection to Galton. It is also surprising when one considers that Peirce's work was published and presented to the American and European scientific communities.

To place Peirce's coefficient of the "science of the method" in some context, we would like to highlight the steps in the modeling of errors and the description of the normal curve as an error model that led to Galton and Pearson's work. After summarizing their work on correlation, we will describe some of the computational forms of the correlation as applied to prediction and association models based on 2×2 contingency tables. These coefficients are still often used as reliability and validity coefficients. We will then describe Peirce's coefficient and describe the circumstances out of which it was developed, showing the striking similarity between that coefficient, the different forms of Q, and the N-coefficient. We will speculate somewhat regarding possible connections among the different players. We will finally suggest that the development of these coefficients by Pearson and Peirce represents another instance of a lifelong disagreement between the two scientists: namely, their respective faith and lack thereof in the normal distribution.

Galton's Antecedents

In the eighteenth century the primary focus of mathematicians creating the new discipline of statistics involved the description of errors in the measurement of the location of celestial bodies and in the description of geodesic phenomena (e.g., the circumference of the earth). With a number of measurements, each one fallible to a certain degree, scientists would consider the best way to combine a set of measurements into a best single measure. Two important questions emerged from this research. First, how could one combine information from all of the measurements to come up with a single best measurement? And second, what form would the distribution of the errors take? The answer to the first question—namely, Legendre's discovery of least squares fit as the "best" way of combining measurements—resulted in the beginning of what might be considered modern statistics. The answer to the second question, Gauss's normal distribution for a single variable and Laplace's multivariate normal distribution for multiple variables, led to the probabilistic basis of the emerging statistical methodology.

In 1805, Legendre published *Nouvelles methodes pour la determination des orbites des cometes* (New Methods for the Determination of the Orbits of Comets), in which he presented the least squares solution to the problem of combining errors to calculate the best value of a measure in the presence of error.[1] For a model with a single parameter (estimate of the best value), the model resulted in the calculation of the arithmetic mean of the observations. Legendre gave no formal requirement for the distribution of the errors of measurement he would combine. He did suggest that if an error were discovered to be too large, it could be dropped from the set of equations to be solved.

Prior to Gauss, the most successful attempt to describe the *error curve*, the probability distribution of the errors of measurement, was put forth by Laplace. Starting from the principle of sufficient reason borrowed from Leibnitz, he reasoned to a curve and then to a method of combining observations. His probability curve was intuitively satisfying in that large errors had a small probability. The probability of smaller and smaller errors increased in a curvilinear fashion, with increasing slope as the error size shrank. His curve, which had the form,

$$y = \frac{1}{2a} \log \frac{a}{|x|} \ for \ x \le a$$

was symmetric for positive and negative errors, and it increased in slope as it approached zero error, leading to an infinite value of the

curve at zero. Gauss extended this curve by maintaining the characteristics of symmetry and decreasing probability for smaller errors
while solving the problem of infinite slope and probability at the zero
error value.

Gauss began by describing the characteristics that a distribution of
errors should have: namely, the distribution would have a maximum
at) = o; it would be symmetric (i.e., overestimates would occur as
frequently as underestimates); and it would be zero outside the range
of possible error. Suggesting that the most probable single value
would be the mean of the observations, he showed that the probability distribution of the errors would have the form,

$$\varphi(\Delta) = \frac{h}{\sqrt{\pi}} e^{-h^2 \Delta^2}$$

which is the form of the normal curve. Here h is a measure of the
precision of the estimate,) is a value of the error, and v is the probability of that error occurring in the distribution.[2]

Laplace, in turn, took Gauss's work, interpreted the results in
terms of his own Central Limit Theorem, which allowed a stronger
theoretical justification for the normal error curve, and immediately
was able to show that the curve implied the simplest method of combination and was equivalent to least squares.[3] In the simplest case of
estimation, the best value—the arithmetic mean—both minimized
the sum of the squared errors and was the expected value under the
condition that the errors followed a normal curve.

By 1812, Laplace had effectively derived the multivariate normal
distribution of two or more least squares estimates. At this point, he
had tied together two important strains of statistical research: the
problem of combining observations in some optimal fashion, and the
probabilistic description of the errors one would make when making
those observations. Laplace presented this work in his *Theorie analytique des probabilites*.[4] With these methods in place and available, scientists would attempt to apply them to social data, and would
eventually use them to describe the association, first, between errors,
and then between variables.

The first applications of these methods in the case of bivariate distributions appeared as attempts to describe the association between two errors of observation. These attempts resulted in formulas for both independent and dependent errors. For the case of dependent errors, these formulas included a product term that would ultimately be named the *correlation coefficient.*

At this point we should mention the role of the circle and the ellipse in the development of the error model. Imagine throwing a dart at a dartboard in the following fashion. There is a dartboard lying flat on the ground below your first-floor apartment window. You are able to reach out the window directly above the bull's-eye. You drop the dart, trying to hit the bull's-eye. If your aim is good, you would be expected to come relatively close to the target more often than not. If we measure whether you miss the target to the right or the left, it is reasonable to think that you would miss to the right as often as you would miss to the left. It is also easy to imagine that far misses would occur less often than near misses. A bell-shaped curve may be a reasonable model for the frequency distribution of these horizontal misses. If we measure whether you miss to the top or the bottom of the bull's-eye, it would reasonable to think that the misses would once again be symmetric, with near misses being more prevalent than far misses. A bell-shaped curve would also suffice for the vertical dimension. It is reasonable to assume that the spread (the variance) of both distributions would be the same.

To determine where one would expect any particular dart to land, we could imagine taking a random miss from the horizontal error distribution and a random miss from the vertical error distribution. Combining these two values would put the dart somewhere on the dartboard: typically nearer to the center than farther from the center. Dropping enough darts would result in a pattern of hits equivalent to the bivariate normal distribution. If the vertical and horizontal spread were the same, this would result in a circle more dense as one moves closer to the center. The two errors (top to bottom and right to left) are, in this case, independent. Now suppose that a wind kicked up that swirled and often changed direction along the right-to-left axis.

This wind would make it harder to land the dart in the center, by pushing it either to the left or to the right. It would not change the top-to-bottom accuracy. Now the horizontal variance would be greater than the vertical variance, and the pattern of darts would form an ellipse with the major (wider) axis running along the horizontal axis. In this case the errors are still independent, but the different variances create an ellipse. Finally, imagine a third scenario in which the wind is blowing northeast (toward the top right). Here we would again have an ellipse; however, errors would be dependent (or correlated), since an error to the right would tend to occur along with an error to the top. The distribution of errors would still form an ellipse, except now the ellipse would be at some angle to the right/left (and to the top/bottom) axis.

Prior to Laplace, Adrain had discussed in an 1808 article the probability of the simultaneous occurrence of two independent errors, arguing that the probability surface should consist of concentric circles when the dispersions of the two errors are equal.[5] He expected the probability surface to consist of ellipses when the dispersions are unequal. He did not consider the case of related errors. In 1811 Plana gave the form of the surface of that integral.[6] His expression was

$$z = \frac{1}{4\pi\alpha\sqrt{E}} e^{\frac{1}{4aE}(CQ^2 - 2BQQ' + AQ)}$$

The product term in this exponent $(-2BQQ')$ indicates the ellipse. Laplace first published a product term in a bivariate distribution in a paper he published on the topic of definite integrals.[7]

In the early 1820s Gauss described the probability of the simultaneous occurrence of two or more errors, and the resulting probability surface, in his *Theoria Combinationis Observationum Erroribus Minimis Obnoxiae* (*Theory of the Combination of Observations Least Subject to Errors*).[8] For two variables, his formula for this surface included a product term. His formula did not express the surface in terms of the correlations and standard deviations. Gauss did not consider the product as the correlation of two observed variables, but instead considered it as representing the geometric relationship between two variables. He gave no substantive interpretation for the elliptical form of the contours of equal probability.

Bravais, apparently independent of Gauss, derived a geometric solution of the normal correlation surface.[9] His equations included a product term, and he mentioned the existence of a relationship, a "correlation," between the variables in question, though he never specifically associated any of the terms in his formula with this notion. In describing the elliptical contour plot, he also described the line segment representing the principal axis. This line would eventually become Galton's regression line. But again, Bravais concentrated on the mathematical properties of the surface and axes and gave no further substantive interpretation of his discovery.

At this point a three-dimensional probability surface would be described for two variables. The base of the surface would represent all possible combinations of variable values. The height of the surface gives the probability of occurrence for that particular combination of variable values. The shape of the surface is described by identifying all values that would yield the same probability. This would be equivalent to passing a plane parallel to the base of the surface. For the bivariate normal distribution, the intersection of the surface and plane would yield the same shape for any given height. This intersection would define a probability contour that decreases in area for variable combinations with higher probability. For two uncorrelated normally distributed variables with identical variances, this contour would be a circle. For uncorrelated variables with different variances, the contour would be an ellipse.

It would remain for Galton to frame a question that resulted in a bivariate normal distribution that had known equal variances for both variables (the same trait measured across succeeding generations). His insight in describing the data led him to suggest correlation as the reason for the elliptical contour.

An earlier attempt to frame a question of social variables in the developing mathematical format appeared in the work of Adolphe Quetelet. Although Laplace had applied his principles of probability to characteristics of people and their behaviors, including a description of the number of letters that ended up in the Paris dead-letter office,[10] it was Quetelet who applied his notion to a wide range of characteristics.[11] Characterizing everything from types of murders to physiological characteristics of different racial groups, he argued that the errors observed for each characteristic could be described using the normal curve. He used his observation that different societal and racial groups appeared to cluster around characteristic averages to argue for his notion of the "average man." The set of characteristics represented by the mean values defined the optimal representative of a class. He used this to argue that a society could be described by delineating its version of the average man. Racial groups could be differentiated by comparing the average man of one group to the average man of another. He called his work the study of *social physics*.

As part of this work, Quetelet attempted to develop an association coefficient that would describe the correlation between two variables.[12] He was dissatisfied with his coefficient and recognized that it did not represent a solution to the problem.

Galton

From his discovery of Quetelet's method for fitting a normal curve, Galton wondered how, if succeeding generations were normally distributed on a given characteristic, that characteristic could possibly be inherited, especially if the population variability of succeeding generations stayed the same. If the offspring of each parent tended to be similar to the parent but with some variability, one would expect that each succeeding generation would be increasingly variable. But for the measures that Galton considered, the variability stayed the same. So, for Galton the existence of the normal distribution seemed to argue against heritability. In 1875 Galton began a study of sweet peas.

In this study Galton categorized a generation of sweet peas into different sizes, from large to small. He then considered the offspring from each size category. He noted that for each group of peas of a particular size, the new generation showed more variability than the

previous generation. He also noted that the overall variability remained constant from one generation to the next. He reasoned that
to reconcile these two apparently contradictory facts, he would observe that the average value of each group in the new generation
would be closer to the overall new-generation average than the same-
size old-generation group average would be to the overall old-generation group average. This *reversion* to the group mean would be the
characteristic that allowed variability to remain constant from generation to generation.

Over the next decade, Galton worked to show that the phenomenon of reversion could also be used to explain the inheritance of
human characteristics between generations—most notably, height.

In his 1885 presidential address to the anthropology section of the
British Association for the Advancement of Science, Galton presented
his conceptualization of reversion (which he would subsequently rename *regression*), which he used to describe concordance of the same
characteristic across generations.[13] This conceptualization included
the description of the association between two variables, the correlation coefficient. Regression was steeped in the tradition of the normal
curve, and Galton's contribution was, in part, his recognition of
the role the normal curve played in the description of the relation
of characteristics between two generations (of peas and of human
beings).

Galton organized his data into a bivariate frequency table and saw
the conditional normality (the existence of small normal distributions on one of the variables for each value of the other variable) and
a characteristic elliptical shape to the table. Since the dispersion was
the same across generations, Galton was able to interpret the elliptical
shape of the data as indicating an association between the two variables. Because he lacked the ability to summarize the results in a formula, he had to wait for Pearson and others who followed to provide
the mathematical realization of his insight.

Although Galton is credited with the use of the bivariate frequency
table to show the association between two variables, it was apparently
Henry Bowditch who first used this graphical method. Bowditch first

presented a bivariate frequency table in his 1877 study of the relationship among growth characteristics of Massachusetts children.[14] In
particular, Bowditch attempted to relate height to weight for the children he measured. The results of those measurements were summarized in a table that dramatically showed the elliptical bivariate
distribution. He presented this table in the same format as did Galton
in his more famous evidence of the existence of reversion. In addition, Bowditch explicitly showed plots of height against weight and
drew what were unmistakably curvilinear regression lines on these
plots. Galton and Bowditch were corresponding at this point, and
there is a record of Galton responding to Bowditch in a letter dated
June 26, 1876 and making some minor suggestions regarding the presentation of the results.[15] This is interesting in the light of Galton's
first public presentation of his early speculation regarding the heritability of traits at an address to the Royal Institution in 1877.[16]

Peirce and Errors

Bowditch represented a notable connection between Galton and
Peirce. Henry Bowditch was the grandson of mathematician Nathaniel Bowditch, who was responsible for, among other things, translat-
ing Laplace's book on celestial mechanics into English. Nathaniel
Bowditch was mentor to Benjamin Peirce, Charles Sanders Peirce's
father. While Benjamin attended Harvard, he helped proofread the
translation. The last volume of this work was issued under his care.
Henry Bowditch was a childhood friend of Charles Peirce and they
remained close through college, both attending Harvard (Peirce grad-
uated two years prior to Bowditch). Bowditch returned to Harvard
for an academic position in 1871, and there he conducted his study of
the growth of children.

Benjamin Peirce produced important work in the area of least
squares and errors. He developed a method for determining whether
an outlier (an extreme value often caused by a mistaken calculation)
was so extreme that it should not be included among the observations. In his work as an astronomer and geographer for the Coast

Survey, the elder Peirce would use least squares to determine the best estimate of the central tendency of a set of measures.[17] Charles continued this family tradition in his work for the Survey, becoming arguably the preeminent *metrologist* of his time. His work in this area involved developing more precise ways to measure certain phenomena, including increasing the precision of the pendulum measures used to assess the force of gravity and developing a more precise determination of the length of a meter based on the wavelength of light. In these pursuits he wrote often on issues regarding the law of errors.

Pearson and the Correlation Coefficient

The correlation coefficient is probably the single most commonly used statistic to describe the association between two variables. Karl Pearson not only developed the statistic, he was its first great proselytizer. In his *Grammar of Science* (1892), Pearson, as was his habit, did not see fit to include a significant reference to Galton.[18] In 1896 Pearson published his formula for the "best value" of the correlation coefficient in his paper "Regression, Heredity, and Panmixia," which appeared in the *Proceedings of the Royal Society*.[19] His formula was:

$$r_{xy} = \frac{\Sigma xy}{N\sigma_x\sigma_y}$$

where x and y are deviations around the means of the respective variables, N is the number of observations, and Φ_x and Φ_y represent the respective variance of each variable.

$\Sigma xy/N$ is the covariance between the two variables, and the product, $\Phi_x\Phi_y$, represents the maximum possible covariance between the variable and limits the maximum size of the coefficient to 1. A correlation of 0 represents no association between the two variables.

Pearson's development represented an appreciation and extension of Galton's work. Pearson was able to take the conditional normal distributions of the bivariate scatterplot and imagine the mathematical form of the ellipse imposed over the plot. Under the assumption that both variables were normally distributed, Pearson was able to determine the major and minor axes of the ellipse as a mixture of two normal distributions.

Pearson's requirement that the observed values of the two variables follow a normal distribution represented more than a statistical assumption. It represented his strong belief regarding the nature of all traits. So strong was his nominalism that he developed a theory of skewed distributions, a way of transforming non-normally distributed variables to retain normality. As noted earlier, since for Pearson natural "laws" were a matter of human creation, in his view it was appropriate to fit nature's results to his description of a normal distribution. This was a consequence of his thoroughly nominalistic understanding of scientific inquiry.

Yule

The first published coefficient of correlation for two dichotomous variables was Yule's Q, which takes the form of

$$Q = \frac{ad - bc}{ad + bc}$$

Yule required any association coefficient to have two characteristics: it would range between $+1$ and -1, and 0 would represent no association. For the case of equally likely events (equal marginal probabilities), this coefficient would be 0, which would occur with equal frequency. The largest association would occur when all values fall in the cells of the main diagonal. In that case, $bc = 0$, and the coefficient is 1. For the situation in which all values fall in the off-diagonal cells, the coefficient would be -1. Peirce's coefficient also satisfied Yule's criteria.

Pearson suggested four other coefficients that differed from Q in the denominator. Pearson changed the name of Yule's Q to Q_2 and presented his own Q_1, Q_3, Q_4, and Q_5.[20] Pearson suggested that the interested researcher look at all of the Q values and, depending on the circumstances, select the most appropriate one.

The computational form of the Pearson correlation coefficient for a 2 × 2 contingency table is the N-coefficient. The N-coefficient is a computational reduction of Pearson's product-moment correlation coefficient formula for the case of two dichotomous variables. If each of two variables can be scored 0/1, the results can be summarized in Table 1.

		X		
		0	1	Total
Y	0	a	b	(a+b)
	1	c	d	(c+d)
	Total	(a+c)	(b+d)	N

where a, b, c, and d are the respective frequencies of each cell. The *marginal* row and column sums, $(a+b)$, $(c+d)$, $(a+c)$, and $(b+d)$ are also included. N is the total sample size.

This table can be reconstructed (Table 2) by replacing the cell frequencies with cell proportions (i.e., dividing through by N).

		X		
		0	1	Total
Y	0	p_{00}	p_{01}	$p_{0.}$
	1	p_{10}	p_{11}	$p_{1.}$
	Total	$p_{.0}$	$p_{.1}$	1

For two such variables, Equation 1 can be simplified to:

$$r_\varphi = \frac{p_{00}p_{11} - p_{10}p_{01}}{\sqrt{p_{1.}p_{0.}p_{.1}p_{.0}}} = \frac{ad - bc}{\sqrt{(a+c)(b+d)(a+b)(c+d)}} \quad 21$$

As we can see, the numerator is again the same. The denominator involves the product of the marginals of the observations and the marginals of the events. As we will see, if the number of observations in which the event occurs equals the number of observations in which the event does not occur (i.e., if the marginals are equal), then this formula is equivalent to the coefficient presented by Peirce in 1884.

Much work followed in the wake of Pearson, including work by Spearman related to developing forms of a correlation coefficient appropriate for established reliability when, for instance, the two variables were the responses of two observers to an event or an observation.[22] In the dichotomous case of whether or not a particular event occurred, the coefficient could be used to assess rater agreement. This work led to a number of different correlation coefficients for a 2 × 2 contingency table.

Peirce's Coefficient

Peirce published his coefficient in 1884, the same year that he left his position as Lecturer on Logic at Johns Hopkins University. He had come to that appointment having established himself as an outstanding scientist, partly through his position as Assistant in the Coast and Geodetic Survey. The British mathematician Arthur Cayley was also in residence at John Hopkins in 1882. In 1858 Cayley had published the influential paper "Memoir on the Theory of Matrices," which represented the culmination of an intense half-century of work in the area of matrix algebra and determinant theory.[23]

Gauss may have presented the first modern use of a determinant in his work on the congruence of quadratic equations.[24] His determinant, $b^2 - ac$, was equivalent to the determinant of a 2 × 2 table with equal values along the main diagonal. He also presented the coefficient of a set of equations in a matrixlike array. Cauchy moved more in the direction of a matrix algebra for quadratic forms, but it was Jacobi who in the 1830s began to develop the modern theory of matrix algebra for the purpose of solving a set of simultaneous linear equations. Throughout the 1840s, these methods were extended to a set of equations of higher degrees by Sylvester and Cayley.[25] Sylvester coined the term *matrix* to represent an array that included the set of equation coefficient.[26] Cayley extended and summarized this work in his important 1858 paper in which he established rules for both square and rectangular matrices.[27] At this point the new results were passed along among the scientific community, especially among those who, like the Peirces, had an abiding interest in developments related to algebra.

Cayley was well aware of Benjamin Peirce's work and reputation, in particular his reputation in linear associative algebra, when he arrived at Johns Hopkins. He discussed a number of topics with Charles Peirce, including characteristics of the 2 × 2 table, which Cayley referred to as his "$ad - bc$" table. In these discussions Peirce noted that the 2 × 2 table could be conceived as a mixture of two algebras (NE, 311). This idea was apparently novel to Cayley. The idea of a mixture provided the mathematical basis for Peirce's coefficient.

The Coast Survey was Peirce's main employer between 1859, when he joined as an aide, and 1879, when he had attained the rank of Assistant. Following in the tradition of his father, Charles worked on a number of different problems related to measurement during his tenure. One concern was the nature of successful prediction. Sgt. J. P. Finley had published data related to his predictions of the occurrence of tornados for different regions in the United States. Finley summarized his success by calculating the number of times he had made an accurate prediction. His correct predictions were of two varieties: those in which he had predicted a tornado and one had indeed occurred, and those in which he had predicted no tornado and none had occurred. His measure of success was the proportion of times he had made a correct prediction. As a result of this estimate, he appeared very successful, since one event—no tornado—occurred much more often than the other. It was, then, possible to appear accurate by always predicting *no tornado*.

This problem was almost immediately recognized. In 1884 G. K. Gilbert responded with an index of predictive accuracy.[28] Gilbert's coefficient was

$$i_G = 2\frac{ad - bc}{(a+b+c+d) - (a^2 + b^2 + c^2 + d^2)}$$

The numerator of the coefficient made use of the determinant of a 2 × 2 matrix as a measure of the degree of association in the table. The determinant of the matrix is a single number that can be used to describe the amount of association in the table. Unscaled, the determinant is symmetric about the value of 0, which represents a random distribution of values among the four cells. The numerator of essentially all coefficients used to describe association in a 2 × 2 table is $ad - bc$.

Rather than report the proportion of successes, Gilbert added a penalty related to the number of incorrect guesses. The denominator scaled the solution, subtracting out the number of correct predictions of no tornado ($-d^2$). This effectively shrank the denominator based on the number of times the observer made the easy prediction. Gilbert's *ad hoc* method for scaling via his denominator seems intuitively interesting; but the rationale for this scaling is unclear.

Peirce's approach to the same question represented a qualitatively different restatement. Although he used the logic and rules of probability to derive his coefficient, he based his model on an imaginary perfect and an imaginary fallible observer witnessing the same event. By describing what each would see and combining those observations into a single table, he invented his new coefficient of predictive success.

Peirce's Coefficient of the "Science of a Method"

Peirce developed a coefficient of predictive success to assess the accuracy of the prediction of a given event (in this case, the successful prediction of the occurrence of tornados). He imagined that an observer was presented with a number of instances in which the event could or could not occur. Peirce would use the number of successful predictions (event was predicted, it did occur; event was not predicted, it did not occur) in comparison to the number of unsuccessful predictions to construct a coefficient. His coefficient was essentially an agreement coefficient;[29] not the agreement of multiple raters, but instead the agreement between prediction and outcome—the accuracy of prediction. This reflected the deductive and inductive moments of Peirce's theory of scientific inquiry, in which the consequences of a given hypothesis are deductively generated and then looked for in experience by way of induction. His work was intended to represent an improvement over other attempts to construct such a coefficient and was specifically suggested as an alternative to Gilbert's coefficient. Peirce's coefficient appeared in a *Science* article titled "The Numerical Measure of the Success of Predictions" and included not only the coefficient, but also a measure of the utility of the prediction, expressed in the form of the "average profit per prediction." He used his coefficient to estimate the predictive success of "Sergeant Finley's tornado predictions."

Although Peirce was not the first to develop a coefficient of predictive success, his restatement of the problem was unique, and it led to a formula of association that anticipated the formula of a correlation coefficient for dichotomous variables by some twenty years. Like the mathematicians who preceded Galton, Peirce was essentially modeling an error distribution.

The European mathematicians modeled the joint distribution of two errors under the assumption that each was normally distributed. The bivariate distribution was then described for both uncorrelated and correlated errors. The presence of the correlation was expressed as a product term in the equation for the probability surface. The mathematicians made no attempt to tie the cross-product term to real data. Peirce, on the other hand, specifically wanted to associate two variables. One variable was the prediction of an event; the other was the observation of the occurrence of the same event. The table crossing these two variables would be used to determine the error of measurement, in the sense of determining the degree to which the predictions could be used as proxy indicators of the event. Rather than consider two position errors, Peirce related a prediction to an observation. The errors appeared in the empirical distribution of the cross-tabulated table.

Peirce considered questions related to the occurrence of an event which presented two possible outcomes. An example would be a situation in which either the event occurred (1) or the event did not occur (o). He more generally considered any event with one of two out-comes, which could easily include questions that could be answered either "yes" or "no," or questions that could be answered "true" or "false."

More generically, we could consider any question in which the codes o or 1 exhaust the universe of outcomes (e.g., yes or no; present or absent). For such a dichotomous item Peirce described four situa-tions. In (aa), the event outcome was 1 (i.e., the event occurred) and the response to the event was 1 (i.e., an observer answers that the event did indeed occur). This led to the observed values:

> (ab), in which the event outcome was 1 and the response to the event was o (e.g., an observer answers that the event did not occur);
> (ba), in which the event outcome was o (e.g., the event did not occur) and the response to the event was 1;
> (bb), in which the event outcome was o and the response to the event was o.

Situations (aa) and (bb) represent correct answers to the question of whether the event occurred, while (ab) and (ba) represent errors. In this conceptualization, a single witness (reliable to a certain degree) makes the judgments summarized by these frequencies.

Peirce then presented two principles. First, "any two methods are to be regarded as equal approximations to complete knowledge, which in the long run would give the same values for (aa), (ab), (ba), and (bb)." This principle is clearly derived from Peirce's concept of pragmatic meaning. In modern statistical modeling, this is expressed as the principle of equivalent models, usually stated as: "any two models that yield the same expectation are indistinguishable." One cannot choose between these two models based on any data collected and tested. This principle is followed by a second, in which Peirce imagines two equivalent situations that could generate the same set of observed values: the first situation refers to whatever true process generated the observed data (e.g., the success of an informed, but fal-lible, observer in predicting the incidence of a particular event); the second situation imagines what the incidence (e.g., of correct predic-tions) would be "if the answers had been obtained by selecting a determinate proportion of the questions by chance, to be answered by an infallible witness, while the rest were answered by an utterly ignorant person at random" (Peirce, W 3:136). The proportion of questions given to the infallible witness, i, is defined as "the science of the method." In more modern terms, this degree of "science" would be the reliability of the observer.

The Galton and Pearson notion of association developed from their study of the bivariate normal distribution. Given two normally distributed variables, one has a joint bivariate normal distribution. With the variance of the two distributions the same, one would see a characteristic shape in the distribution. Under "no association," the shape of the joint distribution would be circular. With increasing association, the shape of the distribution becomes elliptical. With perfect association, the shape of the distribution becomes a straight line. For two dichotomous variables, Pearson imagined categorizing the two-dimensional bivariate plane by bisecting each of the distributions at some center, using lines that were parallel to the major and minor axes of the ellipse. By grouping all of the observations within each of the four resulting quadrants, one ends up with a 2 × 2 contingency table.

Peirce, on the other hand, proceeded to logically determine a set of proportions that would result under his alternative and equivalent model. These logical proportions were based on the empirical distributions of the data. Unlike Pearson, Peirce made no assumptions regarding the underlying distributions of the variables. Given his tychism, however much we might like the symmetry of a normal distribution, actual empirical distributions were not bound *a priori* to reveal normal distribution. This was also consistent with his realism, insofar as the method allowed nature to reveal its own habits. This stands in marked contrast to Pearson's nominalistic and constructivist approach, in which the world is made to fit his notion of normal distribution.

Given the observed values (aa), (ab), (ba), and (bb), Peirce determined the number of correct predictions of the event when it does indeed occur under the second situation. Consider the following: the total number of observations (situations observed in which the event could either occur or not occur) is $\{(aa) + (ab) + (ba) + (bb)\}$, and the total number of possible observations in which the event did indeed occur is $\{(aa) + (ba)\}$. Since the infallible observer sees the proportion, i, of all events observed, then that observer sees $i\{(aa + ba)\}$ of the events that did occur. Since that observer is infallible, each of those observations is correctly place in the (aa) category. The ignorant observer, on the other hand, sees $(1 - i)\{(aa) + (ba)\}$ of the observations in which the event occurs, but only answers correctly j $(1 - i)\{(aa) + (ba)\}$ of those times, and that is the ignorant observer's contribution to (aa). Adding these together gives the number of observations in which the event occurs and is correctly predicted as

$$(aa) = i\{(aa) + (ba)\} + (1 - i)j\{(aa) + (ba)\}.$$

Similarly,

$$(ab) = (1 - i)j\{(ab) + (bb)\};$$

$$(ba) = (1 - i)(1 - j)\{(aa) + (ba)\}; \text{ and}$$

$$(bb) = i\{(ab) + (bb)\} + (1 - i)(1 - j)\{(ab) + (bb)\}.$$

One can compare this imagined second situation to the results obtained from the real observer. If the real observer were perfect, the "science of the method" would be 1, and indeed the proportion i = 1 would have been presented to an infallible observer. This would correspond to the values (ab) = 0 and (ba) = 0. If the real observer were always wrong, then the science of the method would be -1. This would correspond to the values (aa) = 0 and (bb) = 0. If the real observer were completely ignorant and guessing at random, we would expect the pattern of responses to be random (sometimes right, sometimes wrong). We might expect (with equal marginal proportions) that (aa) = (ba) = (ab) = (bb). Then from the above, i would be 0.

This result anticipates the Pearson Π^2 solution to the contingency table problem by some twenty years.

To show the relationship between Peirce's coefficient of "the science of the method" and Pearson's coefficient, we consider Peirce's four categories as a 2 × 2 contingency table. Consider Table 3.

Observation

		1	0	
E		a	b	
v	1	p_{xy}		$p_y(N) = a+b$
e		aa	ab	
n		c	d	
t	0			$(1-p_y)N = c+d$
		ba	bb	
		$p_x = a+c$	$(1-p_x) = b+d$	

where a = aa, b = ab, c = ba, and d = bb and $(1-p_x) = q_x$ and $(1-p_y) = q_y$, then

$$i = \frac{(aa)(bb) - (ab)(ba)}{[(aa)+(ba)][(ab)+(bb)]} = \frac{ad-bc}{(a+c)(b+d)}$$

where the numerator, the difference between the product of the main diagonal (the correct assessments) and the product of the off-diagonals elements (the incorrect assessments), is the determinant of the table matrix and is common to all association coefficients based on the fourfold table. The denominator is the product of the observation marginals and serves the function in all association coefficients of setting the upper bound for the possible values of the determinant of the matrix. Unlike Gilbert's coefficient, Peirce's coefficient would satisfy Yule's criteria for a correlation coefficient.

Peirce also mentioned that he had a solution for the case in which the question considered had more than two possible answers. This would represent a square table with a dimension larger than two. Peirce stated that he had solved that problem, but did not present a formula. The solution would represent the description of a more general contingency table, a problem that Pearson tackled in the early part of the next century.

Peirce's coefficient was apparently well known in the American scientific community. Shortly after its publication, the coefficient was the topic of discussion at a meeting of the Mathematical Section of the Philosophical Society of Washington.[30] The mathematician M. H. Doolittle presented a version of Peirce's coefficient that bore a strong resemblance to what would be Pearson's chi-square.[31] Doolittle argued for expanding the uses of the coefficient beyond predictive accuracy. He argued for the coefficient as a general index of association.

Although Peirce had a strong presence in the European scientific community, his coefficient apparently never crossed the Atlantic. Neither Pearson nor Yule ever indicated any knowledge of Peirce's work in this area. In fact, in 1900 Yule credits Pearson with the notion that $ad - bc$ could be used to describe association in a 2×2 table.[32] Pearson gives little indication of the basis of this insight.

Considering that Peirce was so critical of Pearson's approach to scientific inquiry, in particular of his nominalism and his resultant dependence on normal theory as an indication of true observable population characteristics, it is interesting and somewhat ironic that Peirce anticipated some of Pearson's most important results. It is even more interesting insofar as Peirce's results did not require that the results be dependent on any underlying normality assumptions, but instead relied on his discoveries related to the "mixture of two algebras."

Notes

CHAPTER ONE
PEIRCE ON BERKELEY'S NOMINALISTIC PLATONISM
Doug Anderson and Peter Groff

1. A number of scholars have tracked Peirce's accounts of nominalism and realism in full detail. Among other texts, we recommend John Boler's *Charles Peirce and Scholastic Realism* (Seattle: University of Washington Press, 1963); Rosa Mayorga's *From Realism to "Realicism"* (Lanham, Md.: Lexington Books, 2007); Claudine Engel-Tiercelin's "Vagueness and the Unity of C. S. Peirce's Realism," *Transactions of the Charles S. Peirce Society* 28, no. 1 (1992): 51–82; and Cornelis de Waal's "Peirce's Nominalist-Realist Distinction, an Untenable Dualism," *Transactions of the Charles S. Peirce Society* 34, no. 1 (1998): 183–202. Boler provides good historical background for Peirce's version of realism. Though we think de Waal focuses a bit too exclusively on the distinction between externality and internality, both he and Mayorga show clearly that Peirce's version of realism is more complex than is sometimes supposed. Finally, Engel-Tiercelin's essay develops the crucial links between Peirce's realism and his account of indeterminacy.

2. Realists such as R. B. Perry and R. W. Sellars took nominalism to be at the heart of their thinking. Some recent pragmatists, such as Richard Rorty, make nominalism (at least implicitly) central to their emphasis on contingency.

3. For an excellent treatment of Peirce's realism and its relation to that of Scotus and other scholastics, see Boler, *Charles Peirce and Scholastic Realism,* and his "Peirce and Medieval Thought," in Misak, ed., *The Cambridge Companion to Peirce* (Cambridge: Cambridge University Press, 2004).

4. *Pragmaticism* was a term Peirce used late in his career to distinguish his conception of pragmatism from the pragmatisms of James, Schiller, and others (CP 5.414).

5. It is perhaps important to keep in mind that for Peirce, borders are continua. Thus, nominalism and realism merge into each other; what becomes important, then, at the border between the two, are matters of emphasis, inflection, and direction.

6. Peirce indicated that he understood Berkeley to deny that there is "true continuity in the real world," and he took continuity to be exemplary of generality. See Patricia Turrisi, *Pragmatism as a Principle and Method of Right Thinking: The 1903 Lectures on Pragmatism* (Albany: SUNY Press, 1997).

7. Cornelis de Waal, "The Real Issue between Nominalism and Realism: Peirce and Berkeley Reconsidered," *Transactions of the Charles S. Peirce Society* 32, no. 3 (summer 1996): 437.

8. Ibid., p. 430.

9. Alexander Campbell Fraser, *Selections from Berkeley, Annotated* (Oxford: The Clarendon Press, 1899), p. 45. Peirce noted Berkeley's pragmatism here: "Every concept is a sign. Of what is it significant? It is significant only of its upshot, of the difference between affirming it and denying it. Thus Berkeley says that he does not deny the existence of matter, that he admits it in the only sense in which it has any meaning and is not mere nonsense, that is, in the only sense in which it has any application to practical life" (MS 328, p. 3).

10. Fraser, p. 51.

11. Ibid., p. xxxiii.

12. Peirce's realism also tries to outflank the question of externality by understanding our ideas to be dimensions of a community of thought. Peirce often tried to get at this by stating that we are in thought; thought is not in us.

13. de Waal, "The Real Issue," pp. 433–34; see also Peirce, W 2:240.

14. Peirce draws attention to this internal inconsistency throughout Berkeley's thought. See, for example, MS 641, p. 23.

15. Fraser, p. 74

16. Ibid., p. 229.

17. Because of this movement in Berkeley's thought, Peirce occasionally suggested that his own "conditional idealism" was a modified version of Berkeley's. See, for example, MS 322, p. 20.

18. Fraser, p. 16.

19. Ibid., p. 22.

20. In his fourth pragmatism lecture of 1903, Peirce examined other metaphysical systems by assessing which of his three categories they took into

account. For an extended treatment of his own alternate conception of the real, see these 1903 lectures in Turrisi. See also CP 6.237–28 and 5.430–35. For thorough secondary discussions, see Boler, *Charles Peirce and Scholastic Realism*, 117–44 and Christopher Hookway, *Peirce* (Boston: Routledge and Kegan Paul, 1985), 36–40 and 112–17.

21. For a good discussion of this example, see Engel-Tiercelin.

22. For an extended look at Peirce's evolutionary realism, see Carl Hausman, *Charles Peirce's Evolutionary Philosophy* (New York: Cambridge University Press, 1993). Of course, Peirce took ordinary nominalists such as Pearson to be even more at odds with experience in their belief that the "[u]niverse is a heap of sand whose grains have nothing to do with one another" (MS 641, p. 23).

23. Fraser, pp. 17–18.

24. Ibid., p. xxx.

25. It is worth noting that for Peirce, persons are also signs. That is, our own individuality involves generality in an essential way (see CP 6.344 and W 2:241). For a good treatment of Peirce's conception of persons, see Vincent Colapietro's *Peirce's Approach to the Self: A Semiotic Perspective on Human Subjectivity* (Albany: SUNY Press, 1989).

26. Edward C. Moore, "The Influence of Duns Scotus on Peirce," *Studies in the Philosophy of Charles Sanders Peirce: Second Series*, ed. R. Robin and E. Moore (Amherst: University of Massachusetts Press, 1964), p. 409.

CHAPTER TWO
WHO'S A PRAGMATIST: ROYCE, DEWEY, AND PEIRCE
AT THE TURN OF THE CENTURY
Doug Anderson

1. Josiah Royce, *The Religious Aspect of Philosophy* (Boston: Houghton Mifflin Company, 1885), p. 385.

2. Ibid., p. 433.

3. Josiah Royce, "The Eternal and the Practical," *The Philosophical Review* 13, no. 2 (1904): 137.

4. Ibid.

5. Frank Oppenheim, S. J., *Reverence for the Relations of Life* (Notre Dame: University of Notre Dame Press, 2005), p. 43.

6. *The Middle Works of John Dewey: 1899–1924*, ed. Jo Ann Boydston (Carbondale: Southern Illinois University Press, 1985), 10:88.

7. Ibid., pp. 86–87.

8. Sami Pihlström, "Peirce's Place in the Pragmatist Tradition," in *The Cambridge Companion to Peirce*, ed. Cheryl Misak (New York: Cambridge

University Press, 2004), p. 44. Though Royce was a good historian of Hegel, I take him to be more of a Kantian and a Lotzean than a Hegelian, especially in his mode of inquiry, which is more transcendental than dialectical.

9. John H. Randall, "Josiah Royce and American Idealism," *The Journal of Philosophy* 63, no. 3 (1966): 61.

10. Oppenheim's *Reverence for the Relations of Life* explores this theme in significant detail.

11. Josiah Royce, *Studies of Good and Evil* (New York: D. Appleton and Company, 1898), p. 234.

12. Josiah Royce, *The World and the Individual* (New York: MacMillan Company, 1900), p. 40.

13. Royce, *Studies of Good and Evil*, p. 129.

14. Ibid., p. 248.

15. Oppenheim, p. 31.

16. Mary Mahowald, *An Idealistic Pragmatism* (The Hague: Martinus Nijhoff, 1972), p. 17.

17. Oppenheim, p. 27.

18. Josiah Royce, *The Problem of Christianity* (Chicago: University of Chicago Press, 1968), pp. 348–49.

19. Josiah Royce, *Metaphysics*, ed. W. E. Hocking, R. Hocking, and F. Oppenheim (Albany: SUNY Press, 1998), p. 33.

20. Josiah Royce, *The Principles of Logic* (New York: Philosopher's Library, 1961), p. 34.

21. Ibid., p. 48.

22. Ibid., p. 49.

23. Ibid., p. 50.

24. Oppenheim, p. 36.

25. Royce, *Principles of Logic*, p. 63.

26. Ibid., p. 69.

27. Ibid., p. 63.

28. Ibid., p. 95.

29. Ibid., pp. 53–54.

30. Mahowald, p. 119.

31. Ibid., p. 127.

32. Dewey, *Middle Works*, 3:156.

33. Dewey, *Middle Works*, 10:73.

34. Dewey, *Middle Works*, 3:19.

35. Dewey, *Middle Works*, 3:19–20

36. Dewey, *Middle Works*, 2:223. See also Peirce, EP 2:119–123.

37. *The Later Works of John Dewey: 1925–1953*, ed. Jo Ann Boydston (Carbondale: Southern Illinois University Press, 1985), 6:276.

38. Dewey, *Middle Works*, 4:128 n. 1.

39. Dewey, *Middle Works*, 6:88.

40. Ibid.

41. Dewey, *Later Works*, 6:276.

42. John Dewey, *Human Nature and Conduct* (New York: The Modern Library, 1930), p. 370.

43. Dewey, *Middle Works*, 4:100.

44. Dewey, *Middle Works*, 12:169.

45. *The Early Works of John Dewey: 1882–1898*, ed. Jo Ann Boydston (Carbondale: Southern Illinois University Press, 1967), 2:103.

46. Dewey, *Later Works*, 6:276.

47. Dewey, *Later Works*, 1:47.

48. Dewey, *Middle Works*, 10:43.

49. Dewey, *Middle Works*, 10:45.

50. Dewey, *Early Works*, 4:19.

51. Dewey, *Middle Works*, 3:156.

52. Dewey, *Early Works*, 4:32.

1. Joseph Margolis, "The Passing of Peirce's Realism," *Transactions of the Charles S. Peirce Society* 29, no. 3 (summer 1993): 306.

2. Ibid., p. 295.

3. Ibid., pp. 307, 310–311.

4. Ibid., pp. 306–307, 310–311.

5. Ibid., 307.

6. Ibid., p. 310.

7. Ibid., p. 311.

8. Ibid., p. 314.

9. Ibid., p. 311.

10. Cheryl Misak, *Truth and the End of Inquiry* (Oxford: Clarendon Press, 1991), p. 68.

11. Margolis, p. 311.

12. Ibid., p. 313.

13. For an excellent treatment of the implications of a Peirce-like realism for contemporary science, see Susan Haack, "Extreme Scholastic Realism: Its

Relevance to Philosophy of Science Today," *Transactions of the Charles S. Peirce Society* 27, no. 1 (1992): 19–50.

Doug Anderson

1. For an interesting and amusing exemplification of the tensions between Peirce's and Rorty's versions of pragmatism, see Susan Haack, "We Pragmatists," in *Manifesto of a Passionate Moderate* (Chicago: University of Chicago Press, 1998), pp. 31–47.

2. See Carl R. Hausman, *Charles S. Peirce's Evolutionary Philosophy* (New York: Cambridge University Press, 1993), pp. 144–46.

3. John E. Smith, *America's Philosophical Vision* (Chicago: University of Chicago Press, 1992), p. 29.

4. John Dewey, *Experience and Nature*, in *The Later Works of John Dewey: 1925–1953*, ed. Jo Ann Boydston (Carbondale: Southern Illinois University Press, 1985), 1:8.

5. Ibid., p. 11.

6. Ibid.

7. Ibid., 10.

8. Ibid., pp. 2a–4a, 232f.

9. Ibid., p. 14.

10. Ibid.

11. Ibid., p. 4a.

12. Ibid., p. 16, n. 1.

13. John Dewey, *Logic: The Theory of Inquiry*, in *Later Works*, 12:462.

14. Ibid., p. 249

15. Dewey, *Later Works*, 1:351.

16. Dewey, *Later Works*, 12:248.

17. Dewey, *Later Works*, 1:381.

18. Ibid., pp. 308–09.

19. Smith, p. 6.

20. Richard Rorty, *Consequences of Pragmatism* (Minneapolis: University of Minnesota Press, 1982), p. 73.

21. Ibid.

22. See Richard Rorty, *Philosophy and the Mirror of Nature* (Princeton, N.J.: Princeton University Press, 1979).

23. Rorty, *Consequences*, p. 161.

24. Ibid., p. 165. It should be noted that Rorty's "Platonist" is also a caricature; Plato offered no "theory" of forms, and his outlook is more sophisticated than Rorty's Platonist seems to comprehend.

25. Richard Rorty, *Contingency, irony, and solidarity* (Cambridge: Cambridge University Press, 1989), p. xvi.

26. Ibid., p. 15.

27. Ibid., p. 165.

28. Ibid., p. 343, n. 6.

29. Smith, p. 8.

30. Richard Bernstein, "Philosophy and the Conversation of Mankind: Critical Study of Philosophy and the Mirror of Nature by Richard Rorty," Review of Metaphysics 33, no. 4 (1980): 747.

31. Stanley Rosen, *The Ancients and the Moderns: Rethinking Modernity* (New Haven: Yale University Press, 1989), p. 181.

32. Ibid., p. 182.

CHAPTER FIVE

PEIRCE'S DYNAMICAL OBJECT: REALISM AS PROCESS PHILOSOPHY
Carl R. Hausman

1. William James, *Pragmatism: A New Name for Some Old Ways of Thinking* (London: Longmans, Green, and Co., 1907), p. 54.

2. For more on this claim, and especially its relation to Schelling's work, see Ivo A. Ibri, "Reflections on a Poetic Ground in Peirce's Philosophy," *Transactions of the Charles S. Peirce Society* 45, no. 3 (summer 2009): 273.

3. See Claudine Engel-Tiercelin, "Vagueness and the Unity of C. S. Peirce's Realism," *Transactions of the Charles S. Peirce Society* 28, no. 1 (1992): 51–82.

4. See Cheryl Misak, *Truth and the End of Inquiry: A Peircean Account of Truth* (Oxford: Oxford University Press, 2004).

CHAPTER SIX

ANOTHER RADICAL EMPIRICISM: PEIRCE 1903
Doug Anderson

1. See also Carl R. Hausman, "In and Out of Peirce's Percepts," *Transactions of the Charles S. Peirce Society* 26, no. 3 (1990): 271–308.

2. Bruce Wilshire, ed. *William James: The Essential Writings* (Albany: SUNY Press, 1984), p. 178.

3. This revision began as early as Peirce's 1860s cognition papers.

4. David Hume, *A Treatise of Human Nature*, ed. and with analytical index by L. A. Selby-Bigge, 2d ed., with text revised and notes by P. H. Nidditch (Oxford: Clarendon Press, 1978), p. 636.

5. Richard Bernstein, "Peirce's Theory of Perception," *Studies in the Philosophy of Charles Sanders Peirce: Second Series*, ed. R. Robin and E. Moore (Amherst: University of Massachusetts Press, 1964), p. 177.

6. Bernstein, p. 170.

7. It is important to note that the language of distinctions internal to nature such as ego/non-ego, inner/outer, and so forth are traceable for Peirce not only to American transcendentalism but also to the work of Fichte and Schelling. In this tradition, the "unrelatedness" of subject and object is not a "fact" to be overcome. Rather, in this case, the ego and non-ego are distinct but related.

8. Wilshire, p. 181.

9. For an excellent discussion, see Thomas Short's *Peirce's Theory of Signs* (Cambridge: Cambridge University, 2007), pp. 318–19. For his treatment of the correction of perceptions, see p. 320.

10. Manley Thompson, *The Pragmatic Philosophy of C. S. Peirce* (Chicago: University of Chicago Press, 1953), p. 204.

11. William James, *Manuscript Lectures* (Cambridge: Harvard University Press, 1988), p. 29.

12. Charlene Seigfried, *William James's Radical Reconstruction of Philosophy* (Albany: SUNY Press, 1990), p. 161.

13. John Dewey, *The Essential Dewey*, ed. T. Alexander and L. Hickman (Bloomington: Indiana University Press, 1998), 2:375.

14. Ibid., p. 200.

CHAPTER SEVEN

PEIRCE ON INTERPRETATION

Carl R. Hausman

1. This illustration is offered by Christopher Hookway in his book *Truth, Rationality, and Pragmatism: Themes from Peirce* (Oxford: Oxford University Press, 2000).

2. Hookway, pp. 126–27.

3. For further discussion of whether signs can have dynamic objects, see James Jacob Liszka, *A General Introduction to the Semeiotic of Charles Sanders Peirce* (Bloomington, Ind.: Indiana University Press, 1996).

4. See Collingwood's *The Principles of Art* (Oxford: Oxford University Press, 1963).

CHAPTER EIGHT

PEIRCE AND PEARSON: THE AIMS OF INQUIRY

Doug Anderson and Michael J. Rovine

1. Joseph Brent, *Charles Sanders Peirce: A Life* (Bloomington: Indiana University Press, 1998), p. 8.

2. In 1892 Peirce reviewed the first edition of *The Grammar of Science* for *The Nation*. That review was similarly critical of Pearson's nominalism, but was a bit gentler in tone.

3. Karl Pearson, *The Grammar of Science* (London: Adam and Charles Black, 1900), p. 99.

4. Ibid., p. 103.

5. Ibid., p. 104.

6. Ibid., p. 8.

7. Ibid., p. 9.

8. Ibid., p. 26.

9. Karl Pearson, *National Life from the Standpoint of Science* (London: Adam and Charles Black, 1905), p. 1.

10. Pearson, *Grammar of Science*, p. 26, n. 2.

11. That is, a hypothesis is "valid" just insofar as it potentially, or plausibly, explains the event in question.

12. C. F. Delaney, *Science, Knowledge, and Mind: A Study in the Philosophy of C. S. Peirce* (Notre Dame: University of Notre Dame Press, 1993), p. 22.

13. Brent, p. 279.

CHAPTER NINE

THE PRAGMATIC IMPORTANCE OF PEIRCE'S RELIGIOUS WRITINGS

Doug Anderson

1. See Michael L. Raposa, *Peirce's Philosophy of Religion* (Bloomington: Indiana University Press, 1989).

2. See Hermann Deuser, *Gott: Geist und Natur; Theologische Konsequenzen aus Charles S. Peirce' Religionsphilosophie* (Berlin: Walter de Gruyter, 1993).

3. See also Felicia Kruse, "Peirce, God, and the 'Transcendentalist Virus,'" *Transactions of the Charles S. Peirce Society* 46, no. 3 (spring 2010).

4. For an excellent extended treatment of the role of sentiment in Peirce's thought, see Hookway, *Truth, Rationality, and Pragmatism: Themes from Peirce* (Oxford: Oxford University Press, 2002).

5. Richard Trammel, "Religion, Instinct, and Reason in the Thought of Charles S. Peirce," *Transactions of the Charles S. Peirce Society* 8, no. 1 (winter 1972): 19.

CHAPTER TEN

REALISM AND IDEALISM IN PEIRCE'S COSMOGONY

Doug Anderson

1. Donna M. Orange, *Peirce's Conception of God: A Developmental Study* (Lubbock, Texas: Institute for Studies in Pragmatism, 1984), p. 67.

2. I remind readers that Peirce often roughly equated his three categories of firstness, secondness, and thirdness with quality, fact, and law.

3. There is a question here whether Peirce identified God with the first stage of creation. I have not assumed this identification, though I take it to be a possibility. I leave the question open for now; I have examined the argument from both perspectives and find that our general points concerning Peirce's realism and idealism are unaffected.

4. See Orange, pp. 66ff.

5. See Carl R. Hausman, "Eros and Agape" in *Process Studies* 4, no. 1 (spring 1974): 11–25.

6. See Michael L. Raposa, *Peirce's Philosophy of Religion* (Bloomington: Indiana University Press, 1989), p. 77.

7. Hausman, p. 22.

CHAPTER ELEVEN

LOVE OF NATURE: THE GENERALITY OF PEIRCEAN CONCERN

Doug Anderson

1. See Douglas Anderson, "Peirce's Horse: A Sympathetic and Semeiotic Bond," in *Animal Pragmatism*, ed. Erin McKenna and Andrew Light (Bloomington: Indiana University Press, 2004), p. 86.

2. Joseph Brent, *Charles Sanders Peirce: A Life* (Bloomington: Indiana University Press, 1998), p. 204.

3. Carl R. Hausman, "Eros and Agape in Creative Evolution: A Peircean Insight," in *Process Studies* 4, no. 1 (spring 1974): 22.

CHAPTER TWELVE

DEVELOPMENTAL THEISM: A PEIRCEAN RESPONSE

TO FUNDAMENTALISM

Doug Anderson

1. I would argue that Peirce's response to Christian fundamentalism is useful as a response to any sort of religious fundamentalism. I focus on the Christian version because it was the one with which Peirce was most familiar, and it remains an issue in contemporary American culture.

2. George Marsden, *Fundamentalism and American Culture: The Shaping of Twentieth-Century Evangelicalism* (New York: Oxford University Press, 2006), p. 6.

3. See James Barr, *Fundamentalism* (Valley Forge, Penn.: Trinity Press International, 1981), pp. 1–3.

4. James M. Gray, *Fundamentals*, 3:41. All citations of *Fundamentals* refer to *The Fundamentals: A Testimony*, 12 volumes (Chicago: Testimony Publishing Company, 1910–1915), published "compliments of Two Christian Laymen," by the Bible Institute of Los Angeles.

5. See Barr, pp. 18 and 40–44, and Marsden, pp. 212–20.

6. See Douglas Anderson, "Peirce's Common Sense Marriage of Science and Religion," *Cambridge Companion to Peirce*, ed. Cheryl Misak (Cambridge: Cambridge University Press, 2004), pp. 175–92.

7. Marsden, p. 214.

8. See Marsden, pp. 57, 121.

9. James Orr, *Fundamentals*, 4:103.

10. John Dewey, *A Common Faith*, in *The Later Works of John Dewey*, ed. Jo Ann Boydston (Carbondale: Southern Illinois University Press, 1981–1990), 9:63.

11. Marsden, p. 213.

12. Ibid., p. 217.

13. Barr, p. 162.

14. Marsden, p. 214.

15. Philip Mauro, *Fundamentals*, 2:89.

16. James Burrell, *Fundamentals*, 8:92.

17. F. Bettex, *Fundamentals* 4: 74.

18. Ibid.

19. Ibid., pp. 75–77.

20. Ibid., p. 76.

21. Burrell, *Fundamentals*, 8:90.

22. Ibid., pp. 94–95.

23. Anonymous, *Fundamentals*, 8:33.

24. See George Fredrick Wright, *Fundamentals*, 2: 7–28.

25. Donna Orange, *Peirce's Conception of God: A Developmental Study* (Lubbock: Institute for Studies in Pragmatism, 1984), p. 90.

26. See Donna Orange, "Peirce's Falsifiable Theism," *American Journal of Semiotics* 2 (1983): 85–86, and Richard Trammell, "Religion, Instinct, and Reason in the Thought of Charles S. Peirce," *Transactions of the Charles S. Peirce Society* 8, no. 1 (1972): 3–25.

27. David Pfeifer, "Charles Peirce's Contribution to Religious Thought," *Proceedings of the C. S. Peirce Bicentennial International Congress*, ed. R. J. Roth (New York: Fordham University Press, 1973), p. 369.

28. Vincent Potter, "'Vaguely Like a Man': The Theism of Charles Sanders Peirce," in *God Knowable and Unknowable*, ed. Robert J. Roth, S.J. (New York: Fordham University Press, 1973), p. 253.

ADDENDUM: PEIRCE'S COEFFICIENT OF THE SCIENCE OF THE
METHOD: AN EARLY FORM OF THE CORRELATION COEFFICIENT
Michael J. Rovine and Doug Anderson

1. A. Legendre, *Nouvelles methodes pour la determination des orbites des cometes* (Paris: Courcier, 1805).

2. S. M. Stigler, *The History of Statistics: The Measurement of Uncertainty before 1900* (Cambridge, Mass.: Harvard University Press, 1986), pp. 140–42.

3. Ibid., pp. 143–56.

4. A. Laplace, *Theorie analytique des probabilites* (Paris: Courcier, 1812).

5. R. Adrain, "Research Concerning the Probabilities of the Errors which Happen in Making Observations &c.," *The Analyst, or, Mathematical Museum*, I (Philadelphia, 1808), pp. 93–109.

6. Giovanni Plana, "*Sulla teoria* dell'attrazione degli sferoidi ellittici," *Memorie di matematica e di fisica della Società Italiana delle Scienze* 15 (*1811*): 3–21.

7. See Laplace.

8. K. F. Gauss, *Theoria Combinationis Observationum Erroribus Minimis Obnoxiae* (Gottingen, 1823).

9. A. Bravais, "Analyse mathematique sur les probabilites des erreurs de situation d'un point," *Memoirs presentes par divers savans a l'Academie royale des sciences de l'Institut de France* 9 (1886): 255–332.

10. Louis Menand, *The Metaphysical Club: A Story of Ideas in America* (New York: Farrar, Straus and Giroux, 2002), p. 183.

11. Stigler, pp. 161–81.

12. See H. M. Walker, *Studies in the History of Statistical Method* (Baltimore: Williams and Wilkins Company, 1929).

13. F. Galton, "Presidential Address before the Anthropological Section," *Report of the Fifth-fifth Meeting of the British Association for the Advancement of Science* (London: John Murray, 1886).

14. H. P. Bowditch, "The Growth of Children," in *Eighth Annual Report of Board of Health of Massachusetts* (1877), rpt. in *Papers on Anthropometry* (Boston: American Statistical Association, 1894).

15. See Walker.

16. Stigler, p. 267ff.

17. Menand, pp. 185–86.

18. Karl Pearson, *The Grammar of Science* (London: Walter Scott, 1892).

19. Karl Pearson, "Mathematical Contributions to the Theory of Evolution, III: Regression, Heredity and Panmixia," *Philosophical Transactions*, series A, 187 (1896): 253–318.

20. Karl Pearson, "Mathematical Contributions to the Theory of Evolution, VII: On the Correlation of Characters Not Quantitatively Measurable," *Philosophical Transactions*, series A, 195 (1901): 1–47.

21. J. Cohen and P. Cohen, *Applied Multiple Regression in the Behavioral Sciences* (Mahwah, N.J.: Erlbaum, 1984), p. 37, and W. L. Hays and R. L. Winkler, *Statistics* (New York: Holt, Rinehart and Winston, 1971), pp. 802–04.

22. C. Spearman, "The Proof and Measurement of Association between Two Things," *American Journal of Psychology* 15 (1904): 72–101.

23. See I. Grattan-Guinness, *The Rainbow of Mathematics* (New York: Norton, 1997), pp. 540, 571.

24. Ibid., pp. 354–55, 412–13.

25. Ibid., pp. 540, 571.

26. J. J. Sylvester, "Addition to the Articles, 'On a New Class of Theorems,' and 'On Pascal's Theorem,'" in *Collected Mathematical Papers* (Cambridge: Cambridge University Press, 1850), 1:145–51.

27. A. Cayley, "A Memoir on the Theory of Matrices," *Philosophical Transactions* 148 (1858): 17–37.

28. G. K. Gilbert, "Finley's Tornado Predictions," *The American Meteorological Journal* 1 (1884): 66–162.

29. J. J. Cohen, "A Coefficient of Agreement for Nominal Scales," *Educational and Psychological Measurement* 20, no. 1 (1960): 37–46.

30. L. A. Goodman and W. H. Kruskal, "Measures of Association for Cross Classifications, II: Further Discussions and References," *Journal of the American Statistical Association* 54 (1959): 123–63.

31. M. H. Doolittle, "Association Ratios," *Bulletin of the Philosophical Society of Washington* 10 (1888): 83–87.

32. G. U. Yule, "On the Association of Attributes in Statistics, with Illustrations from the Material from the Childhood Society, etc.," *Philosophical Transactions*, series A, 194 (1900): 257–319.

References

Adrain, R. "Research Concerning the Probabilities of the Errors which Happen in Making Observations &c." *The Analyst, or, Mathematical Museum*, 1:93–109. Philadelphia: William P. Ferrand and Co., 1808.

Anderson, Douglas R. "Peirce's Common Sense Marriage of Science and Religion." In *Cambridge Companion to Peirce*, edited by Cheryl Misak, 175–92. Cambridge: Cambridge University Press, 2004.

———. "Peirce's Horse: A Sympathetic and Semeiotic Bond." In *Animal Pragmatism*, edited by Erin McKenna and Andrew Light, 86–94. Bloomington: Indiana University Press, 2004.

Barr, James. *Fundamentalism*. Valley Forge, Penn.: Trinity Press International, 1981.

Bernstein, Richard. "Peirce's Theory of Perception." In *Studies in the Philosophy of Charles Sanders Peirce: Second Series*, edited by R. Robin and E. Moore, 165–89. Amherst: University of Massachusetts Press, 1964.

———. "Philosophy and the Conversation of Mankind: Critical Study of *Philosophy and the Mirror of Nature by Richard Rorty*." Review of Metaphysics 33, no. 4 (1980): 745–75.

Boler, John. *Charles Peirce and Scholastic Realism*. Seattle: University of Washington Press, 1963.

———. "Peirce and Medieval Thought." In *The Cambridge Companion to Peirce*, edited by Cheryl Misak, 58–86. Cambridge: Cambridge University Press, 2004.

Bowditch, H. P. "The Growth of Children." In *Eighth Annual Report of Board of Health of Massachusetts* (1877). Reprinted in *Papers on Anthropometry* by the American Statistical Association. Boston: American Statistical Association, 1894.

Bravais, A. "Analyse mathematique sur les probabilites des erreurs de situation d'un point." *Memoirs presentes par divers savans a l'Academie royale des sciences de l'Institut de France* 9 (1846): 255–332.

Brent, Joseph. *Charles Sanders Peirce: A Life.* Bloomington: Indiana University Press, 1998.

Cayley, A. "A Memoir on the Theory of Matrices." *Philosophical Transactions* 148 (1858): 17–37.

Cohen, J. J. "A Coefficient of Agreement for Nominal Scales." *Educational and Psychological Measurement* 20, no. 1 (1960): 37–46.

Cohen, J., and P. Cohen. *Applied Multiple Regression in the Behavioral Sciences.* Mahwah, N.J.: Erlbaum, 1984.

Colapietro, Vincent. *Peirce's Approach to the Self: A Semiotic Perspective on Human Subjectivity.* Albany: SUNY Press, 1989.

Collingwood, R. G. *The Principles of Art.* Oxford: Oxford University Press, 1963.

Delaney, C. F. *Science, Knowledge, and Mind: A Study in the Philosophy of C. S. Peirce.* Notre Dame, Ind.: University of Notre Dame Press, 1993.

Deuser, Hermann. *Gott: Geist und Natur; Theologische Konsequenzen aus Charles S. Peirce' Religionsphilosophie.* Berlin: Walter de Gruyter, 1993.

de Waal, Cornelis. "The Real Issue between Nominalism and Realism: Peirce and Berkeley Reconsidered." *Transactions of the Charles S. Peirce Society* 32, no. 3 (summer 1996), 425–42.

———. "Peirce's Nominalist-Realist Distinction, an Untenable Dualism." *Transactions of the Charles S. Peirce Society* 34, no. 1 (1998): 183–202.

Dewey, John. *Human Nature and Conduct.* New York: The Modern Library, 1930.

———. *The Early Works of John Dewey: 1882–1898.* Edited by Jo Ann Boydston. Carbondale: Southern Illinois University Press, 1969–1972.

———. *The Middle Works of John Dewey: 1899–1924.* Edited by Jo Ann Boydston. Carbondale: Southern Illinois University Press, 1976–1983.

———. *The Later Works of John Dewey: 1925–1953.* Edited by Jo Ann Boydston. Carbondale: Southern Illinois University Press, 1981–1990.

———. *The Essential Dewey.* Vol. 2. Edited by T. Alexander and L. Hickman. Bloomington: Indiana University Press, 1998.

Doolittle, M. H. "Association Ratios." *Bulletin of the Philosophical Society of Washington* 10 (1888): 83–87.

Engel-Tiercelin, Claudine. "Vagueness and the Unity of C. S. Peirce's Realism." *Transactions of the Charles S. Peirce Society* 28, no. 1 (1992): 51–82.

Fraser, Alexander Campbell. *Berkeley.* London: Blackwood and Sons, 1881.

———. *Selections from Berkeley, Annotated.* Oxford: The Clarendon Press, 1899.

The Fundamentals: A Testimony. 12 volumes. Chicago: Testimony Publishing Company, 1910–1915.

Galton, F. "Presidential Address before the Anthropological Section of the British Association for the Advancement of Science." *Report of the Fifty-fifth Meeting of the British Association for the Advancement of Science; Held at Aberdeen in September 1885.* London: John Murray, 1886.

Gauss, K. F. *Disquisitiones Arithmeticae.* Leipzig: Fleischer, 1801.

———. *Theoria Combinationis Observationum Erroribus Minimis Obnoxiae.* Gottingen: Dieterich, 1823.

Gilbert, G. K. "Finley's Tornado Predictions." *The American Meteorological Journal* 1 (1884): 156–62.

Goodman, L. A., and W. H. Kruskal. "Measures of Association for Cross Classifications, II: Further Discussions and References." *Journal of the American Statistical Association* 54 (1959): 123–63.

Grattan-Guinness, I. *The Rainbow of Mathematics.* New York: Norton, 1997.

Haack, Susan. "Extreme Scholastic Realism: Its Relevance to Philosophy of Science Today." *Transactions of the Charles S. Peirce Society* 27, no. 1 (1992.): 19–50.

———. "We Pragmatists." In *Manifesto of a Passionate Moderate*, 31–47. Chicago: University of Chicago Press, 1998.

Hausman, Carl R. "Eros and Agape." *Process Studies* 4, no. 1 (spring 1974): 11–25.

———. "In and Out of Peirce's Percepts." *Transactions of the Charles S. Peirce Society* 26, no. 3 (1990): 271–308.

———. *Charles Peirce's Evolutionary Philosophy.* New York: Cambridge University Press, 1993.

Hays, W. L., and R. L. Winkler. *Statistics.* New York: Holt, Rinehart and Winston, 1971.

Hookway, Christopher. *Peirce.* Boston: Routledge and Kegan Paul, 1985.

———. *Truth, Rationality, and Pragmatism: Themes from Peirce.* Oxford: Oxford University Press, 2000.

Hume, David. *A Treatise of Human Nature.* Edited and with analytical index by L. A. Selby Bigge. 2d ed., with text revised and notes by P. H. Nidditch. Oxford: Clarendon Press, 1978.

Ibri, Ivo A. "Reflections on a Poetic Ground in Peirce's Philosophy." *Transactions of the Charles S. Peirce Society* 45, no. 3 (2009): 273–307.

James, William. *Pragmatism: A New Name for Some Old Ways of Thinking.* London: Longmans, Green, and Co., 1907.

———. *The Letters of William James.* Vol. 2. Edited by Henry James. Boston: Atlantic Monthly Press, 1920.

———. *Manuscript Lectures.* Cambridge, Mass.: Harvard University Press, 1988.

Kruse, Felicia. "Peirce, God, and the 'Transcendentalist Virus.'" *Transactions of the Charles S. Peirce Society* 46, no. 3 (2010).

Laplace. A. *Theorie analytique des probabilities*. Paris: Courcier, 1812.

Legendre, A. *Nouvelles methodes pour la determination des orbites des cometes*. Paris: Courcier, 1805.

Liszka, James Jacob. *A General Introduction to the Semeiotic of Charles Sanders Peirce*. Bloomington: Indiana University Press, 1996.

Mahowald, Mary. *An Idealistic Pragmatism*. The Hague: Martinus Nijhoff, 1972.

Margolis, Joseph. "The Passing of Peirce's Realism." *Transactions of the Charles S. Peirce Society* 29, no. 3 (1993): 293–330.

Marsden, George. *Fundamentalism and American Culture: The Shaping of Twentieth-Century Evangelicalism*. New York: Oxford University Press, 2006.

Mayorga, Rosa. *From Realism to "Realism": The Metaphysics of Charles Sanders Peirce*. Lanham, Md.: Lexington Books, 2007.

Menand, Louis. *The Metaphysical Club: A Story of Ideas in America*. New York: Farrar, Straus and Giroux, 2002.

Misak, Cheryl. *Truth and the End of Inquiry*. Oxford: Clarendon Press, 1991.

Moore, Edward C. "The Influence of Duns Scotus on Peirce." In *Studies in the Philosophy of Charles Sanders Peirce: Second Series,* ed. R. Robin and E. Moore, 401–13. Amherst: University of Massachusetts Press, 1964.

Oppenheim, Frank, S. J. *Reverence for the Relations of Life*. Notre Dame, Ind.: University of Notre Dame Press, 2005.

Orange, Donna M. "Peirce's Falsifiable Theism." *American Journal of Semiotics* 2 (1983): 120–27.

———. *Peirce's Conception of God: A Developmental Study*. Lubbock, Texas: Institute for Studies in Pragmatism, 1984.

Pearson, Karl. *The Grammar of Science*. London: Walter Scott, 1892.

———. "Mathematical Contributions to the Theory of Evolution, II: Skew Variation in Homogeneous Material." *Philosophical Transactions*, series A, 186 (1895): 342–414.

———. "Mathematical Contributions to the Theory of Evolution, III: Regression, Heredity and Panmixia." *Philosophical Transactions*, series A, 187 (1896): 253–318.

———. "Mathematical Contributions to the Theory of Evolution, VII: On the Correlation of Characters Not Quantitatively Measurable." *Philosophical Transactions*, series A, 195 (1901): 1–47.

———. *National Life from the Standpoint of Science*. London: Adam and Charles Black, 1905.

Peirce, Charles Sanders. *The Collected Papers of Charles Sanders Peirce.* Edited by Charles Hartshorne and Paul Weiss (vols. 1–6) and by Arthur Burks (vols. 7–8). Cambridge, Mass.: Harvard University Press, 1931–58.

———. The Charles S. Peirce Papers. 30 reels of microfilm. The Houghton Library. Cambridge, Mass.: Harvard University Library Microreproduction Service, 1963–66.

———. *The New Elements of Mathematics.* Edited by Carolyn Eisele. 4 vols. The Hague and Paris: Mouton; Atlantic Highlands, N.J.: Humanities Press, 1976.

———. *Semiotic and Significs: The Correspondence between Charles S. Peirce and Victoria Lady Welby.* Edited by Charles S. Hardwick. Bloomington: Indiana University Press, 1977.

———. *Charles Sanders Peirce: Contributions to* The Nation. *Part Two: 1894–1900.* Edited by Kenneth L. Ketner and James E. Cook. Graduate Studies 16. Lubbock, Texas: Texas Tech University Press, 1978.

———. *Writings of Charles S. Peirce: A Chronological Edition.* Edited by Max Fisch, Nathan Houser, Christian Kloesel, et al. 8 vols. to date. The Peirce Edition Project. Bloomington: Indiana University Press, 1982–2009.

———. *Reasoning and the Logic of Things: The Cambridge Conferences Lectures of 1898.* Edited by Kenneth Laine Ketner. Cambridge, Mass. and London: Harvard University Press, 1992.

———. *The Essential Peirce.* Edited by Nathan Houser and Christian Kloesel. 2 vols. The Peirce Edition Project. Bloomington and Indianapolis: Indiana University Press, 1992–98.

Pfeifer, David. "Charles Peirce's Contribution to Religious Thought." In *Proceedings of the C. S. Peirce Bicentennial International Congress,* edited by R. J. Roth, 367–73. New York: Fordham University Press, 1973.

Pihlström, Sami. "Peirce's Place in the Pragmatist Tradition." In *The Cambridge Companion to Peirce,* edited by Cheryl Misak, 27–57. New York: Cambridge University Press, 2004.

Plana, Giovanni."*Sulla teoria* dell'attrazione degli sferoidi ellittici." *Memorie di matematica e di fisica della Società Italiana delle Scienze* 15 (*1811*): 3–21.

Potter, Vincent. "'Vaguely Like a Man': The Theism of Charles Sanders Peirce." In *God Knowable and Unknowable,* edited by Robert J. Roth, S. J., 241–54. New York: Fordham University Press, 1973.

Randall, John H. "Josiah Royce and American Idealism." *The Journal of Philosophy* 63, no. 3 (1966): 57–83.

Raposa, Michael L. *Peirce's Philosophy of Religion.* Bloomington: Indiana University Press, 1989.

Rorty, Richard. *Philosophy and the Mirror of Nature*. Princeton, N.J.: Princeton University Press, 1979.

———. *Consequences of Pragmatism*. Minneapolis: University of Minnesota Press, 1982.

———. *Contingency, irony, and solidarity*. Cambridge: Cambridge University Press, 1989.

Rosen, Stanley. *The Ancients and the Moderns: Rethinking Modernity*. New Haven: Yale University Press, 1989.

Royce, Josiah. *The Religious Aspect of Philosophy*. Boston: Houghton Mifflin Company, 1885.

———. *Studies of Good and Evil*. New York: D. Appleton and Company, 1898.

———. *The World and the Individual*. New York: MacMillan Company, 1900.

———. "The Eternal and the Practical." *The Philosophical Review* 13, no. 2 (1904): 113–42.

———. *The Principles of Logic*. New York: Philosopher's Library, 1961.

———. *The Problem of Christianity*. Chicago: University of Chicago Press, 1968.

———. *Metaphysics*. Edited by W. E. Hocking, R. Hocking, and F. Oppenheim. Albany: SUNY Press, 1998.

Seigfried, Charlene. *William James's Radical Reconstruction of Philosophy*. Albany: SUNY Press, 1990.

Short, Thomas. *Peirce's Theory of Signs*. Cambridge: Cambridge University Press, 2007.

Smith, John E. *America's Philosophical Vision*. Chicago: University of Chicago Press, 1992.

Spearman, C. "The Proof and Measurement of Association between Two Things." *American Journal of Psychology* 15 (1904): 72–101.

Stigler, S. M. *The History of Statistics: The Measurement of Uncertainty before 1900*. Cambridge, Mass.: Harvard University Press, 1986.

Sylvester, J. J. "Addition to the Articles 'On a New Class of Theorems' and 'On Pascal's Theorem.'" In *Collected Mathematical Papers of James Joseph Sylvester*, 1:145–51. Cambridge: Cambridge University Press, 1850.

Thompson, Manley. *The Pragmatic Philosophy of C. S. Peirce*. Chicago: University of Chicago Press, 1953.

Trammell, Richard. "Religion, Instinct, and Reason in the Thought of Charles S. Peirce." *Transactions of the Charles S. Peirce Society* 8, no. 1 (1972): 3–25.

Turrisi, Patricia. *Pragmatism as a Principle and Method of Right Thinking: The 1903 Lectures on Pragmatism*. Albany: SUNY Press, 1997.

Wachsmuth, A., L. Wilkinson, and G. E. Dallal. "Galton's Bend: A Previously Undiscovered Nonlinearity in Galton's Family Stature Regression Data." *American Statistician* 57, no. 3 (2003): 190–92.

Walker, H. M. *Studies in the History of Statistical Method*. Baltimore: Williams and Wilkins Company, 1929.

Wilshire, Bruce, ed. *William James: The Essential Writings*. Albany: SUNY Press, 1984.

Yule, G. U. "On the Association of Attributes in Statistics, with Illustrations from the Material from the Childhood Society, etc." *Philosophical Transactions,* series A, 194 (1900): 257–319.

Index

Kenneth Laine Ketner, ed., *Peirce and Contemporary Thought: Philosophical Inquiries.*

Max H. Fisch, ed., *Classic American Philosophers: Peirce, James, Royce, Santayana, Dewey, Whitehead, second edition.* Introduction by Nathan Houser.

John E. Smith, *Experience and God, second edition.*

Vincent G. Potter, *Peirce's Philosophical Perspectives.* Edited by Vincent Colapietro.

Richard E. Hart and Douglas R. Anderson, eds., *Philosophy in Experience: American Philosophy in Transition.*

Vincent G. Potter, *Charles S. Peirce: On Norms and Ideals, second edition.* Introduction by Stanley M. Harrison.

Vincent M. Colapietro, ed., *Reason, Experience, and God: John E. Smith in Dialogue.* Introduction by Merold Westphal.

Robert J. O'Connell, S.J., *William James on the Courage to Believe, second edition.*

Elizabeth M. Kraus, *The Metaphysics of Experience: A Companion to Whitehead's "Process and Reality," second edition.* Introduction by Robert C. Neville.

Kenneth Westphal, ed., *Pragmatism, Reason, and Norms: A Realistic Assessment—Essays in Critical Appreciation of Frederick L. Will.*

Beth J. Singer, *Pragmatism, Rights, and Democracy.*

Eugene Fontinell, *Self, God, and Immorality: A Jamesian Investigation.*

Roger Ward, *Conversion in American Philosophy: Exploring the Practice of Transformation.*

Michael Epperson, *Quantum Mechanics and the Philosophy of Alfred North Whitehead.*

Kory Sorrell, *Representative Practices: Peirce, Pragmatism, and Feminist Epistemology.*

Naoko Saito, *The Gleam of Light: Moral Perfectionism and Education in Dewey and Emerson.*

Josiah Royce, *The Basic Writings of Josiah Royce.*

Douglas R. Anderson, *Philosophy Americana: Making Philosophy at Home in American Culture.*

James Campbell and Richard E. Hart, eds., *Experience as Philosophy: On the World of John J. McDermott.*

John J. McDermott, *The Drama of Possibility: Experience as Philosophy of Culture.* Edited by Douglas R. Anderson.

Larry A. Hickman, *Pragmatism as Post-Postmodernism: Lessons from John Dewey.*

Larry A. Hickman, Stefan Neubert, and Kersten Reich, eds., *John Dewey Between Pragmatism and Constructivism.*

Dwayne A. Tunstall, *Yes, But Not Quite: Encountering Josiah Royce's Ethico-Religious Insight.*

Josiah Royce, *Race Questions, Provincialism, and Other American Problems, expanded edition.* Edited by Scott L. Pratt and Shannon Sullivan.

Lara Trout, *The Politics of Survival: Peirce, Affectivity, and Social Criticism.*

John R. Shook and James A. Good, *John Dewey's Philosophy of Spirit, with the 1897 Lecture on Hegel.*

Josiah Warren, *The Practical Anarchist: Writings of Josiah Warren.* Edited and with an Introduction by Crispin Sartwell.

Naoko Saito and Paul Standish, eds., *Stanley Cavell and the Education of Grownups.*

Douglas R. Anderson and Carl R. Hausman, *Conversations on Peirce: Reals and Ideals.*

Rick Anthony Furtak, Jonathan Ellsworth, and James D. Reid, eds., *Thoreau's Importance for Philosophy.*